READING AUDIENCES

WEST SUSSEX
HIGHER EDU
AUTHOR

TITLE
READING

CLASS No
301.161

NOV94

Hardly a week goes by without another sensational story of young people depraved and corrupted by the mass media. Children and young people are often portrayed as passive victims, forcefed violent and dangerous images by the media. Yet this is far from the whole story.

Reading Audiences offers an exciting alternative approach to studying young people's relationships with popular media. It contains detailed qualitative studies covering a range of media, including television, comics, video, and popular fiction. The contributors pay close attention to the diverse roles these different media play in the family and the peer group, and the complex ways in which young people make sense of what they read and watch. Collectively, these studies offer challenging new perspectives on the role of the media in forming the social, sexual and cultural identities of today's youth.

David Buckingham is Lecturer in Media Education in the Department of English and Media Studies at the Institute of Education, London University

EDITED BY DAVID BUCKINGHAM

Reading audiences
Young people and the media

W. SUSSEX INSTITUTE
OF
HIGHER EDUCATION
LIBRARY

Manchester University Press

MANCHESTER AND NEW YORK

distributed exclusively in the USA and Canada by St Martin's Press

Copyright © Manchester University Press 1993

While copyright in the volume as a whole is vested in Manchester University Press, copyright in individual chapters belongs to their respective authors, and no chapter may be reproduced wholly or in part without the express permission in writing of both author and publisher.

Published by Manchester University Press
Oxford Road, Manchester M13 9PL, UK
and Room 400, 175 Fifth Avenue,
New York, NY 10010, USA

Distributed exclusively in the USA and Canada
by St. Martin's Press, Inc.,
175 Fifth Avenue, New York, NY 10010, USA

British Library Cataloguing-in-Publication Data
A catalogue record for this book is available from the British Library

Library of Congress Cataloging-in-Publication Data
Reading audiences : young people and the media / edited by David Buckingham.
    p. cm.
    ISBN 0-7190-3869-3. — ISBN 0-7190-3870-7 (pbk.)
    1. Mass media and youth.   2. Mass media and youth—Great Britain.
3. Popular cuture.   4. Great Britain—Popular culture.
I. Buckingham, David, 1954–
HQ799.2.M35R43 1993
302.23'083–dc20   93-13598
                                CIP

ISBN 0 7190 3869 3 *hardback*
ISBN 0 7190 3870 7 *paperback*

Printed in Great Britain
by Biddles Ltd, Guildford & King's Lynn

CONTENTS

NOTES ON CONTRIBUTORS

MARTIN BARKER is Head of the School of Cultural Studies at The University of the West of England, Bristol. His books include *The Video Nasties* (Pluto, 1984), *A Haunt of Fears* (Pluto, 1984), *Comics: Ideology, Power and the Critics* (Manchester University Press, 1989) and *Reading into Cultural Studies* (with Anne Beezer, Routledge, 1992).

DAVID BUCKINGHAM is a Lecturer in Media Studies at the Institute of Education, University of London. His previous publications include *Public Secrets: 'EastEnders' and its Audience* (BFI, 1987), *Watching Media Learning: Making Sense of Media Education* (Falmer, 1990), and *Children Talking Television* (Falmer, 1993).

MARIE GILLESPIE is a Lecturer in Media Studies at Brunel University, Middlesex. She has contributed to a range of journals, including *Independent Media, Cultural Studies* and *The English Magazine*.

GEMMA MOSS is a Research Fellow at the Institute of Education, University of London. She is the author of *Un/popular Fictions* (Virago, 1989), and has contributed to *The English Magazine, The Australian Journal of Education* and *Women: An International Cultural Review*.

CHRIS RICHARDS is a Lecturer in English at the Institute of Education, University of London. He has contributed to *Screen, Teaching London Kids* and *The English Magazine*, and to the books *Watching Media Learning* (Falmer, 1990), and *English in the National Curriculum* (Kogan Page, 1992).

JULIAN SEFTON-GREEN is a Lecturer in Media Studies and English at the Central School of Speech and Drama in London. He is co-author of *The Music Business* (Hodder and Stoughton, 1989), and contributed to *Watching Media Learning* (Falmer, 1990).

VALERIE WALKERDINE is Professor in the Department of Media and Communications at Goldsmith's College, University of London. Her previous publications include *The Mastery of Reason* (Routledge, 1988), *Counting Girls Out* (Virago, 1989) *Democracy in the Kitchen* (with Helen Lucey, Virago, 1989) and *Schoolgirl Fictions* (Verso, 1991).

JULIAN WOOD is a researcher who is currently working part-time for the British Board of Film Classification. His previous work has been concerned with gender and youth culture. He contributed to *Gender and Generation* (Macmillan, 1985).

Introduction: young people and the media

Teenage mags: stepping stone into womanhood. (handwritten note)

power to morally? (handwritten note)

And the first step, as you know, is always what matters most, particularly when we are dealing with those who are young and tender. That is the time when they are easily moulded and when any impression we choose to make leaves a permanent mark.

... Then it seems that our first business is to supervise the production of stories, and to choose only what we think suitable, and reject the rest. We shall persuade mothers and nurses to tell our chosen stories to their children, and by means of them to mould their minds and characters which are more important than their bodies. The greater part of the stories current today we shall have to reject.

... Nor can we permit stories of wars and plots and battles among the gods.

... Children cannot distinguish between what is allegorical and what isn't, and opinions formed at that age are usually difficult to eradicate or change; we should therefore surely regard it as of the utmost importance that the first stories they hear shall aim at encouraging the highest excellence of character.

Plato, *Republic.*[1]

It might seem inappropriate to begin a book about young people and the media with a reference to the work of an ancient Greek philosopher, written over two thousand years ago. Yet Plato's fears about the influence of the poets on the youth of his time prefigure many contemporary anxieties about the effects of the media.

In devising a programme of education for his ideal society, Plato argues that the poets will play a central role in forming the mind and character of the young. Yet he is also concerned that their power might be misused. He accuses most existing poetry of 'misrepresenting' the nature of the gods, depicting them as quarrelsome and as the cause of evil as well as good. Likewise, the poets are condemned for occasionally presenting heroic characters as 'mercenary and grasping', and displaying 'excessive arrogance to gods and men'. Such moral ambiguity cannot

Teenage mags. (handwritten note)

be tolerated. Ultimately, according to Plato, the poets are 'in error in matters of the greatest human importance': 'they have said that unjust men are often happy, and just men wretched, that wrong-doing pays if you can avoid being found out, and that justice is good for someone else but is to your own disadvantage' (*Republic*, III. 392).

Plato's anxiety is thus partly to do with what we might now term 'poor role-models' or even 'negative images'. Yet he is also concerned that poetry encourages emotional responses, which in turn produce moral weaknesses. 'Horrifying and frightening' accounts of the underworld, for example, would cause a 'thrill of terror [that] will make our guardians more nervous and less tough than they should be'. 'Pitiful laments' could not be placed in the mouths of famous heroes, but should be confined to 'less reputable women characters' or 'bad men', in order to discourage young men from imitating such unworthy conduct. Indulgence in violent laughter is also to be avoided, for fear of the violent reactions it invites. In speaking to 'the lower elements of the mind, to the detriment of reason' and seeking to appeal to 'the taste of the ignorant multitude', the poets will only encourage 'instinct' and 'unreason', and thus cannot be admitted to 'a properly run state' (*Republic*, X. 602–5).

Plato's concern is not solely to do with content, however. He devotes long sections of the *Republic* to a critique of 'mimesis' – a word that covers both imitation or copying and artistic representation more broadly. Plato exploits this ambiguity in the term, arguing that artistic creations are 'at a third remove from reality', offering a mere 'superficial likeness' that cannot possibly produce knowledge of the truth. He is particularly concerned about the dangers of *dramatic* representation, both in plays and in the use of direct speech in poetry, as opposed to indirect speech and narrative. Requiring young people to recite such material, as was the current practice in Greek schools, would encourage them to put themselves into the position of the character, to 'assimilate' themselves to the character's thoughts and feelings. Accordingly, Plato argues, the Guardians (or future rulers) of the society should only act the part of characters 'suitable to them': 'They should neither do a mean action nor be clever at acting a mean or otherwise disgraceful part on the stage for fear of catching the infection in real life' (*Republic*, III. 395).

Plato's criticisms of the popular texts of his time thus derive explicitly from a need to sustain a social order based on an exclusive and hierarchical division of labour. For the Guardians at least, self-control was of the essence. And while poetry might serve as the primary means of moral training, it also held the dangers of 'luxury' and 'indulgence' in the emotions. Like sex, access to it should be rigorously controlled, and the temptations of 'frenzy' and 'excessive pleasure' avoided at all costs. By banning the poets from his ideal Republic, Plato writes, 'we shall thus prevent our guardians being brought up among representations of what is evil, and so day by day and little by little, by grazing widely as it were in an unhealthy pasture, insensibly doing themselves a cumulative psychological damage that is very serious' (*Republic* III. 401).

It is a long way, both historically and intellectually, from Plato's criticisms of the dramatic poets to contemporary debates about the impact of the 'mass' media. As Tory politician John Patten calls for the banning of the Australian soap opera *Neighbours* on the grounds that it 'dulls children's senses', turning them into 'passive, unimaginative voyeurs'; as education ministers cite television as one major cause of allegedly declining standards of literacy, and condemn examination boards for permitting the study of the medium in schools; or as right-wing teachers' leader Peter Dawson denounces the British soap *EastEnders* for its portrayal of 'highly deviant forms of behaviour', it is possible to detect a much cruder conservative agenda at work.[2] Yet while it is certainly tempting to dismiss Mary Whitehouse's criticisms of moral depravity on television, or Prince Charles's attack on the impact of 'screen violence', as merely the unrepresentative ravings of the lunatic fringe, they clearly do reflect anxieties that are much more widely shared.[3]

Such anxieties, and the hysteria that often accompanies them, are rarely absent from contemporary newspaper headlines. The spectre of children narcotised by television, corrupted by video violence and the overt sexuality of popular music, their intellect and imagination destroyed by the mindless products of the culture industry, is one that is routinely invoked in debates about education and the future shape of our society. The 'misrepresentations' of the media are seen to instil false beliefs about the world, and are thus a primary cause of the breakdown of the family, of social unrest and of moral decline – not to mention racism, sexism, militarism, consumerism and manifold forms of discrimination and prejudice. The media are routinely seen as an anti-educational influence, as the deadly enemy of literacy, of morality, of art and culture, and ultimately of childhood itself.

As numerous writers have argued,[4] it is possible to trace this concern about the impact of new popular media on young people throughout history. Contemporary moral panics about the dangers of video violence or computer games are merely part of a long tradition that stretches back, through the campaigns against so-called 'horror comics' in the 1950s and the moves towards greater regulation of the cinema in the 1920s and 1930s, to anxieties about popular literature ('penny dreadfuls') in Victorian times, and indeed to concerns about the depraving influence of the novel itself. Plato's criticisms of the dramatic poets might thus be seen as the earliest recorded example of what has remained a perennial anxiety.

Throughout these debates, the concern has consistently been directed towards 'other people', who are seen to be too immature or simply too feeble-minded to resist the negative influence of the media. And while these 'other people' have invariably been those who hold less power in society, and who are therefore seen to represent a threat to those who do – particularly women, black people and the working classes – it is the young who have inevitably been defined as the most pressing object of concern. Unlike adults, who are presumably immune, young people are seen to be most at risk: their 'tender minds' can be easily moulded, and the damage is indelible. For Plato, and for many of our contemporary critics, these are essentially *educational* issues, which are to do with moral training and with building 'good character'. Yet their response is not to encourage young people to develop their own critical perspectives: on the contrary, the solution is seen to lie in greater control, and indeed censorship, by parents and by the State. Ultimately, what underlies these arguments – quite explicitly in Plato's case – is a concern to preserve the existing social order from threats which might seek to undermine it.

In this respect, these fears reflect broader ideological constructions of childhood and youth. If children are typically defined as innocent and impressionable, they are also seen as potential monsters, who are in need of adult 'protection'. The media are seen to have an extraordinary power to penetrate the thin veneer of civilisation and release the anarchic, anti-social forces that lie beneath. When it comes to adolescence, and to what is typically seen as the precarious transition to adulthood, these fears of collapse into 'primitive abandon' have been the focus of successive moral panics, in which media such as the cinema and popular music have been seen to play a major role.[5] To define young people as merely vulnerable and credulous thus represents a forceful legitimation of adult power and control.

What is particularly striking here, however, is not simply that these anxieties have such a long history. It is also that they seem to recur across such a wide spectrum of political and moral beliefs. Of course, it is important to make distinctions here. Concerns about the impact of televised sex and violence cannot simply be equated with criticisms of gender stereotyping or the celebration of 'consumerism' in advertising. Nevertheless, such arguments about the influence of the media are often based on a shared belief in their extraordinary power, and on assumptions about the vulnerability of the young. Indeed, there are many instances where these very different political perspectives have united, in often quite unexpected and unholy alliances, to condemn media forms that have acquired the status of 'bad objects'. In recent years, for example, 'new wave' TV cartoons and video games have served as a focus for a whole range of concerns about consumerism, violence and sexism – and, in the British context, for a recurrent fear of 'Americanization'.[6] Yet there has been very little attempt to investigate the ways in which young people use these media, and the meanings and pleasures they derive from them: here again, they are defined largely as passive victims of powerful and exclusively negative 'effects'.

On one level, such debates could be seen merely as a reflection of the importance of the media in young people's lives. The media, in their various forms, constitute the major leisure-time activity for the populations of nearly all contemporary societies. Statistically, as many critics are fond of indicating, children in Western countries now spend more time watching television than they spend in school. As the studies collected in this book will indicate, the media play a significant role in young people's relationships with their families and their peers, and in the processes by which their identities come to be formed. In many areas of their lives, the media undeniably exert a considerable 'influence' on the young – even if the nature of that influence and the processes by which it is exerted are more complex, and thus much harder to identify, than is often assumed.

Yet the anxieties which recur in these public debates about young people and the media also relate to much broader concerns, in which the media may in fact have a much less significant – and indeed even a contradictory – role. While the media may play a part in the growth of consumerism, the decline of the family or the rise in violent crime, the causes of these phenomena (assuming that they exist) cannot be reduced to a single explanation. Yet the media routinely serve here as an easy scapegoat, which may actively prevent a more considered, and more honest, appraisal of the issues. To blame the media provides a convenient means of displacing the concern away from questions which are much harder to examine, and which we may actively wish to avoid.[7]

Certainly, the evidence that is offered in support of such arguments is often very limited. In many cases, there is a direct denial of the need for evidence in the first place: it is as if 'common sense' will tell us all we need to know. Given the profound moral and political investments that are often at stake, this is perhaps not surprising. Yet if we are interested in investigating the relationship between young people and the media, we need to begin with some rather more open, and perhaps more modest, questions.

Tracing effects

Academic research on young people and the media has largely been framed by these kinds of anxieties – and indeed it is often on this basis that research is funded in the first place. Perhaps inevitably, many of the studies collected in this book also reflect these concerns, although they do so in a rather different way. The intention here is not primarily to seek evidence of 'effects'. On the contrary, our aim is to investigate the ways in which young people use and make sense of the media in the context of their lived social experiences. In this respect, the book adopts a very different approach from most previous research.

Within the mainstream disciplines of psychology and sociology, research in this area has been heavily dominated by the quest for proof of negative influences. While there has been considerable interest in 'intervening variables' that might mediate between the stimulus and the response, researchers have predominantly conceived of the relationship between media and their audiences as a one-way process of cause and effect. Yet the results of this endeavour have largely been equivocal or inconclusive – a fact which has often occasioned considerable exasperation among popular critics of the media.

The vast body of research on the impact of television violence – which has remained an almost obsessive preoccupation here – is perhaps the most spectacular example of this.[8] Despite decades of research, the proof of any connection between violent television and aggressive behaviour is at best weak, and the conclusions so qualified as to be of little value to potential policy makers. Much of the criticism of the violence research has focused on questions of method. Laboratory experiments, for example, which have been seen by their advocates as a primary source of 'hard' scientific evidence, have often provided the main support for the 'direct effects' hypothesis.[9] Yet, as critics of such work have pointed out, the contexts in which these experiments are conducted, the kinds of media which are used and the kinds of responses which are elicited (and indeed implicitly encouraged) are highly artificial. As such, it is argued, this research bears little relation to the ways in which television is used in the real world, and ultimately proves very little about it.

Likewise, survey research in this area has routinely run up against the confusion between correlation and causality. Put simply, the fact that people who are violent may watch a lot of violent television does not necessarily prove that television causes violence: the causality may work in the opposite direction, and there may be a number of other factors that produce both kinds of behaviour. As in the case of laboratory experiments, it is often assumed that these other variables which might play a part in the process can be 'controlled' – which of course presumes that we know what they all are, and can measure their significance. Despite some highly sophisticated attempts to get around this problem, it has yet to be satisfactorily resolved.

Yet the limitations of this research – and of mainstream effects research more broadly – are not simply to do with the reliability or validity of the methods used. They also reflect a fundamental neglect of the issue of *meaning* – both of the 'stimulus' and of the 'response' it is seen to produce. Both, it is assumed, can be objectively identified, quantified and compared. The question of what 'violence' means, both to those who watch it and to those who perpetrate it (or indeed are victims of it) in real life, has often been answered in highly simplistic terms. Meaning is seen to be inherent in the 'message', and to be transmitted directly into the mind and thence the behaviour of the viewer. As a result, it becomes unnecessary to investigate what viewers themselves define as violent, or the different ways in which they make sense of what they watch.[10] The social processes through which meanings are produced and circulated tend to be reduced to a matter of 'demographic variables', or simply neglected altogether.

These behaviourist assumptions also appear to underlie mainstream sociological research in this area, which has relied heavily on functionalist 'socialisation theory'.[11] Studies of children's acquisition of gender stereotypes from the media, for example, have tended to regard children as passive recipients of 'external' social forces, rather than as active participants in constructing their own social lives and identities. Childhood tends to be regarded here as a kind of rehearsal or preparation for adult life: through the impact of 'models' and stimuli (such as those provided by television), the child progressively overcomes its own inadequacies and enters the social world of adulthood. Statistical content analysis of television 'messages' – for example, counting the numbers of men and women in different occupational roles – is often seen here as adequate evidence of their effects. Yet again, the ways in which children make sense of television, and the social processes through which this occurs, tend to be oversimplified.

Active readers?

The history of media research is far from linear or straightforward. Particularly in the case of young people, there is a sense in which the same issues have recurred again and again as each new medium has arrived on the scene.[12] Here too, the tenacity of received wisdoms about the 'effects' of the media reflects the much more fundamental issues at stake. Nevertheless, within both psychological and sociological research in this area, it is possible to trace a gradual shift away from the notion of 'direct effects' towards the idea of the 'active reader',[13] and a parallel reduction in estimates of the 'power' of the media (although the two are not necessarily causally related). In both cases, these reflect broader theoretical developments within their respective disciplines.

For example, within psychology the behaviourist approach embodied in the laboratory experiments on television violence has largely given way to approaches derived from cognitive psychology.[14] Here, children are seen to be actively constructing meaning from the media rather than simply passively receiving it. They are described as 'cognitive processors', who interpret and evaluate what they watch in the light of their prior knowledge, both of the world in general and of the media in particular.

Likewise, in the case of sociology, the notion of 'direct effects' came increasingly to be questioned as researchers turned their attention to the role of 'intervening variables' (such as the family or the peer group) and acknowledged the significance of 'individual differences'. This led in turn to the advent of 'uses and gratifications' research in the early 1960s, which appeared to make a similar shift towards the notion of the 'active reader'. According to this approach, readers were seen to be actively selecting and using media for their own diverse needs and purposes – for example, as a means of 'escape' from difficult social relationships, or alternatively as a source of information, relaxation or social contact.[15]

Despite the apparent advances of these approaches, there remain significant limitations. Both embody implicit norms of purposeful or mature audience behaviour, against which the understandings of younger audiences tend to be judged and found wanting. Within cognitive psychology, the 'affective' and the 'cognitive' dimensions of media use have been considered as separate, and the former have tended to be neglected. Developmental theories are used to define a rigid series of ages and stages through which children progress as they move towards 'adult' rationality: the child is regarded as a 'deficit system', as more or less incompetent when compared with adult norms. While uses and gratifications research has acknowledged the emotional aspects of media use, it implicitly presumes that readers are self-conscious of their needs, and that needs can be matched against gratifications in a wholly purposeful way. It thus inevitably neglects the possibility of 'unconscious' needs, and the fact that at least some media use may not reflect predetermined needs.

Furthermore, both approaches tend to neglect the social characteristics of audiences and the social contexts and processes of media use. Cognitive psychology predominantly defines 'the child' in ahistorical, asocial terms, with social factors such as class, 'race' and gender only coming into play once the already-formed individual enters the social world. Likewise, very little uses and gratifications research – at least in the USA – pays much attention to social differences, except in the form of 'demographic variables'.[16] Readers are seen as free-floating individuals, possessing inherent psychological needs which vary according to their 'personality types' – an approach which often appears to be little more social than the psychological notion of the reader as an individual 'cognitive processor'. It is in this sense that uses and gratifications research can justifiably be accused of 'psychologizing the social'.[17] In both cases, the 'activity' of audiences is seen in essentially individualistic terms.

Ultimately, then, the relationship between young people and the media has been defined by mainstream academic research as a *psychological* issue – as it was to a large extent by Plato. It is a matter of what the media do to young people's minds – or, more recently, what their minds do with the media. Young people are implicitly regarded here as somehow asocial – or perhaps pre-social – beings. They are merely on their way to becoming something else, something finished. 'The child' is thus defined in relation to 'adult' norms, and in terms of what it cannot do, rather than what it does. Yet, as in the public debates I have considered above, young people are also seen as inherently 'other', and the potential

9

dangers their difference represents have to be incorporated into a rational, cohesive social order. In the process, young people's lived social experiences, and their own voices and perspectives, have effectively been ignored.

Texts, audiences, contexts

The research described in this book emerges from a rather different tradition, although it is one that has seen similar developments to those described above. The main origins of academic Media Studies in this country in fact lie in the discipline of literary criticism – although it has subsequently embraced a complex and occasionally bewildering series of theoretical approaches, including semiotics, Marxist theory, structuralism, post-structuralism and psychoanalysis.[18]

The dominant paradigm within academic Media Studies in the 1970s – which has come to be termed 'Screen theory' – in fact displayed little if any interest in media audiences. This psychoanalytic version of structuralism sought to define the ways in which the film text 'produces' the subjectivity of the spectator, by constructing 'subject positions' from which it is to be read. The emphasis here was primarily on the psychic dynamics of film spectatorship: the act of viewing was defined in terms of psychoanalytic processes such as scopophilia, voyeurism and fetishism, rather than in social terms.[19] According to this approach the language of dominant cinema (for example, 'classical' continuity editing) 'sutured' (or literally 'stitched') the spectator into the text, and thereby into the 'dominant ideology' – a process which the spectator was seen as largely powerless to resist.

During the late 1970s and early 1980s, Screen theory came under attack from a number of directions, for its neglect of the political economy of the media, its reliance on the 'patriarchal' psychoanalytic theories of Freud and Lacan, and its privileging of the elite avant-garde.[20] However, perhaps the most damaging limitation of Screen theory from the point of view of audience research was its exclusive emphasis on texts – and in this respect at least, there is a considerable degree of continuity with the literary origins from which it emerged. While the analytic methods developed by Screen theory were much more sophisticated than the statistical content analysis favoured by most US researchers, both approaches tended to assume that the meanings identified by critics would be 'swallowed whole' by audiences. Screen theory, it was argued,[21] tended to conflate the 'inscribed' reader, constructed by the text, with real readers, living in real social and historical formations.

It was David Morley's study, *The 'Nationwide' Audience*,[22] that represented the most significant shift towards an engagement with real – as opposed to 'inscribed' – audiences. Morley's work derived from the more sociological perspective of 'Cultural Studies', developed initially at the University of Birmingham Centre for Contemporary Cultural Studies.[23] Drawing on previous analysis of an early evening television news magazine programme,[24] Morley identified some of the ways in which the text sought to promote a 'preferred' reading which was in line with the 'dominant ideology' – for example, in how items were framed and defined, the kinds of people chosen as 'experts' or 'ordinary people', and how studio discussions and interviews were conducted. The readings of viewers drawn from a broad range of social and occupational groups were then classified in terms of the degree to which this preferred reading was accepted, negotiated or rejected.

In retrospect, the significance of this work lies more in its critique of *Screen* theory, rather than in the empirical study itself – which, as Morley and others have acknowledged, suffers several limitations.[25] Morley claimed that *Screen* theory amounted to a form of 'textual determinism', in which the audience was 'reduced to the status of an automated puppet pulled by the strings of the text'. He argued that the viewer was 'interpellated', not by a single 'dominant ideology', but by multiple discourses – brought into play by virtue of the subject's other social, cultural and institutional experiences – which were diverse and potentially contradictory. The viewer was not only a 'subject of the text', but a social subject with multiple 'subjectivities'.

Morley's work effectively paved the way for a series of empirical studies of television audiences, both in relation to news and other non-fictional genres,[26] and increasingly in relation to television fiction, particularly soap opera.[27] While such studies have certainly emphasised the diversity of audience readings, they have typically combined this with detailed study of the texts themselves. More recently, however, there has been a growing emphasis on research into the domestic viewing context, using broadly 'ethnographic' methods:[28] here, the focus of study has shifted away from readings of specific texts, towards the nature of television viewing as an activity, and the social relations which surround and constitute it. Yet despite the focus on family groups, the specific nature of young people's uses and experiences of the media has remained largely neglected here.[29]

Youth culture

Nevertheless, within the broader field of Cultural Studies, there is a tradition of work on 'youth culture', which is drawn upon in a number of the contributions included in this book. This research attempted to recast dominant sociological explanations of young people's transition to adulthood embodied within theories of 'secondary socialisation'. Rather than regarding youth culture merely in pathological terms, as a matter of 'deviance' or 'delinquency', it sought to emphasise its political potential as a form of resistance to adult authority and to dominant social norms – while acknowledging that in other respects, it may have served to reinforce these. The focus of this research, then, has been on the ways in which particular forms of cultural expression (for example, fashion, music and 'style') and the social activities that surround them offer opportunities for young people actively and collectively to construct their own social identities.[30] Youth subcultures were seen to offer 'magical' solutions to the real, inherent contradictions of the socio-economic system, particularly as experienced by working-class youth; yet they were also seen to enable young people to develop self-images that allowed them to 'escape' – however temporarily – from their pre-determined class position.

As a number of critics have noted, this research on youth culture has been quite narrowly focused. The emphasis on 'spectacular' working-class youth cultures has led to a comparative neglect of the more ordinary, everyday cultural activities in which the vast majority of young people participate.[31] At least in the 1970s, the more domestic (and thus less immediately 'visible') cultures of girls were neglected in favour of male street cultures – and male researchers were accused of glamourising their 'machismo', while ignoring their inherent sexism and racism.[32] 'Race' and cultural difference also appeared rather belatedly on the research agenda, and again with a focus on more 'spectacular' subcultures at the expense of others.[33] Finally, much of this research concentrates on 'youth' – and in effect, on teenagers – while tending to neglect the social and cultural worlds of younger children: here again, it is as though children have implicitly been regarded as pre-social. The 'sociology of childhood' remains an underdeveloped – although emergent – area of study,[34] and the problematic issue of 'children's culture' has barely begun to be explored.

Although studies of youth culture have concentrated in some detail on particular media forms – notably, of course, popular music – others have tended to be neglected. While this may reflect the relative lack of significance of the media in the lives of older teenagers (they are, for example, the age group that watches the *least* broadcast television), it again reflects a neglect of the 'ordinary' in favour of the 'spectacular'. On the other hand, however, these studies do point to the need to situate young people's media use within the context of their other social activities and experiences. The media are seen here, not as a powerful source of dominant ideologies, but on the contrary as a 'symbolic resource' which young people use in making sense of their experiences, in relating to others and in organising their daily lives. The media offer material for experimentation with alternative social identities, if only at the level of fantasy or aspiration – although of course the identities and perspectives they make available are far from neutral. To this extent, therefore, there may be a growing convergence between work on media audiences and work on youth culture within the Cultural Studies tradition: this is certainly reflected in many of the contributions here, and it will be taken up in more detail in my conclusion.

The situated audience: possibilities and problems

As a framework for studying young people's relationships with the media, the approach developed within Media and Cultural Studies appears to have a number of advantages when compared with those described earlier. At least in principle, it offers an alternative to the psychological notion of young people as individual 'cognitive processors', while also avoiding the danger of regarding them merely as representatives of given demographic categories. On the contrary, this approach *situates* media use within the wider context of social relationships and activities, which are by definition diverse and particular. In this respect, 'being an audience' (or a member of an audience) is seen as a *social practice*, not as a fixed state of existence: it is something you *do* rather than something you *are*.

While this approach has much in common with the notion of the 'active reader', it does offer a more complex view of meaning, and of media texts themselves. Rather than regarding meaning as something contained within the text, it draws attention to the possibility of ambiguity and contradiction. While the text might 'prefer' or 'invite' a particular reading, and thus prevent or restrict others, it might also invite multiple readings – although the limitations and the ideological consequences of that diversity cannot be guaranteed or determined in advance. At the same time, readers are not seen simply as free-floating individuals, able to make meanings of their own choosing. Reading will inevitably rely upon established strategies for making meaning, and on orientations and expectations about texts, which are socially shared. The discourses – or ways of defining and making sense of the world – which are available to readers, and which are brought into play by the text, are not infinite, nor are they equally available to all. Readers do indeed make meanings, but they do so under conditions which are not of their own choosing.

This, at least, is the theory. In practice, audience research within Media and Cultural Studies has often been caught in an uneasy tension between perspectives that proclaim 'the power of the reader' and those that insist on 'the power of the text'. In recent years, this tension has resulted in a great deal of unproductive theoretical debate, in which positions have become unduly polarised, and there has been a considerable degree of mutual caricature. The recent work of John Fiske – which has widely (and to some extent unfairly) been seen to celebrate 'the power of the audience' at the expense of 'the power of the text' – has precipitated a kind of counter-reaction, in which audience study has been equated with a kind of simple-minded populism.[35] Yet the problem with this debate (and, it must be acknowledged, with some of Fiske's own work) is that it has been conducted primarily at the level of abstract polemic. Despite the renewed emphasis on 'real audiences', there remains a remarkable lack of detailed, empirical work in the field. Cultural Studies appears to have developed its own form of 'common-sense wisdom' about audiences on the basis of very limited evidence: small-scale studies have been made to carry much broader theoretical implications than their authors would claim, and findings which relate to very specific aspects of media use have been taken as evidence for much broader generalisations.[36]

One of the aims of this book is to help rectify this imbalance, by offering detailed analyses of specific audience groups, and of their readings of particular media forms or texts. While these studies are inevitably informed by broader theories of the 'power' of the media, they regard that power not as a *possession* either of texts or of audiences, but as something which is embedded in the *relationship* between them.[37] Power is, in this sense, not something which can be identified in the abstract, or apportioned according to some generalised theoretical equation. On the contrary, it is very much an empirical issue, that needs to be addressed in relation to specific audiences, specific media and specific social contexts of use.

In the case of research on young people and the media, these points have two additional implications. Firstly, they should caution us against a view of young people as a unitary or homogeneous social group, with specific psychological characteristics. Most obviously, this involves paying close attention to gender, 'race' and social class, although we need to avoid regarding these simply as 'demographic variables'. On the contrary, we need to consider the diverse ways in which young people themselves construct the *meanings* of those differences, and how they are defined and mobilised in different social contexts.

Yet the same is true of age itself. As sociologists and historians have shown, childhood is not merely a biological phenomenon, or a particular state on the way to physical maturation:[38] it has been constructed in very different ways in different cultures and in different historical periods. What it means to be a child (or a youth, or indeed an adult) is the subject of a constant process of negotiation, both between adults and children and between children themselves. Likewise, as some psychologists have now begun to acknowledge, 'development' cannot adequately be understood without situating it within the social contexts and relationships in which it occurs, and which essentially bring it about.[39] Age is, in this sense, a *social* category, not merely a biological one and it interacts with other social categories in complex and diverse ways.

Furthermore, while it may make sense to talk about 'youth culture' or 'children's culture' as somehow separate and distinct, these cultures are not hermetically sealed. On the contrary, they are formed through their relationships with the dominant 'adult cultures', and through the institutional contexts in which – and against which – they occur. As many of these studies will indicate, young people's use of the media is heavily determined by its regulation by adults such as parents and teachers, and by the more distant control of the State. However successful young people may be in their struggle to avoid this kind of regulation, the meanings and pleasures they derive from the media are bound to be at least partly defined by it.

The second issue here concerns our own position as adult researchers, and indeed as adult readers. Perhaps to a greater extent than in other forms of social research, the relationship between adult researchers and their young subjects is bound to be unequal. While we may seek to reduce this power differential – for example, by attempting to appear extremely knowledgeable about what young people enjoy – it can never be completely eliminated.[40] Children are inevitably 'other', and any attempt to speak on their behalf is bound to be highly problematic. As Matthew Speier has argued:

> [traditionally] sociologists have been going about their study of children mainly like colonial administrators who might be expected to write scientifically objective reports of the local populace in order to increase their understanding of native culture, and who do so by ideologically formulating only those research problems that pertain to native behaviours coming under the regulation of colonial authority.[41]

While researchers in Cultural Studies have generally attempted to avoid this approach, they have sometimes gone to the opposite extreme. In the case of research on youth culture, for example, the attempt to identify oneself with the 'other' has occasionally led to a romanticisation of forms of 'resistance' which are politically far from progressive. As Simon Frith has noted,[42] this celebratory approach may hold a particular attraction for intellectuals and academics: identifying oneself with 'the kids' and thereby seeking to proclaim one's own street credibility is undoubtedly an occupational hazard, but it is one that holds significant dangers. In the case of younger children, it is often hard for researchers (and their readers) to avoid a Wordsworthian marvelling at children's innate wisdom and sophistication, or a vicarious identification with their anarchic – but nevertheless terribly cute – rejection of adult norms. The difficulty many adults experience in listening to children without patronising them is a direct consequence of their own power.[43] This questioning of the relationship between the researcher and the researched has recently been the focus of considerable debate within ethnography and Cultural Studies,[44] and is reflected in many of the studies included here.

An overview of the contributions

While the contributions collected in this book all derive from the Cultural Studies perspectives outlined above, they are extremely diverse, both in terms of the areas of study and the broader theoretical issues which are raised. Neither 'young people' nor 'the media' are here seen as homogeneous categories. On the contrary, the contributions cover a broad range of media – including television, video, comics and popular fiction; and they investigate very different audience groups, in terms of age, gender, ethnicity and social class. The focus throughout is on the *specific* and highly *situated* nature of particular young people's interactions with particular media forms or texts. The studies are largely based on small-scale qualitative research, and on the detailed analysis of spoken or written data. Nevertheless, in many instances, they form part of broader, longer-term research projects, of which the present contributions represent necessarily brief instances.

Across the eight chapters included here, a number of shared themes emerge. Many of the pieces address the domestic contexts of media use, and consider how young people's access to the media is regulated and controlled by parents and other adults. The role of the peer group, and the ways in which the meanings of young people's experience of the media are established and circulated within it, are also a central focus of study. In many instances, gender is very much the central issue here, although the role of the media in helping to construct gendered identities is seen as a complex and contradictory process, in which young people themselves are far from passive victims. In this respect, many of the contributions seek to re-frame broader public anxieties which surround and define young people's use of the media – and in particular the recurrent preoccupation with sex and violence. In addition, for many of the contributors, the question of *what* we know about young people cannot be separated from that of *how* we know: many of the pieces reflect directly on the practice of research itself, and the relationships between adult researchers and the young people whom they study. Broadly speaking, the book moves outwards from the domestic context to the peer group and thence to the wider field of 'youth culture' – although, as many of the contributors acknowledge, these fields should not necessarily be seen as separate or distinct.

Chris Richards's chapter 'Taking sides? What young girls do with television' considers the domestic use of television and television-related material by young girls, and its role in their acquisition of gendered subjectivity. The chapter analyses detailed examples of girls' readings of television, and of the ways in which they make sense of material they find frightening; yet it also seeks to situate these within a broader account of their social relationships, both with each other and with their parents and friends, in which girls are actively seen to choose 'feminine' tastes and identities.

In 'The *Mahabharata*: from Sanskrit to sacred soap' (Chapter 3), Marie Gillespie offers an ethnographic account of the use and interpretation of two televised versions of one of the foundation myths of Indian society, by the children of a Hindu family in Southall, West London. The chapter analyses how the viewing of the *Mahabharata* is integrated into domestic time; how specific religious rituals accompany the viewing of such 'sacred' texts; and how its moral code and philosophy are perceived and incorporated into the everyday lives of the children, thereby serving to maintain Hindu norms and values within the wider context of British society.

Valerie Walkerdine's chapter 'Daddy's gonna buy you a dream to cling to ...' (written with the assistance of June Melody) is also concerned with family viewing, although in a different context again. Using a psychoanalytic approach, this chapter explores the simultaneously psychic and social processes which are involved in one working-class family's viewing of the film *Annie*. Walkerdine argues against the 'pathologisation' of working-class viewing practices, which she detects in previous psychological research, and raises challenging questions about the role of research as a form of voyeuristic surveillance.

In 'Boys' talk: television and the policing of masculinity' (Chapter 5), I consider some of the ways in which boys negotiate definitions of their own masculinity in discussing popular film and television. The chapter describes some general findings from a broader research project, setting these within the context of recent debates about masculinity, and goes on to consider detailed case studies of two discussion groups. By analysing the discursive strategies which are employed here, the chapter seeks to identify some of the ways in which definitions of masculinity are put at risk, as well as policed and reinforced.

In Chapter 6, entitled 'Girls tell the teen romance', Gemma Moss focuses on how girls understand the place for popular romantic fiction alongside other kinds of reading. Drawing on interviews with twelve-year-old romance readers, it shows where romance fits in a social system of reading based on contrasts between adult and child, male and female, 'soppy' and 'dirty' forms of fiction. Moss offers a broader argument for the importance of addressing young people's reading histories, in which their understanding of reading as a social practice mediates the meanings they make from texts.

'Untidy, depressing and violent: a boy's own story' (Chapter 7), by Julian Sefton-Green, examines the ways in which boys' fictional writings appropriate the imagery and narrative forms of popular cultural genres. Based on a detailed analysis of a single story, it explores the narrative pleasure provided by films such as *The Terminator* and comics such as *Death's Head* and their role in boys' construction of their own masculine identities. In common with the other studies included here, the role of the media in young people's acquisition of gendered subjectivity is seen not as a process of 'conditioning', but as a matter of considerable tension and uncertainty.

In 'Seeing how far you can see: on being a "fan" of 2000 AD' (Chapter 8), Martin Barker considers how readers relate to the comic 2000 AD and its anti-heroic central figure Judge Dredd. Based on a questionnaire and three detailed case studies of 'fans', it explores the meanings imputed to Dredd, the way the comic and its stories relate to other activities, and readers' perceptions of the relationship between fiction and reality. This analysis is framed by a broader argument, based on historical and textual analysis, about the comic as a subcultural response to changing perceptions of the contemporary socio-economic climate.

'Repeatable pleasures: notes on young people's use of video' by Julian Wood (Chapter 9) raises questions about the specific characteristics of video viewing as a social practice, particularly among working-class teenage boys. Through an account of data gathered through participant observation and an analysis of interview material, the chapter examines young people's responses to adult regulation, by both parents and censors. It considers the possibility that adult regulation may have unintended consequences, in constructing a notion of 'forbidden fruit', against which children may be encouraged to test themselves.

Finally, in 'Re-reading audiences' (Chapter 10), I consider some of the broader implications of these studies in terms of future research in the area, and in relation to education. Developing some of the broad themes raised in the different contributions, this chapter emphasises the limitations of a merely 'celebratory' approach to young people's use of the media, and argues for the importance of detailed empirical study. It also points to the need for a more considered basis for teaching about the media, which acknowledges the complexity and diversity of young people's experience, while also enabling them to reflect systematically upon this, and to move beyond it. In this respect, we hope that the contributions contained in this book will come to inform future developments, not merely within academic research, but also in the educational lives of the majority of young people themselves.

Notes and references

1 Plato, *The Republic*, trans. Desmond Lee, 2nd ed (revised) (London, Penguin, 1987), II. 377–8.

2 For John Patten's comments, see the *Sun*, 14 May 1991; on the study of popular television in schools, see the *Mail on Sunday*, 24 May 1992 and the *Daily Mail*, *passim*; for the text of Peter Dawson's comments (from the *Guardian*, 2 August 1989), see Peter Fraser, 'How do teachers and students talk about television?', in David Buckingham (ed.) *Watching Media Learning: Making Sense of Media Education* (London, Falmer, 1990).

3 On Mary Whitehouse, see Michael Tracey and David Morrison, *Whitehouse* (London, Macmillan, 1979); on Prince Charles, see David Buckingham, *Children Talking Television* (Falmer, 1993), Chapter One.

4 For example, Geoffrey Pearson, 'Falling standards: a short, sharp history of moral decline', in Martin Barker (ed.), *The Video Nasties* (London, Pluto, 1984); David Lusted, 'A history of suspicion: educational attitudes to television', in D. Lusted and P. Drummond (eds), *TV and Schooling* (London, British Film Institute, 1985).

5 On children, see Martin Barker, *Comics: Ideology, Power and the Critics* (Manchester University Press, 1989); on teenagers, see Iain Chambers, *Urban Rhythms* (London, Macmillan, 1985).

6 For further discussion, see Buckingham, *Children Talking Television*. On 'Americanization', see Dick Hebdige, 'Towards a cartography of taste 1935–1962', in B. Waites, T. Bennett and G. Martin (eds) *Popular Culture Past and Present* (London, Croom Helm/Open University Press, 1982). There are certainly historical parallels here with the moral panic over 'horror comics' in the 1950s, which united the moral right and the Communist Party in a shared concern over the evils of American culture: see Martin Barker, *A Haunt of Fears* (London, Pluto , 1984). A contemporary example, in relation to adults, would be the alliance between some feminists and the 'moral majority' in opposition to pornography: see Lynne Segal and Mary McIntosh (eds), *Sex Exposed: Sexuality and the Pornography Debate* (London, Virago, 1992).

7 Ian Connell argues that this is the case for many on the Left in his piece 'Fabulous powers: blaming the media', in L. Masterman (ed.), *Television Mythologies* (London, Comedia/MK Media, 1985).

8 This research has been amply reviewed elsewhere. See, for example, David Buckingham, *Children and Television: An Overview of the Research*, mimeo (London, British Film Institute, 1987); Guy Cumberbatch and Denis Howitt, *A Measure of Uncertainty: The Effects of the Mass Media* (London, John Libbey, 1989).

9 For one of the most uncompromising statements of this position, see H. J. Eysenck and D. K. B. Nias, *Sex, Violence and the Media* (London, Maurice Temple Smith, 1978).

10 See Barrie Gunter, *Dimensions of Television Violence* (Aldershot, Gower, 1985) for an interesting investigation of this issue.

11 For examples and criticisms of this approach, see Chris Jenks (ed.), *The Sociology of Childhood: Essential Readings* (London, Batsford, 1982).

12 See Byron Reeves and Ellen Wartella, 'Historical trends in research on children and the media, 1900–1960', *Journal of Communication*, 35: 2 (1985), 118–33.

13 This development is traced in many of the standard histories of mass communication research, such as Denis McQuail, *Mass Communication Theory: An Introduction*, 2nd edn. (London, Sage, 1987) and Melvin de Fleur and Susan Ball-Rokeach, *Theories of Mass Communication* (London, Longman, 1982). The concept of the 'active reader' remains ill-defined, however, and often appears to amount to little more than a slogan.

14 For reviews of this area of research, see Aimée Dorr, *Television and Children: A Special Medium for a Special Audience* (Beverley Hills, Sage, 1986) and Jennings Bryant and Daniel R. Anderson (eds), *Children's Understanding of Television* (New York, Academic, 1983).

15 For examples of this research in relation to children, see Ray Brown (ed.), *Children and Television* (London, Collier Macmillan, 1976).

16 This is much less the case, however, with British uses and gratifications research, which draws on sub-cultural theory: see, for example, R. Dembo and R. McCron, 'Social factors in media use', in Brown (ed.), *Children and Television*.

17 See Carmen Luke, *Constructing the Child Viewer: A History of the American Discourse on Television and Children, 1950–1980* (New York, Praeger, 1990).

18 For summaries of these developments, see Rosalind Coward and John Ellis, *Language and Materialism* (London, Routledge and Kegan Paul, 1977) and Kaja Silverman, *The Subject of Semiotics* (Oxford, Oxford University Press, 1983).

19 Annette Kuhn, in her piece 'Women's genres' (*Screen*, 25: 1 (1984), 18–28) makes a useful distinction here between notions of spectatorship, embodied in film theory, and notions of the 'social reader' in television research.

20 For instances of these arguments, see respectively Nicholas Garnham, 'Subjectivity, ideology, class and historical materialism', *Screen*, 20: 1 (1979), 121–33; Jane Gallop, *Feminism and Psychoanalysis: The Daughter's Seduction* (London, Macmillan, 1982); and Sylvia Harvey, *May '68 and Film Theory* (London, British Film Institute, 1978).

21 Notably by Paul Willemen in 'Notes on subjectivity: on reading Edward Branigan's "Subjectivity Under Siege"', *Screen*, 19: 1 (1978), 41–69.

22 David Morley, *The 'Nationwide' Audience* (London, British Film Institute, 1980).

23 For overviews and histories of this area, see Stuart Hall *et al.* (eds), *Culture, Media, Language* (London, Hutchinson, 1980); and Graeme Turner, *British Cultural Studies: An Introduction* (London, Unwin Hyman, 1990).

24 Charlotte Brunsdon and David Morley, *Everyday Television: 'Nationwide'* (London, British Film Institute, 1978).

25 See David Morley, 'The *Nationwide* Audience: a critical postscript', *Screen Education*, 39 (1981), 3–14; Justin Wren-Lewis, 'The encoding/decoding model: criticisms and redevelopments for research on decoding', *Media, Culture and Society*, 5: 2 (1983), 179–97; and Martin Jordin and Ros Brunt, 'Constituting the television audience: a problem of method', in P. Drummond and R. Paterson (eds), *Television and its Audience: International Research Perspectives* (London, British Film Institute, 1988).

26 For example, Justin Wren-Lewis, 'Decoding television news', in P. Drummond and R. Paterson (eds.), *Television in Transition* (London, British Film Institute, 1985); John Corner, Kay Richardson and Natalie Fenton, *Nuclear Reactions* (London, John Libbey, 1991); Greg Philo, *Seeing and Believing: The Influence of Television* (London, Routledge, 1990).

27 For example, Dorothy Hobson, *'Crossroads': The Drama of a Soap Opera* (London, Methuen, 1982); Ien Ang, *Watching 'Dallas': Soap Opera and the Melodramatic Imagination* (London, Methuen 1985); David Buckingham, *Public Secrets: 'EastEnders' and its Audience* (London, British Film Institute, 1987).

28 For example, David Morley and Roger Silverstone, 'Domestic communication: technologies and meanings', *Media, Culture and Society*, 13: 1 (1990), 31–55; James Lull (ed.), *World Families Watch Television* (Newbury Park, CA, Sage, 1988); James Lull, *Inside Family Viewing* (London, Routledge, 1990).'Ethnographic' is a term which has become extremely fashionable in media research in recent years, yet is in my view often misused. Very little media audience research is based on the kind of long-term immersion in the lives of particular cultural groups that is traditionally associated with ethnography in the field of anthropology. Marie Gillespie's study in this volume, however, does represent an instance of this kind of research.

29 The major exceptions to this are Patricia Palmer's study, *The Lively Audience* (Sydney, Allen and Unwin, 1986), which adopts a symbolic interactionist approach; and Bob Hodge and David Tripp's important and influential book *Children and Television: A Semiotic Approach* (Cambridge, Polity, 1986), which is an ambitious attempt to unite some very diverse theoretical perspectives.

30 See, for example, Stuart Hall and Tony Jefferson (eds), *Resistance Through Rituals: Youth Subcultures in Post-War Britain* (London, Hutchinson, 1975); Mike Brake, *The Sociology of Youth Culture and Youth Subcultures* (London, Routledge and Kegan Paul, 1980); Angela McRobbie and Mica Nava, *Gender and Generation* (London, Macmillan, 1985).

31 See Gary Clarke, 'Defending Ski-jumpers: A Critique of Theories of Youth Subcultures', stencilled occasional paper, (University of Birmingham Centre for Contemporary Cultural Studies, 1982).

32 See Angela McRobbie, 'Settling accounts with subcultures: a feminist critique', *Screen Education*, 34 (1980), 37–49.

33 See Centre for Contemporary Cultural Studies, *The Empire Strikes Back: Race and Racism in 70s Britain* (London, Hutchinson, 1982).

34 See Chris Jenks, *Sociology of Childhood*, and Allison James and Alan Prout (eds), *Constructing and Reconstructing Childhood: Contemporary Issues in the Sociological Study of Childhood* (London, Falmer, 1990).

35 See John Fiske, *Television Culture* (London, Methuen, 1987) and, among others, Jim Bee, 'First citizen of the semiotic democracy?' *Cultural Studies* 3: 3 (1989), 353–9; Meaghan Morris, 'Banality in Cultural Studies', in Patrician Mellencamp (ed.), *Logics of Television: Essays in Cultural Criticism* (London, British Film Institute, 1990); and Alan O'Shea, Television as culture: not just texts and readers', *Media, Culture and Society*, 11 (1989), 373–9. These criticisms are, however, more fairly applicable to Fiske's more recent work, for example *Understanding Popular Culture* and *Reading the Popular* (both London, Unwin Hyman, 1989). See Martin Barker's review in *The Magazine of Cultural Studies*, 1 (1990), 39–40. For a discussion, see Buckingham, *Children Talking Television*, Chapter Eleven.

36 This is, in my view, particularly true of the reception of David Morley's *Family Television* (London, Comedia, 1986), which has been seen to support some enormous and highly problematic generalisations about the different ways in which men and women use television.

37 In a sense, this represents a move towards a Foucauldian conception of power: see, for example, Michel Foucault, *Power/Knowledge*, ed. C. Gordon (Brighton, Harvester, 1980).

38 For example, Philippe Ariès, *Centuries of Childhood* (Harmondsworth, Penguin, 1973); Lloyd de Mause (ed.), *The History of Childhood* (New York, Souvenir, 1974); and James and Prout (eds), *Constructing and Reconstructing Childhood*.

39 See, for example, Valerie Walkerdine, *The Mastery of Reason* (London, Routledge, 1989); Martin Richards and Paul Light (eds), *Children of Social Worlds* (Cambridge, Polity, 1986).

40 This point is well made by G. A. Fine and B. Glassner in 'Participant observation with children: promise and problems', *Urban Life*, 8: 2 (1979), 153–74.

41 Matthew Speier, 'The child as conversationalist: some culture contact features of conversational interactions between adults and children', in M. Hammersley and P. Woods (eds), *The Process of Schooling* (London, Routledge and Kegan Paul/Open University Press, 1976).

42 Simon Frith 'The cultural study of popular music', in Lawrence Grossberg, Cary Nelson and Paula Treichler (eds), *Cultural Studies* (London, Routledge, 1992).

43 Perhaps the most strongly felt – and almost chastening – critique of adult power over children remains Shulamith Firestone's account in *The Dialectic of Sex* (London, Cape, 1971).

44 See J. Clifford and G. E. Marcus (eds), *Writing Culture: The Poetics and Politics of Ethnography* (Berkeley, University of California Press, 1986). Examples in television audience research include Valerie Walkerdine's influential piece 'Video replay: families, films and fantasy', in V. Burgin, J. Donald and C. Kaplan (eds), *Formations of Fantasy* (London, Routledge and Kegan Paul 1986); and Ellen Seiter, 'Making distinctions in TV audience research: case study of a troubling interview', *Cultural Studies*, 4:1 (1990), 61–84.

Taking sides? What young girls do with television

> the differential entry of men and of women into language and into semiosis has a real history, a history of specific experiences in particular social institutions ... a history which may also be a significantly differentiated one for different individuals from differing social origins. At any rate it is not the pseudohistory posited in asocial, ahistorical psychoanalytic accounts. The entry into semiosis has that institutional specificity, a specificity which attends to class, gender, ethnicity. Children's construction of meaning, their reconstruction of texts, their construction of their semiotic systems always takes place in contexts of this kind, not in some decontextualised or contextless fantasy of 'childhood'.
>
> Robert Hodge and Gunther Kress, *Social Semiotics*[1]

This chapter is concerned with the way in which young girls talk about television in the midst of family life. An interest in the domestic contexts of television use has been prominent in recent research. However, to have access to children, away from school classrooms, has often been difficult for researchers. To make formal approaches to families through the parents often results in adults emerging as the dominant, almost exclusive, 'informants'.[2] For the purposes of this study, therefore, I have resorted to my own immediate familial situation as one which could be considered somewhat from within, if also from a position of difference, distance and uncertainty. What I write here will remain tentative and partial. I have not assumed some already secure and privileged knowledge of the everyday world of my own daughters: however familiar, it remains puzzling and sometimes obscure.

What I document here may contribute to a broader understanding of 'cultures of childhood'. However, it should perhaps be read more specifically as evidence of one such 'culture' – that of middle-class girls, less than ten years old in 1991, and attending a school which, though ethnically diverse, is broadly, if not exclusively middle-class. The institutional setting is that of a 'nuclear' family, geographically separated from any consistent involvement with others belonging to the familial network. This household is, of course, middle-class and is located in a relatively affluent middle-class area of north London: most neighbouring households are sustained by people who belong to the professional middle class. The street, and the immediate area, is almost exclusively white. For both my daughters, current friendships have been made through their school and, in that context, with other children occupying broadly similar social positions. As both their parents are employed full-time in higher education, there is some intermittent dependence on various forms of 'domestic help' – references to young women employed as part-time cleaners and childminders occasionally enter into the talk recorded here. Some material is also derived from the girls' friendship networks though this draws in more, mainly middle-class, girls and virtually no boys at all.

My title, 'Taking sides?', by posing a question, defines the concerns of this chapter in terms which are tentative, suggesting possible understandings of what I describe. There is, I suggest, the taking of sides in the divisions of gender: here girls take up the 'side' of girls, explicitly, forcefully, and unambiguously. There is also the taking of sides within a familial nexus of power relationships; this often involves negotiations of what are perceived to be parental positions, but is also a matter of sisters defining their relation to each other across an age gap of more than four years and from within quite distinct age/friendship groups. Broadly, my intention is to consider how children use television and other media in their enactment and exploration of possible identities. However, the emphasis is on how these girls use television and not on how television, as a medium, or as a diversity of programmes and genres, simply positions them. The rhetorical force of television as it is invoked in girls' engagements with each other is of central concern.

It is a familiar method of domestic television research to conduct interviews, with varying degrees of pre-planning and perhaps contrived informality. I have used this approach and have complemented it with being around, noting what I could through listening and observation. This is a diffuse and discontinuous process and could be compared to the lengthy commitment involved in forms of ethnographic enquiry. My own prior experience of taking up the position of participant observer in a domestic context comes from living in a Japanese village, in Kyushu – being around people's homes and participating in their lives, and taking photographs, was a regular part of my daily life for a period of six months. It is a difficult and contradictory activity because it feels intrusive even when invited, parasitic though hospitality is offered and, particularly with a camera in hand, like a form of surveillance and appropriation despite photography's place as a part of the popular cultural practice of the people concerned. At first, I thought of the present task as different because I am not a stranger to the people with whom I live and do not relate to them as members of a different and 'exotic' culture. But of course forms of estrangement, of distancing and of appropriation enter into even the most intimate relations and become accentuated when the purposes of those involved are not shared, not common, not even mutually understood. Documenting the familial lives of children (those I live with or any others) and thus making their lives an object of study and a part of the work that I do in a public, institutional domain of which they have only slight knowledge, cannot be made a matter of shared understanding and negotiation. What the meaning of this work might be for them is elusive; but in taking up positions in relation to my enquiries, they inevitably imply particular understandings of my intent and the frameworks in which it might 'make sense'.

I have attempted to enable the children involved to be more active subjects in the process of enquiry, engaged in a dialogue, reflecting on and to some extent investigating their own everyday practice. But I do not pretend that this eliminates the inequality of the social relations through which research gets done at all. Conducting interviews seemed at least to address children on terms more comparable to those which prevail where adults are made the respondents in research. It is usual to assume that adults possess the capacity for memory, self-reflection, rational self-knowledge, a capacity to distinguish between levels of reality and fantasy, and coherent verbal articulation – precisely those characteristics which young children are often thought to lack.[3]

Identity, gender, agency

One precedent for the research presented here comes out of an article by Myra Barrs, 'Maps of Play'.[4] Her study reports the play of a five-year-old boy over a period of several days and in the context of a holiday where other children were absent. The study draws on observation, on recorded audible speech, on the comments of a man with whom the boy played, and on the drawings which the boy produced in the course of his play. Barrs outlines aspects of his play which suggest how television cartoons are drawn into the boy's elaboration of a male self. In a further argument she pursues an emphasis on the constructive value of play, in this case invoking Vygotsky.[5] Barrs stresses the boy's active use of available characters and narrative elements in a process which is seen as combining an exploration of literacies with an assertive entitlement to male mastery. The implication of Barrs's study is that the formation of the boy's gender identity draws upon, but is not determined by, narratives in which male protagonists pursue quests and victories in conflict with other male figures. Here her stress on the active, self-constructive subject, seeking out and making choices of narrative material for himself, seems to confirm the boy hero in his fantasy. The energetic and almost obsessive pursuit of masculine forms is read, perhaps too unequivocally, as optimistic, confident and assertive.

Offering a different inflection, in her consideration of writing by an adolescent boy, Gemma Moss has argued that a preoccupation with violence and with overcoming enemies and threats suggests a more defensive masculinity, a fear and need to manage the consequences of being read as male in a social context where competition and the risk of violence between men prevails: 'behind the figure of the assertive and powerful male lurks the frightened adolescent peeping between the lines'.[6] Moss emphasises the way in which popular genres provide material for the exploration of being positioned as male or female. My own priority here is to hold open the possibility that activities or utterances which imply an unproblematic acceptance of gender positions might be more uncertain and complex. In a way, Barrs's stress on the active subject leads her to collude with the meanings masculinity claims for itself; Moss usefully opens up the notion of an active subject engaging with, but not simply reproducing, the meanings of a pre-existing genre.

There are, of course, some exceptionally complex issues to be negotiated in thinking through what might be meant by the 'active subject' where, otherwise, theories of social and cultural reproduction seem to bear down with undue authority. Elsewhere,[7] I have suggested that the tendency to hold the popular media responsible for the reproduction of rigidly demarcated gender identities can be challenged from a position informed by Nancy Chodorow's sociological reading of psychoanalysis.[8] Her view that what is most fundamental about the formation of gendered identity has its 'origins' in particular intra-familial relations, not in 'universal structures' and not just in the consumption of 'cultural stereotypes' offers a position from which to contest both the ahistorical tendencies of psychoanalysis and the simplistic determinism of some ideological analysis of texts. But there is a risk that Chodorow's argument represents forms of gendered subjectivity as settled so early in the lives of individuals that subsequent reworkings of the self through, for example, processes of reading and learning, appear merely superficial. The reproduction of gendered identities might thus seem even more inexorably determined. I want to retain the argument that gender identity is not so tenuous as we might wish and, equally, to emphasise that such identities have a deeply embedded history in particular social relations. However, it is also necessary, and hence this study, to investigate the relation between children's early assumption of gender positions and their engagement with gendered discourses present to them in their immediate familial scenes and beyond – to explore how individuals live through the particular social meanings of gender available to them.

Unwilling to 'write off' psychoanalytic perspectives in favour of either the simplifying determinism of some sociology or a common-sense humanism, I want to reference the discussion pursued by Anthony Giddens in *Central Problems in Social Theory*.[9] He proposes a 'stratification model' of personality, 'organised in terms of three sets of relations: the unconscious, practical consciousness, and discursive consciousness'. Giddens's model is an attempt to understand consciousness and agency as layered rather than moved by either, simply, the force of the unconscious or the discursive. He argues that:

> A 'stratified' model of personality, in which human wants are regarded as hierarchically connected, involving a basic security system largely inaccessible to the conscious subject, is not at all incompatible with an equivalent stress upon the significance of the reflexive monitoring of action, the latter becoming possible only following the 'positioning' of the actor in the Lacanian sense.[10]

The importance of this perspective here is to hold open questions of the relation between determination and agency, and to do so by questioning the customary exclusion of psychoanalysis from sociology.

From another position, within a feminism informed by Lacan, several writers have refused the perspective developed by Chodorow precisely because it appears to do no more than collapse psychoanalytic understandings of gender into familiar, and weak, sociological categories. Juliet Mitchell and Jacqueline Rose suggest that Chodorow produces too closed a notion of identity – of gender identities established and secure:

> displacing the concepts of the unconscious and bisexuality in favour of a notion of gender imprinting ('the establishment of an unambiguous and

unquestioned gender identity' ...) which is compatible with a sociological conception of role. Thus the problem needing to be addressed – the acquisition of sexual identity and its difficulty – is sidestepped in the account. The book sets itself to question sexual *roles*, but only within the limits of an assumed sexual *identity*.[11]

Valerie Walkerdine and Helen Lucey adopt a similarly critical view.[12] They argue that Chodorow wrongly assumes a set of real conditions to be defined and ameliorated and that she thus reiterates the 'guilt' of women held to be really responsible for what 'goes wrong' in the formation of their children. As elsewhere in Walkerdine's work, the category of 'fantasy' is of central importance – 'fantasy' as, at least, a powerful set of structures not amenable to change only through intervention in 'real conditions' informs an argument which refuses any easy politics of personal agency.[13] Despite what I take to be the relative pessimism of their account, I have found the emphasis they place on affectivity, on regulation, conflict and power to be of central importance in reading the transcripts which I consider here. But a different view of agency emerges from my reading – a view which implies that more sustained strategies of assertion are possible for young girls, though of course from positions of subordination.

Taking sides? – an 'interview'

Perhaps even the most oblique and seemingly 'unmarked' means of enquiry transform the meaning of otherwise routine social situations and constitute new relations and new positions for the participants. Certainly any attempt to record what people say defines the status of the talk as something other than ephemeral and inconsequential. To ask direct questions is to place 'respondents' and their replies as credible, coherent and worthwhile. Here I want to begin to identify some of the ways in which an attempt to ask direct questions about television was understood by Cesca, eight, and Fay, four: what kind of interaction is this, how is it understood and how, accordingly, do they position themselves and negotiate the positions they feel they should maintain? I recorded a conversation with both of my daughters on a Sunday morning, lying on the living room floor and using what is more often routinely referred to as 'the radio' rather than an unfamiliar tape-recorder. The situation seemed to me very informal, almost haphazard, with no prepared list of questions and no explicit articulation of my expectations. Nevertheless, it was known to both of them that I was interested in what they had to say about television and they had expected me to ask direct

questions of them and to record their comments. They also knew that
the interest had some basis in my work and that I might well incorporate
some of their responses in what I write. The term 'interview' as a means
to name the occasion for asking questions may well have been introduced by me but, whatever its source, it certainly became a frame for the
expectations of the elder girl. My initiating admonition may also have
underpinned and enlarged the implications of being 'interviewed':
'Speak properly because if you don't I can't hear you'. Thus, despite the
informality of the physical setting, they are immediately called upon to
be clear and articulate, to take this seriously; the situation is marked as
special. Cesca, particularly, engages with this and thus, towards the end
of the session, reminds Fay, and me, what this is about:

> Fay: But Daddy can we listen to ... the radio now? [Cesca sings]
> CR: You want to listen to it.
> Cesca: Fay but Daddy's interviewing.
> CR: I'm not I'm just chatting to you.
> Cesca: Why are you putting it on tape then? ... you said we are ...

Throughout the session Cesca also appears anxious to be the provider of
reliable and coherent answers and seems also to take it upon herself to
speak for Fay, whom she positions as too young to engage properly with
the questions. But she is also sometimes a little ill-at-ease and, for
example, apologises in a whisper: 'I just hit the machine' or is cautiously
reticent.

Fay, to the contrary, actively subverts the seriousness of the interaction and competes against her sister's verbal dominance by offering
memories and fantasies which connect with the agenda I implicitly
prescribe. My preoccupation with a particular film, Solarwarriors,[14] and
particularly with moments which may have been frightening, seems to
invite quite a disparate array of fearful experiences, some of which are
only tenuously associated with film and television. Fay's interventions
are also markedly different from the replies-framed-by-the-question to
which her sister almost entirely adheres: again and again Fay attempts to
develop a narrative account of her experience. For Fay, the formal rules
of response appropriate to an 'interview' are either unknown or disre-
garded. Moreover, she consistently addresses me as her father, whereas
Cesca ranges across a variety of modes of address, often seeming to
speak as pupil to teacher. My identity, identified as variable in Cesca's
responses, is for Fay confined within particular familial terms.

The following utterances all come from Cesca and, directly addressing me, claim to speak for Fay:

> She does ... do you like *Lovejoy*, Fay? No, she doesn't exactly like *Press Gang* and *Wonder Years*.
> She doesn't even like watching *Newsround* ... it's a special children's news thing.
> Yeah, *Newsround* 'cos it's a children's one, it's not, it's not babyish like for Fay ... it's like for my age ... but it Fay, erm, by Fay, erm, underst ... [15]

Cesca both positions herself as older and more knowing and attempts to sustain the continuity and seriousness of the 'interview'. By contrast, Fay voices a variety of aberrant and sometimes disruptive utterances:

> Daddy, my, this nail needs cutting.
> I've got a friend Beverly I have ...
> ... germs on your ... . But you were putting your hand down your bottom.
> ga ga goo goo

Clearly these are utterances of different types but they each suggest the extent to which she is orientated towards the situation and towards me in terms which have little to do with a knowledge of 'interview' rules implicit in, for example, its televisual and radio forms or, say, in encounters with doctors. These verbal utterances, variously inflected and sometimes mixed with laughter, make reference to her own body (and a service she can expect her parents to provide), to a friend (unknown to me), to my body (perhaps the most knowingly disruptive strategy, as she sees an opportunity to voice an injunction to which she is often subject) and, finally, to the pre-verbal babbling of babies (again a knowing disruptive strategy). It could be argued that she is simply bored, but the contexts of these utterances each suggests an impatience with Cesca's dominance, both in terms of volume and topic, and an intention to make space for her own discourse. She insists, for example:

> And now you've got to listen to the shark ...
> Daddy I ... Cesca's been talking much ...
> Daddy, shall I tell you why I like *'Allo, 'Allo* ... 'cause 'cause the police says 'Good moaning'.

Fay has a repertoire of themes which differs from that of her sister, but it is invoked selectively in relation to the range of topics which I map out as of interest. To that extent, she is speaking within the framework of the 'interview' and, justifiably, attempting to insist on a more equable division of time between them. She is also able to counter her sister's assertions and lapses directly:

> But Cesca, actually you're wrong.
> Yes, but Cesca there's no more televisions.
> Cesca, there wasn't ...
> Why don't you 'xplain it to yourself?

Cesca you absolutely sing that all the time.
Blue Peter is boring.

The modes of response displayed by her sister are largely unavailable to Fay but she is nevertheless determined to mark out her own right to speak – to struggle, with suppressed anger, to counter her lack of power in relation to a sister more than four years her elder. In this respect, her narratives, though interrupted, carry a kind of expanded claim to a more sustained presence in the 'interview'. Telling a story enables her to develop, and return to, a structure which may at times intersect with the sequence of questions but which acquires an autonomy from the 'interview' and enables her to re-enter on her own terms when Cesca hesitates or lapses in her articulation. The narratives she offers facilitate her negotiation of the social relationships between participants and the 'interview' form in which the particular occasion was constituted. But, at the same time, they also pose some problematic formulations of modality and suggest important ways of thinking through being positioned as a girl.

Three narratives: sharks, thunder and the horrible man

There are three main narrative strands which need to be considered here. I have labelled them as 'sharks', 'thunder' and 'the horrible man inside the television'. The first, 'sharks' and the second, 'thunder', surface together early in the 'interview' in the context of questions about the fear and revulsion provoked by the film *Solarwarriors*, questions which were framed by the issue of my power/responsibility to curtail their viewing and send them off to bed. Cesca's spontaneous comment prior to the 'interview' was 'It was the vilest film we watched last night, wasn't it? Lucky it didn't give me nightmares.' At the time of viewing she got up and walked out of the room on several occasions. Fay, coming to sit on my knee, said 'This is an absolutely horrible film.' In the 'interview' both Cesca and Fay refuse the suggestion that they should have been prevented from watching and argue that 'the end was OK' (Cesca) and 'the music was nice' (Fay). At this point, both display a knowledge of broad narrative and generic conventions, and use that knowledge to contest my implied power to curtail their viewing. Cesca follows these observations:

Cesca: Luckily I didn't have nightmares ... I usually do.
Fay: Well ... I had a 'mare of a shark I did and some thunder.
Cesca: A shark?
CR: Why did you ... what, last night ... was it a nightmare or not?

Fay: I didn't have a nightmare tonight ... I was just ...
Cesca: You mean last night, Fay
CR: So why did you have a nightmare about a shark, then?
Fay: Because I just dreamed ... I don't know ...
CR: But you've never seen a shark, have you?
Fay: Na ...
Cesca: But she has on films.
Fay: I have, I have seen a shark on *Home and Away*.
Cesca: I remember seeing *Jaws* when I was three years old ... it was dreadful.
Fay: Daddy you remember Rory got eaten by a shark? On *Home and Away*.
CR: Who got eaten?
Fay: Rory on *Home and Away*
Cesca: Yeah, Rory and he got eaten by a shark.
CR: Did you see him getting eaten?
Fay: Yeah, no I didn't really ... I can ...
Cesca: We saw the shark and him going ... 'na ... na' like that.
Fay: And he was drowning he was falling ... and he tried to get up, he did.

The exchange continues but Fay is marginalised as Cesca speaks more loudly and rapidly. Eventually Fay regains my attention with 'But anyway I was frightened of the shark.' I respond by asking 'Were you? So what was your dream?' but rather than elaborating on the 'shark-mare' at this point she takes 'dream' as an invitation to speak not of television but of a frightening dream involving thunder. The connection between television and dreams, which entered Cesca's discourse, appears to be absent from Fay's. In response to a direct question – 'Have you ever had a bad dream after you'd seen something on TV?' – Fay answers, without hesitation, 'No.' Rejecting that line of questioning she insists, 'And now you've got to listen to the shark ... ' and, hurriedly excluding Cesca, she offers her shark story:

> and now but now when, on the shark day I was sleeping and then and then me and Daddy went into the boat ... and we were near some sharks ... we could feel the shark's skin but the sharks didn't eat us so we swam back into the boat but we weren't eaten but I was still scared.

The modality status of this is unclear. It might be argued that there is some confusion in that she moves from speaking of sharks on television, in a fictional drama, to dreams and, further, into what appears to be an entirely imaginary event. However, as I have suggested, she is responding to an agenda construed as 'what makes you afraid' rather than one narrowly focused on television. She is also able to articulate quite complex modality distinctions. Thus with reference to the dream of thunder she says: 'when I was asleep I was thinking it was real'; a comment which suggests a capacity to reflect upon and distinguish shifts in the modality of subjective experience. On other occasions she has remarked, it seems with some pleasure, 'You can think about thinking, can't you?' With the shark story the opening moment – 'on the shark day I was sleeping' – is ambiguous; it could mean that what follows was experienced or dreamt while asleep or that what follows comes after having slept. Fay positions herself in the story as 'we', 'me and Daddy', embarking on and returning from a venture involving danger and, though safe, lingering fear. This is not without some precedents in her real experience: in the preceding summer, when she was still three, she had been taken out, on several occasions, in a canoe and once, in shallow water, I had momentarily touched, almost held, a trout. Fay was afraid of being out in a canoe and resisted further repetitions of the trip. Apart from the transformation of trout into shark, which could be said to draw on a fishy repertoire made available by television, this dreamlike story appears to have little to do with images derived from the media. It does however employ a narrative structure which is familiar in many children's stories – that of an adventure and safe return.

The second narrative, 'Thunder', is more clearly and explicitly presented as a dream and, again, with no obvious reference to television. This is Fay's account:

> Er ... One night I had a dream of er thunder and it was really scary (-ed). ... And Mummy and Daddy were at Helen's and the babies and Tatjana was looking after us and it was so thunder and we couldn't get to sleep so we stayed up late and so and when Mummy and Daddy came and but when the doctor came and Mummy and Daddy came home another day ... [*draws breath*] The doctor said you've got to stay home because something wasn't right ... Mummy 'nd Daddy had to go out for dinner together, just the two of them and the doctor was and the doctor said 'I'll come back as fast I can' but he didn't come and instead of coming tonight ... but he didn't he didn't.

There is an evident concern here with the question of who is responsible for her, who has the task of 'looking after us', particularly when there is 'thunder'. Anxiety, arising out of her own lack of power to control the actions of adults, appears to motivate this scenario. Again there are fragments of real situations and remembered comments by adults, but they acquire different meanings in this presentation: it may be, for example, that the doctor's injunction 'you've got to stay home' is addressed to 'Mummy and Daddy' and voiced by the doctor as one of the few adults with some apparent power over parents. The narrative is disjointed and incomplete, like the memory of a dream, but is reported rapidly, and almost without pause, in order to hold open the space she has provisionally secured within the frame of the 'interview'.

The third narrative engages with the film *Solarwarriors*, an 'absolutely horrible film' in which Fay identified one figure with particular distaste – 'I hate that man ... he's absolutely horrible ... he's horrible to ladies'. Fay's narrative develops in the following way:

> Daddy I ... Cesca's been talking much ... as I wanted ... and Daddy last night when I was watching that film and, do you know what, the man, the man, horrible man that had, looked like a police, and then he, and then a little bit of skin then all his skin came off and all it was all red he ... looked disgusting and then it close ... and then the skin camed on again ... . That was scary to me ... . Yeh and that's a horrible man. ...
>
> ...
>
> But Daddy I would like to cut the telly open ... and jump in ... and pretend I'm in there ... .
> I think it's really scary ...
> And that man did it to me ...
> *CR*: You don't want to be in that film do you?
> It'll be better, it'll be better with all the boys and girls ... who're escaping ...
>
> ...
>
> 'cause I saw some more girls ... I can see one or two other girls ... friends ... I saw one ... a ... I saw a lickle (little) ... I saw a girl that had er, er, yellow hair and ... like this and curly hair all down and that was a girl and she was 'scaping with somebody else but ...
>
> ...
>
> But anyway, Daddy ... this is really horrible ... the man who looked like a police [*drops voice very low*] kicked one of the ... [girls?] and he was really horrible and one of her boyfriends came to help ...
>
> ...
>
> He was absolutely nasty, nasty and I wouldn't go near him ... if I saw him I would ...
>
> ...
>
> And, and Daddy, but if I saw him I would open the television and get out and under the carpet and sit on the settee and take my things off ... the skating things ...
>
> ...
>
> Yes but Cesca but there's no more televisions because I would be in this house if I got out of there if I got out ...
>
> ...
>
> And but er, but if the man didn't see me and I tiptoe, tiptoe like a mouse, and then if he, if he turned his head 'round, could see, like a mouse, then I'd do, so I'd run away ...

This summary transcription omits many of my questions and several interjections from Cesca, but it is Fay's most sustained contribution to the whole interview. She expresses strong feelings of revulsion, shock and excitement in retelling and extending in fantasy the events she had observed. It is possible to speculate that she displays an innocence of distinctions between reality and fantasy, and perhaps an inability to separate out threats to characters within the filmic diegesis from the threat to herself as a viewer in the same room as the television 'containing' the horrible man and his actions. But Fay embarks on this narrative with a clear distinction marked in her account: ' I would like to cut the telly open ... and jump in ... and pretend I'm in there.' This use of 'pretend' is a common feature of children's play and, in this case, might suggest a wish to heighten the modality of her viewing experience to such an extent that it is 'as if' she were herself one of those girls escaping from their pursuers. Moving into the 'pretend' mode of play often signals Fay's assumption of some position of power over others, particularly adults. Fay claims more of a presence for girls than her sister, who remembers the film as lacking in female agents and judges it, on such a demographic imbalance, 'sexist'. Given Fay's modal shift – 'pretend' – this is irrelevant to her fantasy of adventure in the world of the *Solarwarriors*. Of course, it could be argued that Fay is unable adequately to judge the modality of the film, that she takes it to be a reality separate from, but coexisting with, the one she inhabits. To move from one to the other might be very frightening and hence the 'pretence' of the transition. Certainly this is an instance of a continuing attempt to explore and make sense of the modalities of experience across a range which, though including television and film, clearly also embraces dreams, memories and everyday 'present' experience. But through her own control of modality, she rearticulates the space of the film as one in which she can take action.

An exchange between Fay and her sister on an earlier occasion may clarify this. When Fay was four years and two months old, they were watching *The Trials of Life*, a natural history series known for its vivid presentation of often 'violent' animal behaviour:

> *Fay (addressing a doll)*: Don't watch this darling, it's horrible.
> *Cesca (to Fay)*: Babies don't watch television.
> *Fay (to Cesca)*: I'm just playing a game.
> *Fay (to doll)* : Baby, don't watch this.
> *Fay (to Cesca)*: Put *Brookside* on. It's horrible, it's about eating.
> *Cesca (to Fay)*: I want to watch this.

Here Fay is determined to maintain her fantasy, not because she is 'lost' in it, but because it enables her to be a powerful figure. She is entirely clear about the status of her quasi- maternal utterances and ignores Cesca's attempt to disrupt them. As Walkerdine and Lucey suggest in their study, she appears to take 'in fantasy the position of the mother who can discipline a daughter ... thus a form of resistance and a bid for power'.[16] At the same time, however, she is actually also refusing scenes which, if they are about eating, are also about being eaten. For a child 'to be eaten' is one instance of subjection to the power of parents and other adults – and many adults express their relations with children in exactly such ambiguous terms: 'I could eat you up.' So the modal status of the *Trials of Life* is by no means weak, but neither does it seem appropriate to argue that Fay, at four, cannot herself manipulate modality.

A further aspect of this issue centres on the modality of human actors in film and television. Fay may recognise actors collecting their children from the school she attends and she does sometimes see a familiar newsreader with her child in a local park. She knows that some people do move between the two domains of everyday reality and of television. After seeing *Teenage Mutant Ninja Turtles* at a local cinema, Fay, in considering their difference from the familiar television cartoon turtles, remarked that 'They weren't real, they weren't coming up to us' – again, this is ambiguous, for it could mean that their modality status is thus judged less than that of those people in the everyday real world who can and do 'come up to us', but it may also be consistent with the view that their reality status is the same as that of people in the everyday real world but that they are somehow contained in another, separate, space from which they cannot easily cross.

In Fay's fantasy of entering the television, and of encountering the 'horrible man' within that space, there is an important stress upon her own agency and, to some extent therefore, her capacity to evade what is threatening. The fantasy is one which involves putting herself at risk but, necessarily, so that she can work through her anxieties about what might happen to her: 'He was absolutely nasty, nasty and I wouldn't go near him ... if I saw him I would ... open the television and get out and under the carpet and sit on the settee and take my things off ... the skating things.' Escape is a matter of crossing from the domain of television back to the safety of the living-room, and it seems therefore that she is confident that he cannot make this transition even though the need to conceal herself 'under the carpet' implies that he can see out of the television and into the living room. Of course newsreaders, and many other 'presenters', do collude in the construction of precisely this pretence and it may be that the insertion of film into the domestic medium of television confuses what in a cinema seems distant, to be looked at, with the experience of television as a 'way in' to domestic space, a medium from which others look out at us. 'If the man didn't see me and I tiptoe, tiptoe like a mouse, and then if he, if he turned his head 'round, could see like a mouse, then I'd do, so I'd run away'. Here Fay extends her exploration of what it might be like to be caught by the look of the horrible man but stresses, again as a strategy of evasion which perhaps helps to control the anxiety this provokes, her ability to escape, by becoming small and silent and by running away. It is not clear in this final utterance in the narrative if she positions herself still within the space of the television or if, and this does seem more likely, she is elaborating on her escape to 'this house' where there is only one television, one 'way in' or vantage point from which she might be seen

Taste: 'I like all lady things ... I don't like men things'

It is common for Fay to voice a strong identification with girls and with all that is feminine and, also, to express considerable doubt, sometimes disgust, in relation to men and boys. On one occasion, as Cesca skimmed through the advertisements in the middle of *Roseanne*, Fay urged her to move on quickly through an advertisement addressed to men (for aftershave, I think), saying, with her tongue out, making violent noises of disgust: 'I like all lady things ... I don't like men things' (Fay at 4 years 10 months). It was as if Fay had tasted something which had to be spat out.

Taste is a powerful term in common-sense discourse: 'taste' naturalises cultural preferences through its physical connotations and is further secured by association with the powerful affective expression of oral tastes in infancy. Infancy, understood as less social than later phases of childhood, can easily be invoked as evidence of how 'inexplicable' taste can be. But, wary of this, I want to devote some space to the different ways in which Fay's 'taste' might be understood. She voices her taste in terms which suggest a fantasy of oral ingestion and, because what is offered for consumption is so markedly male, of forceful expulsion and disgust. I suppose that her revulsion might be grounded in her experience of men and boys, myself included.

Bourdieu's perspective on taste, though largely framed by questions of class, also extends to gendered differences within particular class categories :

> Taste classifies, and it classifies the classifier. Social subjects, classified by their classifications, distinguish themselves by the distinctions they make,

between the beautiful and the ugly, the distinguished and the vulgar, in which their position in the objective classifications is expressed or betrayed.[17]

In matters of taste, more than anywhere else, all determination is negation; and tastes are perhaps first and foremost distastes, disgust provoked by horror or visceral intolerance ('sick-making') of the tastes of others.[18]

This perspective suggests how the strongly bounded gender preferences of young children serve them in their efforts to position themselves unambiguously in the division between male and female. Clearly there are 'blurrings' of this division which are accepted, or perhaps also insisted upon, by children. But though the division may be contested, and particularly by girls whose perceptions of the power differentials inscribed in the division give them ample motive, it is also the case that children do speak from one position or the other and do not often question their positioning as such. If gendered identity is experienced as ambiguous or precarious, in speech and in play such 'experience' is largely denied.

Whatever might follow from the division of gender, and however much particular forms may be struggled over, the division itself, and being on one side or the other, is a basis for the fundamental work of identity and of social orientation. As they are constituted, most social worlds 'make sense' from gendered positions and would be bewildering and perhaps overwhelming if no secure gender location was available within them. For the children here, no other classification of the social world is both so immediate and enduring: they are male or female now and will be when they grow up. The division of children from adults is of comparable concern, but they develop towards, and actively project themselves into, futures where the power of adulthood will be available to them. Distinctions of class, and of race, though also powerful determinants of identity are not, in this social context, elements in a system of difference sustained by a single binary, and primary, distinction. So, for Fay at four, being a girl and being a child matter most in her negotiations of the everyday world. To negotiate power within the relations thus prescribed is a viable strategy; to question the basis of those relations, for young children, is remote and inconceivable.

Fay, and her friends of four, five and six, are preoccupied with nurturant play in relation to babies and their substitutes, with clothes and looking pretty, with Sindy and Barbie dolls. Her list of desirable Christmas presents for 1991 included: a Barbie wedding-dress, a Barbie man in a wedding suit and some other clothes for him, Baby Shivers, an ironing board and Li'l Miss Magic Hair. Many of these were advertised on television in the pre-Christmas period. Perhaps many who read this will, if not for the first time, now recoil in horror at such tastes. These objects and their packaging come in gendered colours; if this is unfamiliar, a walk around Toys-R-Us offers profuse evidence of the distinctions currently in play. Colours are coded unequivocally as 'boy colours' and 'girl colours' (as Fay would say). Fay shares and insists on this coding. She tolerates no loosening of the most rigid, and seemingly arbitrary, categories and complains, for example, that a jigsaw has 'too many boy colours in it'. *The Care Bears* and *My Little Pony*, which are among the most popular of the videos available to her, are clearly marked by a predominance of the 'girl colours' which are 'to her taste'. If this voicing of taste expresses an affective commitment to gendered classification it is, at the same time, an assertion of her gender, and that of her friends, in a context where gender loyalty and, equally, mistrust of men and boys, could be a necessary strategy.

Bourdieu's emphasis on social classification needs to be complemented with an account of agency which allows for more than active acquiescence in pre-existing social divisions. The psychoanalytic concepts of fantasy and of the unconscious do usefully complicate those theories which collapse subjects into the 'objective' social relations in which they are constituted.[19] But they may not provide much which enables a more precise grasp of agency to be produced. 'Intra-psychic' determination may be written into such an account but, in some versions of psychoanalysis, this can seem a more complete determinism.

The fantasies which are presented in Fay's narratives are also social acts: a 'taking of sides'. The narrative of the 'horrible man' is not at all unfamiliar in terms of its simple structure: a journey into a dangerous, uncertain but exciting place (the television/the diegesis of *Solarwarriors*) an encounter with a monster/danger (the 'horrible man'), escape and safe return home. *Where the Wild Things Are, Outside Over There*, and *In the Night Kitchen* (all by Maurice Sendak) are popular stories of this kind, and many others with a similar structure could be cited here. Fay's fantasy is both a reworking of the particular narrative of the film in question and, in that reworking, a quite effective use of generic knowledge derived from hearing and seeing the many narratives of adventure, threat and escape available to her (not just Sendak and other books but also many television cartoons, *Thundercats*, for example). It is consistent with her knowledge of narratives beyond those specifically addressed to children that the threat should be embodied here in male form and that, in this case, escape rather than combat is the principal means to evade capture. Fay, as female agent, goes for escape from rather than confrontation with, the threatening male figure. Her fantasy works with a discourse which, in its numerous textual repetitions, defines relations between girls and men as doubly fraught with the inequalities of power consequent on gender and age. It is useful, but not sufficient, to read this fantasy as an instance of the social reproduction of gender appropriate knowledge: it is rational, coherent and confirms a kind of social knowledge which is widely legitimated. Girls (and boys too, but differently) are repeatedly warned not to go near strangers, particularly strange men, if not always specifically men in quasi-fascist uniform. For girls, running away is supposedly unproblematic; for boys, there is an imperative to imagine more aggressive alternatives. For Fay, at four, this fantasy seems to suggest a working through of what it means to be a girl and a child in a social world where vulnerability and a lack of power are central facts of everyday life.

The emphasis of my reading is that young girls learn to be wary of men and to locate their security in being able to escape and return home. The risk here is that subjectivity is thus represented as no more than a sum of the social relations and the socially available discourses in which subjects come to be, and to know, their positions. But Fay's use of fantasy is perhaps comparable to that exploration of identity through the terms of an available genre described by Gemma Moss. Fay's wish to produce her fantasy scenario, and the evident emotional excitement in doing so, suggest a taking hold of this generic mode in a social situation where otherwise the space to speak and to be someone might have eluded her. Of course, to retain a notion of the 'unconscious' implies that individuals are subject to structures which escape consciousness, both practical and discursive. However, without contradicting this, I want to stress that fantasy is a mode in which Fay is able to assert the reality of her own agency – as both speaker and, in the drama she articulates, actor.

The voicing of taste and the production of fantasy seem to be related strategies. In comparing taste to fantasy, I intend neither to dismiss it nor to render it asocial. The vehemence with which tastes are expressed suggests a marking-out of the self, though with terms of difference which are, of course, social. Both the articulation of fantasies and of tastes are important challenges to accounts of 'socialisation' which stress transmission from those who are social to those who are not.[20] The insistent activity of children, in play, in fantasy and in their negotiation of social relations exceeds the learning of pre-existing positions. The forceful voicing of taste matters because, in its excesses, children define themselves. Mostly, the objects of pleasure or of disgust, be they 'yum' or 'yuk', do not seem rationally related to the responses they evoke. But in the complicated selections and demonstrations of pleasure in toys, in colours, in clothes, in music and in television, there is a constantly reworked pattern of self-delineation. Taste, like fantasy, serves in the elaboration of social identity. It is one of those continuing strategies of assertion in the immediate familial context and, beyond that, in the social space of classrooms and playgrounds.

Some conclusions

Taste, as a powerfully naturalised discourse in which fantasies of social difference are secured, has been discussed in the preceding account largely with reference to age and gender. The question of taste arose between Fay and Cesca, as sisters divided by an age gap of more than four years. *Solarwarriors* was for neither an object of much pleasure and, for Cesca, it was of less interest than the numerous comedies to which she enthusiastically attached herself, and which she set against all that was 'gruesome', 'awesome' and 'gory'. In fact Fay may have worked up more of an interest in talking about *Solarwarriors* just because she saw a way of appearing to cope with something which had upset her much older sister. On a subsequent occasion, at the age of five, Fay stayed up to watch a review of horror-film techniques, including clips from *The Fly* and the *Nightmare on Elm Street* cycle.[21] Meanwhile her sister curled up in a chair, covered her face and, after a few moments, went off to bed. Fay was thus able to maintain a presence and a relation to me, in the absence of her sister, and to make a claim to both greater maturity and intimacy. Horror, for Fay, had acquired a specific strategic advantage. However, at other times, Fay voiced anxieties suggestive of the realisation that with adulthood comes the loss of dependence and a greater proximity to death. Thus, while watching *Sesame Street*, she once remarked, 'I don't want to die, I don't want to be grown up, I just want to stay a child.' On another occasion, on a Sunday afternoon, Fay was playing by the television as we watched *Tokyo Story*. She became more attentive towards the end, got up from the floor to sit on her mother's knee and, obviously concerned by the death of grandparents, remarked 'My grandfather died but I wasn't born so I didn't cry.'

Cesca's rejection of horror appeared to turn, in part, on a more general refusal of genres identified too unequivocally as adult. The generic knowledge she brought into play in the 'interview', where she positioned herself as more mature, was not of sex or violence or horror. It was, rather, of comedies such as *Lovejoy* and *Butterflies*. As Cesca moved on from talking around *Solarwarriors*, Fay struggled to keep up with Cesca's flow of references and recollections which, on the whole, constituted a repertoire incompletely available to her; she conceded, in a tone suggestive of frustrated resignation, 'I like everything that Cesca likes.' Thus, though Cesca was able to present herself as older and more knowledgeable, she accomplished this without compromising her distance from programmes marked too sharply as adult, particularly by their gravity or sexual content. Situation comedies appeared to provide a precarious compromise for Cesca and her friends in the 'middle years' of childhood. Requiring greater social and generic knowledge than most 'infants' have accumulated, they seem to mark out an ambivalent self-location, as knowing more than the babies but much less than the grown-ups.

There are other dimensions of taste which need to be examined more fully and which emerge even from the limited material I gathered in preparing this chapter. In particular, there is the high culture/low culture distinction which is perhaps invoked as much between children as by their parents. In this connection, I want to introduce the brief transcript of a dialogue between Cesca and one of her friends, Miriam. With Miriam, Cesca is in a different position. The following comes from a brief discussion of *Neighbours*:

Cesca: I watch it anyway [*Cesca laughing*].
Miriam: It's still gossip ... all soap operas have gossip.
Cesca: What do you mean exactly ... 'gossip'?
Miriam: Gossip, don't you know what gossip means?
Cesca: Yes.
Miriam: Well they all have gossip ... *Neighbours* has gossip ... *Coronation* ...
Cesca: Well what do you exactly mean by 'gossip'?
Miriam: They all have like ... well talk about ... well 'Charlene dropped her bucket last night' ... everyone's saying ... what's interesting about that? ... nothing exciting ...
Cesca: Well ...
Miriam: ... it's all like well 'Charlene did that and Charlene did this'...
Cesca: Charlene went away a year ago.
Miriam: 'Charlene ...
Cesca: [*laughs*]
Miriam: 'Charlene had a baby and ...
Cesca: No she never.

> *Miriam*: Oh maybe she did I don't know ... I don't watch it ... 'Charlene had a baby and
> *Cesca*: No she didn't
> *Miriam*: I know she didn't ... but they always gossip on about each other – [*in mocking rhythm*] 'someone had a baby, someone didn't do ... someone dropped a bucket last night and someone didn't ... [*All of this interrupted by laughter and protests from Cesca*] ... someone ... [*drowned out by Cesca's laughter*]
> *Cesca*: Where's that needle Mummy had for me?

Like most of Cesca's friends, Miriam comes from a household with a more high cultural orientation (with parental involvement in visual arts and art education) and a relatively marginal commitment to television. Miriam finds it easy to ridicule something of which she has a generalised generic knowledge: the detail of the kind which committed viewers accumulate hardly counts as knowledge at all in her discourse. There are other examples that could be given – of a friend whose parents confined her viewing to children's BBC, the news and occasional films – but it is important to note that even within a well established friendship group there is not necessarily any shared discourse around television or shared repertoire of viewing experiences. The repetitions, disjunctions and eventual escape into laughter which characterise the transcript above indicate that there is no simply homogeneous 'culture of childhood' here. Of course these girls do share many objects with equal enthusiasm – situation comedies and the books they read, for example – and, to some extent, Cesca was keen to counter the implication that division and difference were characteristic in her network. Perhaps in relation to me, and this writing, it became important to define the shared enthusiasms of the group.

Nevertheless, the formation of taste is in part regulated by families in terms of their relation to wider cultural hierarchies, and many of these girls have their time away from school highly organised around the demands of music ('classical' violin and piano) and ballet lessons or the private tuition their parents seek to facilitate their daughters' entry to selective schools. Certainly time watching television must, in such a context, seem time wasted when otherwise the more valued forms of cultural capital might be secured. In the making of young middle-class girls popular culture has only a peripheral place, if any, in these parentally-managed childhoods. Of course what I describe here is no more than the scaffold which these parents seek to construct. With girls of eight, nine and ten, there does appear to be a high degree of dependence on such scaffolding but there is also a measure of involvement with popular film and television, if not yet with music, which may well acquire a greater presence as they move into adolescence.

In this chapter, I have argued that the 'cultures of childhood' are, unsurprisingly, enmeshed in the larger divisions of the social world. In conclusion, I want to suggest that these divisions, and particularly their relation to individual fantasies of taste, should be central to a school curriculum in which hierarchies of taste are still too secure, passing unquestioned too often. It may be, for example, that in some respects even progressive policies, such as those which intend to challenge sexism in representation, effectively collude with an essentialism of taste in proscribing or patronising the tastes of young girls. The meanings attached to some objects, Barbie dolls, Kylie Minogue or Li'l Miss Magic Hair, may seem both self-evident and unambiguously undesirable to adults, but their meanings for young children are not simply available to us and need to be approached in terms of children's negotiations of difference and unequal power in the social worlds in which they are placed.

The need, then, is for educational strategies which address the social meanings of taste, not as an awkward impediment to the study of popular cultural forms in school, but as integral to an understanding of the cultural domain. The meanings of taste in terms of negotiated social difference should be central here. If the 'taking sides' motif has its value in examining intra-familial relations, I see little difficulty in similarly reading classroom talk in terms of situated social relations, marked by conflicts and struggles to sustain, or secure, a presence and a degree of power in relations with others. The central problem will be, however, that of enabling students to reflect on matters of taste when, as I have suggested, they are understood as personal and permanent, perhaps as idiosyncratic as tastes in food, where revulsion is often claimed to be an entirely physical, and non-negotiable, matter. As much of what I have described in this chapter suggests, the tasks of teaching are mostly a matter of working with what is already formed, and sometimes seemingly fixed. Nevertheless, it is unwise to prejudge the meaning and purpose of tastes and their gender and class dynamics are neither predictable nor simple. Indeed, detailed explorations of why tastes matter and of the broader social relations in which they are implicated could provide a valuable starting point for more distanced reflection. In this respect, qualitative and ethnographic research into audiences should be an invaluable resource for teaching about popular culture.

Notes and references

This chapter is a revised version of a paper presented to a Media, Culture and Curriculum symposium at the Annual Meeting of the American Educational Research Association in San Francisco, 20–4 April 1992. Thanks to Fay and Cesca for putting up with this; Elizabeth for reading and commenting on an early draft; and thanks to various friends of Fay and Cesca who talked, from time to time, of how they watch television – Lucy, Miriam, Paloma, Jenny, Handé and Che.

1 Robert Hodge and Gunther Kress, *Social Semiotics* (Polity, 1988), p. 249. See particularly the last chapter, 'Entering Semiosis: Training Subjects for Culture'.

2 See David Morley, *Family Television: Cultural Power and Domestic Leisure* (Comedia, 1986); and James Lull, *Inside Family Viewing* (Comedia, 1990). The work of Patricia Palmer is a notable exception as she more successfully engages with children's television use in terms which they themselves define: Patricia Palmer, *The Lively Audience* (Allen and Unwin, 1986) and 'The Social Nature of Children's Television Viewing', in *Television and its Audience*, ed. P. Drummond and R. Paterson (British Film Institute, 1988).

3 See Bob Hodge and David Tripp, *Children and Televison* (Polity, 1986); David Buckingham, *Children Talking Television: The Making of Television Literacy* (Falmer, 1993)

4 Myra Barrs, 'Maps of Play', in *'Language and Literacy in the Primary School* ed. Margaret Meek and Colin Mills (Falmer 1988).

5 See L. Vygotsky, *Mind in Society* (Harvard University Press, 1978).

6 Gemma Moss, *Un/popular Fictions* (Virago 1989), p. III.

7 Chris Richards, 'Intervening in Popular Pleasures: Media Studies and the Politics of Subjectivity', in *Watching Media Learning*, ed. D. Buckingham (Falmer 1990).

8 Nancy Chodorow, *The Reproduction of Mothering* (University of California Press, 1978).

9 Anthony Giddens, *Central Problems in Social Theory* (Macmillan, 1979), p. 2.

10 *ibid.*, p. 123.

11 Juliet Mitchell and Jacqueline Rose, *Feminine Sexuality* (Macmillan, 1982), p. 37.

12 Valerie Walkerdine and Helen Lucey, *Democracy in the Kitchen* (Virago, 1989), p. 143. See also V. Walkerdine, *The Mastery of Reason* (Routledge, 1988) and Carolyn Steedman, *The Tidy House* (Virago, 1982).

13 Walkerdine and Lucey, *Democracy in the Kitchen*.

14 *Solarwarriors*, directed by Alan Johnson, starring Jami Gertz, Jason Patric, Richard Jordan, Charles Durning, and Lukas Haas. *The Radio Times* for 16–22 March 1991 comments, with some accuracy, that it is 'A derivative space fantasy adventure about rollerskating teenage orphans, held prisoner by an evil ruler on a parched planet'.

15 *Lovejoy* is an early/mid-evening drama series (BBC); *Butterflies* (cited later) is a situation comedy made by the BBC and shown originally in the 1970s. *Press Gang* is transmitted during the late afternoon/early evening for a young, probably teenage, audience (Central TV); *The Wonder Years* is a US import shown on Channel 4 in the early evening; *Newsround* is a children's news programme (BBC); *'Allo, 'Allo* is a very popular early-evening comedy (BBC); *Home and Away* is an imported Australian soap directed at a young audience (ITV); *Brookside* is a Liverpool-based soap (transmitted on Channel 4); *The Trials of Life* is a natural history series made by David Attenborough (BBC).

16 Walkerdine and Lucey, *Democracy in the Kitchen* p. 123.

17 Pierre Bourdieu, *Distinction* (Routledge and Kegan Paul, 1986), p. 6.

18 *ibid.*, p. 56.

19 J. Laplanche and J-B. Pontalis, *The Language of Psycho-Analysis* (Hogarth, 1985), p. 280. In their comments on post-Freudian 'object-relations' analysis Laplanche and Pontalis legitimately query an undue stress on 'real relations' with others, reasserting an understanding of particular social relationships as always also constituted in the unconscious and through its characteristic modes. My concern is with the detail of how subjectivity is constantly remade in and through real relations with others. See, by the same authors, 'Fantasy and the Origins of Sexuality', in *Formations of Fantasy*, ed. V. Burgin, J. Donald and C. Kaplan, (Methuen, 1986); also, in the same volume, see V. Walkerdine's 'Video Replay: families, films and fantasy'. Alice Miller, *The Drama of Being a Child* (Virago, 1988), is also of some interest.

20 Giddens, *Central Problems in Social Theory*, p. 130. In concluding a discussion of 'socialisation' he argues this:

> *The unfolding of childhood is not time elapsing just for the child*: it is time elapsing for its parental figures, and for all other members of society; the socialisation involved is not simply that of the child, but of the parents and others with whom the child is in contact ... . Socialisation is thus most appropriately regarded not as the 'incorporation of the child into society', but as the *succession of the generations*.

This suggests a dynamic model of socialisation. My emphasis is upon the affective and relational continuities – people have histories and histories of relations with each other – which constantly inform the choice of positions in discourse.

21 *Moving Pictures*, 25 January 1992, BBC2.

The Mahabharata: from Sanskrit to sacred soap
A case study of the reception of two contemporary televisual versions

Introduction

The Mahabharata is one of the foundation myths of Indian society. It is said to permeate every aspect of Indian social life and to enshrine the philosophical basis of Hindu religion, culture and tradition. It is the longest poem ever written. The first versions, which were written in Sanskrit, date back to the fifth and sixth centuries BC but by the third and fourth centuries AD it began to take more definitive forms. Variations abound according to regional traditions and to the interpretations of the writers. Maha in Sanskrit means 'great' or 'complete'. Bharat is the name of a legendary character, a family and a clan. In a more extended meaning bharat means Hindu, and even more generally, 'mankind' or 'race'. So 'Mahabharata' is variously interpreted as the 'The Great History of Mankind' or as 'The Great History of the Indian "race"'. It tells the story of the long and bloody quarrel between two groups of cousins: the Pandavas, who were five brothers; and the Kauravas, of whom there were a hundred. The family quarrel over who will rule ends with an earth-shattering war, an Armageddon, where the fate of the world is at stake and millions are left dead.[1]

For centuries The Mahabharata and its sister epic The Ramayana have been communicated in a variety of forms; in Sanskrit, as well as in folk and classical theatre; by village storytellers and mass-produced cartoon strips. But now it is principally through TV that it is communicated to people in India and to Indians in the diaspora. The popularity of the TV serials – broadcast by the government monopoly channel, Doordarshan – is unparalleled. On Sunday mornings all India stops still while 115 million people tune in simultaneously to view these 'sacred soaps'. The uproar that ensues if a community set breaks down or if viewing is interrupted by a power-cut is well documented. Fans of these epic TV serials claim they have enormous social benefits as they encapsulate Hindu religious beliefs and reinforce traditional values while providing popular entertainment for the masses. However, critics claim that they are exacerbating the trend towards religious fundamentalism, intolerance and ritualism which is seen to characterise religious communities in India today. It is argued that Doordarshan, in broadcasting such religious epics, is contravening the Constitution of India and eroding the basis of the secular State. But as ever the dividing line between religion, culture and politics remains elusive.[2]

This chapter is part of a more extensive study which examines the ways in which young Punjabi Londoners use TV as a resource in negotiating issues of cultural difference and identity.[3] The research involved intensive, long-term ethnographic fieldwork in Southall, a predominantly Punjabi town in west London and one of the largest 'Asian' communities in Europe. Since the first phase of migration from the Punjab in the 1950s Southall has developed into a thriving commercial and cultural centre. Its demographic majority is of Sikh religion although Muslims, Hindus and Christians of various denominations are also represented. Rather than being a homogeneous 'Asian community', social boundaries are marked by cross-cutting differences in national, regional, religious, caste and linguistic heritage.

In much of the literature produced by the 'race-relations industry' young 'Asians', born and brought up in Britain, are seen to be trapped in a 'clash of cultures', torn by a confused sense of identity and troubled by conflicting allegiances.[4] This study problematises and undermines the time-worn dichotomies of the 'culture-clash' thesis. It uses ethnography to examine their everyday talk about TV and the role of TV in their lives. The study highlights how, through their everyday talk about TV, young people articulate conceptions of cultural differences and negotiate issues of national, local, ethnic and religious identities.

This chapter is based on a case-study of the Dhanis, a Hindu family living in Southall. It compares their responses to two versions of *The Mahabharata*, the 91-part serial produced by India's state channel, Doordarshan, and broadcast on BBC2 over two years, and Channel 4's six-hour broadcast of Peter Brook's theatrical production. In the first part of the chapter I describe the Dhani family, their viewing of religious films and the fieldwork itself. A brief description of the key distinguishing features of the two TV productions of *The Mahabharata* is also presented. In part two I present a parallel textual and ethnographic account comparing the family's readings of the two texts. The issues of casting and characterisation and visual representation, the narrator's role and the narrative weighting of particular incidents in both versions will be examined. These areas were chosen because they dominated the family's responses to both texts. They offer a good insight into the frames of reference that were drawn upon in making sense of the productions and highlight the specificity of the cultural and symbolic codes mobilised in their readings. Some of the deeper philosophical aspects of the young Dhanis' engagement with *The Mahabharata* are also explored, in particular their negotiation of some of the moral paradoxes in the epic.

Part one: Setting the context

The Dhani family

At the start of fieldwork, the household consisted of nine people: mother and father in their late forties; five female children: Munni age 23; Sewanti aged 21; Sefali aged 19; Malati aged 14 and Lipi aged 12; and two male children: Dilip aged 17 and Ranjit aged 11. The parents originate from Bangladesh and came to England twelve years ago, shortly after the war. The father, mother and two eldest daughters are employed in low-paid, semi-skilled jobs in local catering firms. They live in a comfortably furnished three-bedroom terraced house in Old Southall. The main living-room is a through lounge with TV set in the window bay and a sideboard with family photos. Large pictures of Krishna, Shiva, Vishnu, Lakshmima and other gods, draped with tinsel, line the top of the sideboard.

Upstairs the family have their own domestic shrine and here *puja* or prayers are performed three times a day. Visits to the temple are reserved for special occasions and religious festivals. Worship and leisure take place principally in their home. Unlike most families in Southall, the Dhanis have no other relatives living nearby. Their main leisure activity is watching television and at the weekend they watch two or three popular Hindi movies as well as several 'god films'. The girls and youngest boy are keen viewers of Australian soaps, such as *Neighbours* and *Home and Away*, as well as game shows and comedy programmes which are their main weekly viewing. The eldest son hires English and American videos which the family view two or three times a week, especially when the father is working late and the mother is busy.

The family watch more Hindi than English TV and films since the whole family can understand these. They have a video library of about 200 films mainly in Hindi, which includes a complete set of *The Mahabharata* (which was taped from broadcast TV) and of *The Ramayana* (which was taped from cable TV) as well as a collection of various blockbuster and religious films. Favourite episodes of both these epic TV serials are viewed again and again and often discussed with the mother or among the children. The children speak in English together and in Bengali to their parents. Mr Dhani understands and speaks more English than his wife, who communicates mainly in Bengali.

Family viewing of religious videos

The mother is the keenest viewer of religious videos and will stay up, accompanied by her children, until the early hours of the morning watching them. There is a tone of guilty pleasure in her voice when she admits to having hired five videos at the weekend and watched them all (15 hours' viewing) at least once. Such admissions are usually accompanied by playful reprimands by her husband or children who complain that she cannot get up before midday following a session of religious movies. They are also quite expensive to hire in such quantities.

For her, religious films provide comfort and solace from life's everyday anxieties. When she or a member of her family is ill or when she is worried, she will view them compulsively. But they also function as part of her and her family's religious practice itself. Such viewing is a form of religious ritual. Incense is lit at the start of the film and a salutation to God is made. Often a *puja* will be performed before or during viewing. Once a 'god' film is put on, it must be viewed until the end. No food is allowed to be eaten whilst viewing, except *prasad* (or holy food) and if, for example, Krishna appears on screen, the mother encourages her children to sit upright with toes pointing towards the screen and to join their hands, as in acts of worship at the temple.

In fact, the viewing of 'god films' is regarded, by the mother especially, as an act of pleasurable devotion in itself. The appearance on screen of favourite gods such as Krishna, in close-up, gazing direct to camera, with eyes seemingly penetrating the viewer's inner core, is for them like a divine apparition in itself. It is as if the gods speak directly to the viewer. Such viewing is considered to 'bring the gods into you' and if, after watching, 'you can bring the gods into your dreams', then it is considered to be a divine visitation whereby blessings are bestowed and favours may be requested.

This highlights the importance, in any analysis of TV, of taking into consideration the context of viewing as well as the various contexts in which discussions about viewing take place. The meaning of the text and of viewing are not pre-given, but are created by viewers. *The Mahabharata* and *The Ramayana* are important because they are perceived as sacred texts. There is an a priori acceptance of their religious and cultural authority which is a product of this family's religious beliefs and world view. These TV programmes are not seen as representations of the texts but as synonomous with the ancient Sanskritic texts. They are endowed with an aura of factuality.

Prior to the advent of video technology, anything more than the most rudimentary knowledge of *The Mahabharata* in Southall would have been unusual, unlike *The Ramayana* which is much more popular, accessible and well-known. Similarly, in India, deeper access to it could only be gained through a reading of the Sanskritic texts which would exclude the majority of women of Mrs Dhani's generation, who are illiterate. Her understanding of *The Mahabharata* is derived mainly from oral traditions, religious instruction in the temple and through its various popularisations in theatrical and print forms in India. Despite the enormous popularity of the cartoon-strips, TV has enhanced her ability to communicate its deeper meanings. She exploits the entertainment and the instructional aspects of the texts and the medium to inform her children and negotiate with them the beliefs and values inherent in *The Mahabharata*. It is primarily through the family, and the mother in particular, that the foundations of religious beliefs and of a religious world view are established. Maternal and cultural authority unite to strengthen and confirm the status of these texts as both sacred and real.

Competing claims of greater knowledge and understanding of Hinduism are made by the children. The youngest boy Ranjit, who is eleven years old, whispered to me:

> Well, I know most really about the gods because I sleep downstairs with my mother and she always tells me stories before I go to sleep and when she's watching late at night she'll keep waking me up and saying 'watch this, Ranjit, it's important'. So often, I go upstairs and splash my face with cold water and then we sit up until 3 or 4 in the morning with her.

Malati, who is fourteen, claims a better understanding of the films and of Hinduism, because she studies Hindi at school and so has better access to the language. Her ambition is to read *The Mahabharata* in Sanskrit like her grandfather. Sefali, who is nineteen, claims greater knowledge because she is older and is taking English A level, and she often relates aspects of *The Mahabharata* to Shakespearian texts such as

King Lear and to Greek tragedies such as *Antigone*.

In fact, few Hindus young or old are very familiar with *The Mahabharata* in its entirety due to its length and complexity, although they are very familiar with parts of it, particularly *The Bhagavad Gita*, one of the most sacred texts of Hinduism which recounts a dialogue between Krishna and Arjuna (the eldest Pandevas brother) before the great battle in the epic took place. There is also a superstition, common in India, that having the *The Mahabharata* in one's home or reading it may bring bad luck into the family. Some say this is because the story concerns war and conflict but I suspect that it has more to do with its provocative and complex moral philosophy, a point we shall examine in much greater detail later. This same superstition, however, does not appear to extend to the televised version, partly because it is made so much more accessible due to its popular, serialised 'soap' format. In Southall, each episode is avidly followed in many Hindu homes, especially by women, but I know of Sikhs and Muslims who also watch it regularly. It appears to be less popular generally among many young people, especially those who do not understand Hindi and therefore find reading the subtitles tedious: they find the narrative pace too slow, the production style unrealistic, the acting styles too melodramatic and the special effects ridiculous.

The fieldwork

The ethnographic data upon which this account is based was gathered over a three-year period. I got to know the Dhani family through Malati (then aged fourteen), whom I had previously taught. We had on previous occasions discussed *The Ramayana* and then one day she told me that friends at the temple informed her that *The Mahabharata* was going to be on TV at the weekend (November 1989) and that she was looking forward to watching it. I asked her if I might join her family to watch it since I was doing a project on TV and was interested in religion. After consulting her parents, she agreed. The children were curious about my motives. 'Why are you interested in *The Mahabharata*?' asked Ranjit upon my arrival. 'Because I've heard it is a great story which has a lot of wisdom in it, if you can understand it', I replied. 'If you can understand the Mahabharata, you can understand life itself,' he retorted with the air of an elderly sage.

It was thus in the hope of understanding some of its wisdom that we set out to watch Brook's version together. However, the experience was so bewildering and disconcerting, for reasons which will be explained later, that we abandoned it altogether after a couple of hours and watched the more reassuring *Sita's Wedding*, a 'god film' centred on an episode from *The Ramayana*. Thereafter, I visited the family regularly on Saturdays and in school holidays. We watched Brook's production again, over several visits, on video. This gave the added advantage of being able to pause it when they wanted to discuss something or explain things to me. They welcomed me openly into their home and were clearly amused by the teacher who had come to learn from them. My presence obviously led them to express responses, ideas and views about which they might otherwise have remained silent. We soon became friends, which was not difficult given the kindness and warmth that the family showed me.

Two months later, BBC2 started televising Doordarshan's *The Mahabharata* on Saturday afternoons and over the two years I visited regularly and we viewed it together. It was taped every week, so if I missed an episode that the children or mother considered important we later watched it on video. Comparing and contrasting the two versions, therefore, arose quite naturally. The children led the discussions which prioritised certain parts of the story and this is reflected in the data presented. The hospitality of the Dhani family was such that they soon accepted me as a member of the family and thankfully talked to me or ignored my presence as they wished. They got used to my naïve and probing questions, my notebooks and my fondness for tea and chapatis. In return I contributed to the family in different ways as opportunities arose. It is difficult to convey my affection, appreciation and gratitude to the Dhanis for what they have taught me and for their continuing friendship. It has also been difficult to select from the rich data that they enabled me to collect and inevitably some of this richness has been lost in the writing.

The storyline

The central storyline of *The Mahabharata* is of the family feud between two groups of rival cousins, the Pandevas and the Kauravas. They are brought up together by Bhisma but they are always fighting. Bhisma is the rightful heir to the throne who, out of love for his father, vowed to remain celibate. This was to enable the son of his father's second marriage to succeed him. However, this son dies childless but Vyasa, the second son of this marriage (and the narrator of *The Mahabharata*), is asked to sleep with two princesses. Two sons are produced; Dhritharashtra, the blind man, and Pandu, 'the pale one'. Pandu is king but, due to a curse, he has to renounce the throne. He has five sons by divine birth through Kunti – Yudhishtira, Bhima, Arjuna, Nakula and Sandeva. These are the Pandevas. Dhritharashtra (who has become king despite his blindness) marries Gandhari and after an extraordinary birth, she mothers one hundred sons, the Kauravas. The first-born, Duryodhana, is full of hate and destruction and responsible for much of the conflict. The five Pandevas marry the same woman, Draupadi, because of an irrevocable slip of the tongue on the part of their mother beseeching her sons to share everything. Since no word uttered in *The Mahabharata* can ever be undone, they are compelled to share a wife. The Pandevas try to avert war but Duryodhana cannot stand Yudhishtira's wisdom and so invites him to a game of dice, knowing his weakness for gambling. Yudhishtira loses everything – kingdom, brothers, even Draupadi. She is about to be stripped naked before the court, when she calls on Krishna who performs a miracle. She swears vengeance in war.

The Pandevas are condemned to twelve years' exile in the forest and a thirteenth year in disguise so that no one may recognise them. In their exile they meet with many obstacles and threats from the Kauravas. However, the god Shiva comes to the aid of Arjuna, the chief warrior of the Pandevas, and gives him the supreme weapon, capable of destroying the entire world. In the thirteenth year of exile, Yudhishtira predicts the coming of the dark age, the age of Kali. Further warnings of the destruction of the world, and of its salvation in the belly of a child, are given by Vyasa.

War approaches. Duryodhana refuses to give back his cousins their kingdom because they came out of hiding before the agreed time. Duryodhana and Arjuna ask Krishna for support but Krishna decides to give support to the Pandevas. The blind king fears his sons and the consequences of war and so asks the ageing Bhisma to take supreme command of the battle. Just before the battle begins, Arjuna, seeing the relatives he is going to kill, breaks down. Krishna encourages and fortifies him with advice about resolute action in the world – the text of *The Bhagavad Gita*. The battle ensues leaving millions dead.[5]

The drama functions on two planes: first, the will of the gods who can change into whatever form they wish to take; and second, the will of humans on earth to fulfil their destiny. Among the humans, the key tension arises between sons and nephews (cousin rivalry) and between fathers and uncles (male sibling rivalry). To redeem humans one needs women. They act as mothers, stepmothers, adoptive mothers, rearing aunties, mothers-in-law and daughters-in-law. It is their sacrifice which guides men towards their duty to the gods. Thus men fulfil the will of the gods; men owe their pride to the gods and their existence to female humans.

The film of the play and the sacred soap

Brook's TV production is based on his theatrical version of *The Mahabharata*. An international co-production, spearheaded by Channel 4, it was shot on 35mm film at the Joinville studios, Paris. The visual style of the film and its mode of realism were thus crucially determined by the studio setting. The sets, which are sparse, bare and earth-coloured, match the costumes which are equally simple and sombre. There are no realistic exteriors, no batallions of warriors. Close-ups and photographic precision convey a certain realism. Costumes, lamps, weapons and furnishings were brought from India in order to ensure 'close-up' realism. The result is the cinematic equivalent of the stage version.[6] The cast of Brook's production is international and drawn from each of the five continents, no doubt to emphasise the universal nature of the story and to ensure international appeal.

Brook's production is theatrical, authored and targeted at a middle-class, educated audience. Although screened in six consecutive hours on a Saturday evening, it defies any simple generic classification. If it falls into any generic category, the 'single play' tradition of British television would be most appropriate. It is divided into three main parts: The Game of Dice; Exile in the Forest; and The War.

In sharp contrast, Doordarshan's production is not specifically authored. It is televisual and aimed at a mass, national audience, many of whom are illiterate. However, it appeals across class, caste, regional, and even religious boundaries, and it bridges 'high' and 'low' cultural forms. As a genre it most resembles the continuing serial or soap in its length (approximately 70 hours), its preoccupation with family conflicts and kinship ties and in the intimacy and familiarity with the characters which develops alongside the unfolding narrative.

The sets are majestic and palatial, inhabited by kings and queens, gods and goddesses. We are transported from the heavens to earth, from magnificent palaces to epic battlefields. The costumes and jewellery are opulent, regal and highly colourful. Special effects are employed to convey the actions or miracles of the gods. At one moment, thousands of arrows are seen darting across the heavens and goddesses magically appear from the sea; while at the next moment we are invited to share in the splendour of the gods in paradise. Dramatic moments in the story are powerfully reinforced by music, song and special effects. The earth is made to tremble and shake, lightning and thunder split the sky asunder in order to convey the solemnity of a promise or the anger of the gods. In accordance with Hindi film conventions, the narrative moves through

successive modes of spectacle, action, emotion, song and intense dialogue in circular rather than linear fashion.

As I shall indicate, the Dhani children's perceptions of the striking
differences between these two productions provide a valuable insight
into the frames of reference and reservoirs of knowledge and experience
which they draw upon in making sense of them.

Part Two: Making sense of The Mahabharata

Characterisation and visual representation

It is difficult to convey the bewildering confusion which accompanied
our first viewing of Brook's *Mahabharata*. To set the scene, ten people
were present, the family and myself. Unused to viewing in such a large
group, I was surprised by the amount of talk and comment and thus
found it difficult to hear and follow the narrative. From the outset, the
children were shouting 'who's that?', simultaneously trying to identify
and explain who was who! The international casting and the representation of the characters had the immediate effect of rendering their dearly
loved gods and goddesses unrecognisable, and this confusion was voiced
in an unceasing barrage of argument:

> *Ranjit*: Look! that's Ganesha!
> *Sefali*: No it isn't, be quiet!
> *Lipi*: There's Vishnu!
> *Malati*: Don't be silly, its Vyasa.
> *Ranjit*: But Vyasa is Vishnu.
> *Sefali*: No he isn't, he's Krishna.

The children appealed to their mother for help, but she was even more
lost than they because she understands very little English. The father and
elder son went out after thirty minutes or so, muttering, 'it's no good, it
doesn't carry the meaning'. The international casting was greeted variously – the younger children found the black character playing Bhisma
amusing, whilst a certain unvoiced disapproval on the part of the mother
could be detected. Sefali, the 19-year-old daughter, thought it emphasised the universal nature of the story's appeal:

> *Sefali*: They've chosen actors from so many different races, it sort of brings
> all the world together, it makes you feel as if all the human race is one. I
> suppose they want to show that *The Mahabharata* relates to the whole
> human race.

But the whole dilemma on the first viewing revolved around identifying the characters. They were familiar with the basic storyline and the main characters and their attributes from the cartoon-strips and from a three-hour Hindi film of *The Mahabharata*. They felt that if they succeeded in recognising and naming the character, they would then be more likely to be able to situate them within the narrative. Viewing became a frantic guessing game, but they had few visual clues to help them. Whilst the dialogues were simple and clear, they demanded a degree of concentration difficult to achieve amidst the noise. After confusion, irritation set in:

> *Sefali*: You can't even recognise Krishna here, normally he's blue.
> *Malati*: And Gunga and Bhisma normally wear white because it's a symbol of purity and truth.
> *Ranjit*: All the strong characters are black, like Bhisma and Kunti but Bhisma should look more physically strong.
> *Sefali*: Black seems to symbolise strength.
> *Malati*: But they've chosen the right kind of actor to play Karna because he's strong and has a certain meanness about him.
> *Ranjit*: Duryodhana should wear red, shouldn't he? Red stands for blood, anger and fire.

Certain conventional visual codes had been flouted, such as the use of colours, usually symbolic of certain qualities and associated with particular character attributes. Such colour classification and symbolism is to be found in many ancient religions and provides a kind of primordial classification of reality.[7] But this was simply the tip of the iceberg. More disarming than the disruption caused by the visual codes was the transgression of deeply-rooted cultural codes. But this only became apparent upon viewing the Indian version, for it was not until then that they were able to articulate the difference between these quite distinct styles of representation.

> *Sefali*: All the gods are born into royal families. In the Indian one you can tell the gods from humans but not in the English one. In the Indian one you can tell who is the king from what he wears, how he talks and behaves, you can tell by his strength. Like the gods, they actually show their strength and also when Krishna appears there's always joyful music. There are other details, like the king will always wear gold and the prince silver.
> *Sewanti*: Like in the Indian one you can tell a baddy because he will be wearing black clothes and the music will have an evil feel to it, but in the English one you can't tell who's who, they've left it all to language, whereas in the Indian one everything contributes to the meaning, the way they speak and how they are spoken to, how they behave, what they wear, their clothes, jewellery, their actions, everything has meaning.

Malati: The respect is missing, like you would never hear Krishna being called by his name like that, it would always be Lord Krishna, you would never hear someone call their elder by their name, you would have to show them respect by using their proper title. Like in the Indian one people show Krishna respect by kneeling and kissing his feet. The way you greet someone, how you sit and talk, all these things are missing. These might seem like little things but they are very important.

The casting, the visual representation of the gods, the flouting of well-established visual and cultural codes made it difficult for the Dhani family to 'read' and therefore enjoy the Brook production. They expressed their distaste at its profanity:

Munni: It doesn't, you know, concern me.
Sewanti: They show the culture as if people lived in the jungle.
Lippi: Some of the actors can't act or speak properly, they've got funny accents.
Sewanti: They've spoilt the picture of the culture, they've done us disservice, really.
Munni: There's no, you know, no feeling in it, you can't feel for the characters.
Malati: They borrowed the story but not the culture, the culture is missing.
Ranjit: Mum says it left a bad taste in her mouth and that she had to watch the Indian one to get her taste back.
Sewanti: You see, we can't accept Krishna being shown like he was just anybody. He's not given any dignity.

The lack of distinction between gods and humans is distasteful to them because the gods are not portrayed with due status, dignity and respect. In contrast, the representation of the gods in the Indian version conforms to conventional portrayals in which they are seen to emanate a sacred aura. Consequently, they can be worshipped on the screen.

The visual codes associated with the representation of Hindu deities have developed over centuries. However, the introduction of popular, mass-produced prints has resulted in fixed stereotypical portrayals of the gods. Tapati Guha-Thakurta has traced the changing iconography of popular religious picture production in India. He describes how the introduction of lithography presses and colour printing in the domain of artisanal picture production led to the increasing turnover of gaudy chromolithographs of Hindu deities

with loud flamboyant colours, dazzling costumes and majestic backdrops as their main trademark. These pictures have a rather tenuous basis in realism except in the solidity and roundedness they imparted to all forms ... the humanisation and domestication of divinity, theatrical postures and expressions became part of the fixed stereotype of the gods.[8]

These popular mass-produced prints were important in establishing conventional portrayals of Hindu deities in filmic and televisual forms. The power and authority of such 'sacred' representations cannot be ignored. Small wonder that the apparent profanity of Brook's version should surprise and disorientate spectators. However, it is when questions of narrative are discussed that one gains deeper insight into the cultural frames of reference which the Dhani children have at their disposal.

Narrative

The experience of viewing a six-hour televised drama is hardly comparable to the weekly viewing of a 45-minute episode of a 92-part serial. The Indian version is seen to resemble various soap operas. The young Dhanis claim that the Indian version is like a soap because it allows for greater identification with the characters and their dilemmas and a deeper affective engagement in the narrational processes:

> Malati: You get to know the characters much better in the Indian one and the funny or special things about them. Like Bhisma, in the Indian one whenever he gets a chance he is eating, he's playful and silly but aggressive when he wants to be.
> Sefali: Another thing is that you can identify with the characters better, because it's slower, you get to know the characters you like and dislike, you can put yourself in their shoes, but not with the English one, they all seem far away, distant, but in this one you feel you're in it, you're involved.

The frequent moments of 'high' melodrama, often involving the uninhibited expression of heightened emotion, are compared with similar moments in weekly American soaps like Dallas and Dynasty. Furthermore, they are compared not only in terms of their luxurious settings (the palatial homes in Dallas and Dynasty and the dazzling opulence of courtly life in The Mahabharata) but also in terms of their central preoccupation with good and evil. Other parallels with soaps are made: the complex interweaving of plots; the cliffhanger endings; the pleasurable anticipation of viewing; intense involvement while viewing; subsequent discussions about what has happened in an episode; the mobilisation of knowledge about past events in making sense of the unfolding story; and predictions about what might happen. The addictive pleasures of the soap format are highlighted with reference to Neighbours, the most popular daily soap among the Dhani children. At the same time, the serial narration is contrasted with the economy and density of the narration in the English version which condenses and inflates the main narrative events, eliminating the many subplots.

Malati: It's like *Neighbours*, you get hooked on it.
Sefali: The English one has a beginning and an end but the Indian version seems to have no beginning and no end.

Despite the apparent 'profanity' of such comparisons with soap operas, it is clear that the serial narrative of the Indian version is better able to represent epic, cyclical and mythical notions of time which constitute the philosophical core of *The Mahabharata* – which in turn enables the Dhani children to mobilise their formidable repertoire of cultural knowledge in constructing the narrative.

The role of the narrator

The role of the narrator is also different in both versions. In Brook's *Mahabharata*, the story is narrated by the god Vishnu through Vyasa and transcribed by Ganesha (the elephant god who is an incarnation of Vishnu). A young Indian boy accompanies Vyasa and Ganesha. The children most closely identify with the boy:

> *Malati*: I think the boy is an example of a human being and he's there to show us what we can gain from watching. The story is being told to the boy by Vyasa and he asks the questions that we would.
> *Sefali*: You see, when the boy asks, 'Do I have the same blood, do I come from the gods?', that is how the story starts, that is how the human race came about and we are like the boy, a part of the human race, it is telling us that we are all one.

In the English version we see Vyasa the narrator whereas in the Indian version the narrator is given a divine quality. The story is directly narrated by Vishnu who does not appear in person but as a disembodied voice emanating from heaven:

> *Sefali*: In the Indian one you see the shadow of the world going round, that symbolises time and destiny, which goes on and on, because time waits for no one. It is the shadow that is telling the story. It is Vishnu. Vishnu is time and time rules the gods and the universe. Time is eternal.
> *Malati*: When there's something important, like Bhisma's vow, he interrupts the story and explains things because some people might not understand the importance of it. The Indian one explains everything to you. It helps you understand the meaning of the story. The English one doesn't really explain the important things to you.
> *Sefali*: Vyasa is Krishna and he is the only one who can tell the story. Without him there would be no story because Krishna is Vishnu and Vishnu is time, that's why Krishna's got the Chakkar around his wrist, that's how you always recognise Krishna, by the Chakkar.

The Chakkar is a bracelet, a distinguishing feature of Krishna, symbolising the circle of time or eternity. Time is one of the central themes of *The Mahabharata* – although in contrast to the Western notion, it is not conceived of as linear but as cyclical. The children struggle to understand and express such complex philosophical notions with the help of the narrator. The narrator takes on a much more interventionist and didactic role in the Indian version. Unlike conventional soap operas in the West, this 'sacred soap' does not allow the viewer to adopt a shifting point of view. The narrator provides the dominant discourse, guiding and leading the viewer to a 'proper' understanding of themes and events. These didactic passages, which explain notions of time or the interchangeability of the gods, narrated from the heavens, are rewound and reviewed and listened to by the family again and again until they arrive at some understanding of what is being explained.

One of the most beneficial features of the Indian version is the subtitles. If something is not understood in Hindi, they can read the subtitles in English. Although the Dhanis' mother-tongue is Bengali, they understand Hindi very well, partly as a result of their long-term exposure to Hindi films. Hindi is also the language of religious worship in the temple. Nevertheless, there are gaps in their understanding of Hindi which impede their full understanding of the Indian *Mahabharata*. In contrast, the language register of Brook's production is, for the most part, accessible to them. In this version, it is the casting, foreign accents and the condensation of narrative events which impede comprehension. However, being able to switch from one language to the other (Hindi, English and Bengali), and from spoken to written language, mobilises and assists the development of the full range of their linguistic competences which are applied to the task of 'reading' these texts.

While Bengali is used to discuss the finer points of interpretation with their mother, the young Dhanis will use English among themselves. They learn Sanskrit by memorising the songs in the Indian version, practise their Hindi by imitating the characters' dialogues and are able to translate the private world of their religious beliefs and practices into what is for them the more public language of English. Furthermore, in their eagerness to understand the full intricacies of the story and plumb the depths of *The Mahabharata*, the gaps in their understanding of the TV serials have encouraged them to read various versions of the story in English and in Hindi. The interaction of various kinds of literacies (visual, oral, aural and written), of different linguistic registers and of different cultural systems allows the Dhanis to develop and intellectually benefit from their multilingualism. It also helps them to integrate their religious world view into their everyday life more effectively. I also suspect that being able to articulate their religious views in a sophisticated manner in English allows them to feel a greater sense of pride in the religion. The Dhanis would be the first to acknowledge that these cultural and linguistic competences have been developed through their viewing of *The Mahabharata* over a two-year period.

Narrative weighting

One further difference between the two versions is in the dramatic weighting given to events. As I shall indicate, this has significant consequences for the Dhanis' readings. In general, the children perceive narrative events in the English version as unrealistic, magical and metaphorical, whereas in the Indian version they are understood morally and literally. The perceived realism of events is a function not only of the different modes of representation employed but also of the religious beliefs they bring to the text and of their conviction that *The Mahabharata* recounts actual historical events. This has profound implications for their engagement in the dramaturgical process. The weighting given to events and actions, and the moments of tension, dramatic climax and resolution are entirely different in the two versions. In order to demonstrate this point more fully, let us compare how both versions deal with the same sequence, which occurs at the beginning of *The Mahabharata*.

BHISMA'S VOW

Santanu, the king, is married to Gunga. They are gods who were cursed by Brahma (Gunga's father and The Creator) and sent to earth to suffer as humans. Upon marrying Santanu, Gunga made him promise that he would never question any of her actions. She gives birth to seven sons and she drowns each of them to save them from human suffering. The king is broken-hearted but he cannot ask her why she drowns their sons. On the birth of the eighth son he breaks his promise and saves his child. That child is Bhisma, who is witness to the entire story. The children are able to interpret this seeming act of cruelty as being for the greater moral good. Gunga sacrifices her children since she knows they are cursed to suffer as humans. She is seen as possessing greater moral strength than her husband who, cursed to suffer as a human, acts with human frailty.

Years later, Gunga having disappeared and Bhisma a grown man, King Santanu falls in love with Satiavati and asks her father for her hand. Her father will only agree to their marriage if King Santanu forbids

Bhisma to claim his right to the throne, thus allowing Satiavati's son to be the king's successor. The price is too high for the king because he loves and respects his son and rightful heir, Bhisma. But in an act of supreme self-sacrifice and devotion to his father, Bhisma makes a vow, renouncing the throne and promising to remain celibate forever. He hopes to prevent any contest over the throne in future generations. To reward his son for such moral strength, Santanu blesses Bhisma with the power to choose the time of his own death.

The dramatic weighting given to these events in the two versions is entirely different. In the Indian version the moral order is disturbed by Santanu breaking his promise never to question his wife and this is given dramatic effect by the music, acting style and the narrator's interventions. Moral order is restored when Bhisma makes his vow. It is hard to convey the emotion and awe that this act inspired in the children.

> *Ranjit*: In the English version they make it seem like it's just a little promise but in the Indian version, Bhisma's vow shakes the earth, thunder and lightning open up the skies. No human would be able to make a promise like that just to please his father. I love that bit, it's pure! If he does that for his father, imagine what he would do for his mother!
> *Lipi*: In the English version you don't get all the background so you don't really understand the importance of the vow. If Bhisma had been king, the whole history of the world would have been different. There wouldn't have been a fight for the throne.

Furthermore, in order to underline the significance of this vow, the narrative flow is interrupted by shots of the heavens, accompanied by the narrator's voice saying 'Never has there been such a man.' Thereafter follow scenes of intense emotional power, intimate exchanges between father and son revealing the king's guilt for his son's suffering which causes him to die a broken-hearted man. His father's death leaves a void and opens up the further problem of his succession; a theme which dominates the entire narrative. The movement of the narrative, from disruption to resolution to further disruption, is moral in nature. The intense emotional exchange between Bhisma and his father, which powerfully expresses the strength of kinship bonds and duty, has a profound affective impact on the Dhani children. Scenes such as these function as normative guides to conduct in the family and serve to reinforce established values of respect, loyalty, honour and obedience in their own family life.

By contrast, the English version emphasises narrative events which are not very significant to them. For example, Brook's production gives enormous weighting to the divine births of the Pandevas and

Kauravas. Indeed the births form the dramatic high point of the first part:

> *Malati*: In the Indian one, Kunti never tells you where she gets her children from, it's taken for granted that the Pandevas are gods, not like in the English one where they had to explain that to English people because they probably wouldn't understand that they are superhuman, so you have to adapt it to them.
>
> *Sefali*: It's like the idea of Dharma. Every Hindu person will know the importance of this word. It means law and duty. It's, like, the law upon which the order of the world rests, and if you don't get that, you can't understand *The Mahabharata*. It's like the idea of Karma as well. We know something about these ideas but they have to explain it for English people.

In the Indian version, certain cultural knowledge is assumed. In constructing and responding to the narrative, the children are able to draw upon this knowledge whilst also being able to position themselves as English spectators who need certain 'taken for granted' things explained. But it would be a mistake to assume that this knowledge or cultural competence is somehow complete or equally shared and agreed upon among the Dhani children. On the contrary, they constantly battle with each other over differences in comprehension and details of interpretation.

DRAUPAUDI'S HUMILIATION

Another episode which was much discussed by the Dhani children was that of Draupaudi's humiliation. Draupaudi is the wife of the five Pandevas. Yudhishtira, the eldest of the Pandevas, is cajoled into a game of dice with Duryodhana, the eldest of the Kauravas. His weakness for gambling leads him to lose everything the Pandevas possess. He even bets and loses his wife Draupadi. The Kauravas attempt to humiliate her and violate her honour by stripping her of her sari in public. Krishna intervenes and magically bestows upon her a sari of infinite length, thus safeguarding her honour. This is a turning-point in *The Mahabharata*, but again the lack of narrative significance attributed to this event and its portrayal in Brook's version is considered inept and even shocking by the Dhani children:

> *Malati*: In the English version, when they drag her into the court, she lets everyone know that she shouldn't be seen in public because she has her period. In the Indian version they just hint at it. It's understood, because she's wearing yellow clothes and she's segregated – normally she's all dressed up like a queen.
>
> *Sefali*: In the Indian version (...) the true strength of her character comes

out. She questions all the men in the court (...) she thinks they're being weak.

Ranjit: And in the English one Bhisma looks at Duryodhana trying to strip her clothes off her. He would never do that.(...)

Malati: they call her a prostitute and insult her really badly but the hurt of all this doesn't come across in the English one (...).

Sefali: (...) in the Indian one, there's that amazing vision of Krishna (...) Krishna performs the miracle. They don't show miracles properly in the English one.

Ranjit: She swears she will get her revenge and after that she keeps the wound alive.

Sefali: It's this incident which really leads to the war.

According to the Dhanis, the deep insult of Draupadi's humiliation, her self-defence and Krishna's divine intervention in this episode are not given due weight and authority in Brook's version. To them, Draupadi represents a powerful symbol of female strength and authority. In the Indian version she rejects silence and explodes her anger in court. In doing so she raises a whole series of questions concerning her status as woman, as wife, as property, as slave, as subject and as object, which Brook misses.

It is of interest that critical commentaries on Brook's version, which I have come across more recently, also highlight Draupadi's humiliation as exemplifying Brook's 'orientalist' misinterpretation of the epic. For example Rustom Bharucha[9] is clearly seething at what he calls Brook's 'inter-cultural experiment', his 'cultural appropriation' of *The Mahabharata*, as he writes: '(...) not once are we made to feel that Draupadi has been seriously wronged. (...) One never really senses the threat of rape in Duhsassana's handling of Draupadi (...) When Draupadi wails, "Where is Dharma?", it seems like pointless hysteria, a case of a woman not being able to shut up on time' (p. 244).

The coincidence of viewpoint between Indian cultural critics, the Dhanis and others whom I interviewed in Southall about *The Mahabharata* would suggest that such negative responses to Brook's 'Westernised' production are perhaps more widespread than this case study can convey. The lack of a clearly defined religious framework of reference; its lack of contextualisation within the social and ritual processes of Hindu society; the loss of humanity which Draupadi and Yudishthira undergo are but three of the other criticisms that Bharucha makes which correspond with those of the Dhanis. According to both, Brook does not have a sufficient grasp of the religious and philosophical basis of *The Mahabharata* nor of Hinduism to convey the dramatic significance of certain events. Cultural codes and conventions which have powerful symbolic meaning are so frequently flouted that the plausibility of the production is destroyed.

The Bhagavad Gita

As I have mentioned, the first viewing of Brook's *Mahabharata* was accompanied by confusion and a sense of alarm. The TV was switched off at the point when Krishna persuades Arjuna to go to war and fight his cousins the Kauravas. Krishna is a god, an incarnation of Vishnu, and yet he engineers deceit and provokes war. As Malati said, 'You don't know who're the goodies and the baddies in this one.' This was so disconcerting for them that the elder daughter and mother went upstairs to pray, returned downstairs, lit incense and decided to watch *Sita's Wedding*, a religious film which recounts an episode in the life of Krishna from *The Ramayana*, the main source of the Dhani children's knowledge of Krishna. In *Sita's Wedding*, Krishna is presented as 'sweet' and unambiguous. He is portrayed in an almost monotheistic way, demonstrating 'goodness' in his every word and deed. His character inspires the greatest love and devotion. Little wonder, therefore, that Krishna as he appears in *The Mahabharata* should so disturb and disarm the Dhani children. It was not until later that I realised that, at this point of Brook's *Mahabharata*, it became very difficult for Malati and her family to continue believing in the divinity of Krishna.

> *Sefali*: Why does Krishna persuade Arjuna to go to war if he is a god?
> *Ranjit*: Why didn't he prevent the war from happening?
> *Malati*: He throws away the Chakkar [the bracelet representing the circle of time] at the battle. He's no longer in control of time. He lets the war happen.
> *Ranjit*: He shouldn't have done that.

In an attempt to overcome their bewilderment at Krishna's incitement to war, the episode of Doordarshan's *Mahabharata* which covers the battlefield dialogue between Krishna and Arjuna (otherwise known as *The Bhagavad Gita*) was obtained from the video shop and we viewed it several times. A copy of *The Bhagavad Gita* was also borrowed from the library. This is perhaps the most sacred of Hindu texts and is said to contain the essence of Hindu wisdom. Through repeated viewings, reading and discussion the Dhanis learned to rationalise the moral paradox that confronted them and to articulate some of the more profound philosophical themes of *The Mahabharata*. The didacticism of Doordarshan's *Mahabharata* enabled them to learn the discursive register of The *Gita*'s teachings and to take pleasure in explaining its principles to each other and to me:

Malati: The *Gita*, it's strange because it makes you see good in bad and bad in good.

Sefali: That's because everything depends upon time. In the early stages of time, human beings lived close to the gods and things were in harmony. But then time moves on to a stage where humans move away from the gods and then chaos comes. Krishna was born into the Age of Destruction.

Malati: You see, Krishna is starting the war off, he says to Arjuna that he must take the kingdom even though it means killing his own family. But you can't say Krishna is being bad, he's doing the best for mankind in the long run.

Through reviewing various episodes of *The Mahabharata*, an understanding emerges which accepts that whilst the actions of the gods may seem immoral in the short term, in the long term, they will be for the good.

Ranjit: If the world doesn't have Yudhishtira for king then the world will be bad anyway. Krishna's intentions are good. He knows that you have to go through a bloody war, all because of justice. He does it to fulfil Dharma.

Sefali: You see, human are ruled by time and so is the world. Not even the gods can prevent some things happening. The world has to fulfil its own destiny *in time* like human beings. That is our fate, to be reincarnated until we attain Nirvana.

Thus we see here that repeated viewings of *The Mahabharata* enable them to articulate a cosmic view of the world which challenges and negates some of the certainties of their pragmatic everyday world. But these distinctive world views interact, coexist and even contradict one another. This is evident when the radical nature of the ideas expressed about time, the ambiguity of good and evil and the paradoxical actions of the gods are taken back and *The Mahabharata* is reduced to a battle between 'goodies and baddies':

Malati: Krishna has taken sides with the Pandevas because before the battle he sees Duryodhana and says, 'what do you want, my army or me?' and Duryodhana replies, 'your army' because be thinks that will help him win the battle. Then he goes to Arjuna and asks 'what do you want, my army or me?' and he replies 'you'. The Pandevas brothers are more holy than the Kauravas. They make the right decision. That's why Krishna drives their chariot for them.

This is a consolation. By giving a reason why Krishna protects the Pandevas – they are good, unlike the Kauravas, and are worthy of his protection – the everyday pragmatic world view rears its head again and the notion of good and bad are reinstated as categories.

Sefali: *The Mahabharata* makes you see life like it's a battle between good and evil that everyone fights (...) a battle for, sort of, justice or Dharma, and when the equilibrium is lost you have chaos, like in *King Lear*.

For the Dhanis, the possibility for human beings in any stage of history to escape chaos by moral action becomes a necessity for pragmatic, everyday living. Thus in the short term, through honesty, devotion and performing one's duty, moral action is possible but, in the face of eternity, the distinction between good and evil disappears. However, the consequences of moral actions can never be presumed:

Sefali: Human beings have a free will, they can choose between different actions. Destiny or fate don't control everything, neither do the gods, people have some freedom to choose their path. But you can't do something good with the hope of getting a reward. You must first know what is right and then do it. But if you do something good you can't be sure the outcome will be good.

Ranjit: We're created by the gods, but in the war if the Kauravas had won it, all the world would have been bad. But when Arjuna and Krishna won the battle, they gave good people to the world and even though there are always some bad people in the world but there are always good people to show them the way. Anyway, [he chuckles] that's what the gods thought!

The application of ideas and beliefs derived from their religious world view and undoubtedly developed and refined by their viewing of *The Mahabharata* is evident in many aspects of the children's everyday lives. But the examples in the data are too rich in detail and too numerous to recount here. Suffice it to say that notions of time, fate, destiny, enlightenment, self-knowledge, reincarnation and salvation are deeply embedded in their consciousness and frame their perceptions of everyday reality. The Dhanis' responses to *The Mahabharata* have helped to make explicit the connections and interactions between their belief, action and value systems. The integration of religious and commonsense world views is made apparent in they way that notions of time, in particular the Age of Destruction, are linked to the contemporary threats of nuclear and ecological disasters:

Sefali: Time moves in circles and there are times when the world moves away from god, don't you think it's a bit like that now? We have the ultimate weapon, like the Pandevas, we have nuclear weapons. Humans are destroying the environment. Birds and fish are dying because humans don't respect them. Money is God today. The *Gita* teaches us that our real wealth is our soul because that is eternal and that if you act upon knowledge and do good then you can't be destroyed, ultimately.

Malati: If you think about it, why do holy men meditate? It's to get their soul pure, so that the body becomes immaterial. You have to lose desire and when you get to this state, Krishna takes your senses, he comes into you and you see through him, hear through him, everything you touch is

69

through him, everything. It is then you become harmonious with god – that's Nirvana.

The high point of the entire 92 episodes of *The Mahabharata* came during the *Bhagavad Gita* sequence when Krishna shows Arjuna his Universal Form. The sheer awe with which this sequence was viewed by the family was as stunning as the images on the screen. Krishna can only reveal himself to those who are enlightened and when Arjuna, full of self-doubt before the battle, asks Krishna 'How should I recognise you?' a shaft of light shoots out from Krishna's hand into Arjuna's eye. A low-angle tracking shot follows Krishna, surrounded by a golden aura, and, as he moves gracefully through air, his figure expands to dominate the screen and his multifarious incarnations successively appear around him amidst flames and shafts of water. These images represent to the believing viewer the transmigration of souls. Small human bodies float into the mouth of one of Krishna's incarnations and out of another as if on a waterfall. It represents, for the Dhanis, the nearest thing on earth to a divine vision. Inside Krishna's mouth one is offered a view of eternity and the cosmos. It is as if Krishna makes an appearance in the living room. This is Nirvana on TV.

Conclusions

Five propositions are woven through this chapter, which are summarised below. First, the Hindu children in this family come to *The Mahabharata* with two distinctive reservoirs of cultural knowledge and experience: one based on Indian culture and religion (acquired through socialisation in the home and local neighbourhood) and the second based on socialisation in British institutions, particularly in school and among their peers. In both contexts, young people use TV to negotiate issues of cultural identity and difference. However, these reservoirs of knowledge and experience (like the ideological categories, British and Indian culture, upon which they are based) are neither mutually exclusive nor necessarily oppositional but interact with, support and condition each other. They are the symbolic and material systems through which young people in Southall actively and creatively construct, integrate and transform their social lives.

Secondly, the juxtaposition of the English and Indian versions of *The Mahabharata* in the domestic context generates comparative readings of the texts. These comparative readings provide a key to unlock the cultural specificity of the interpretative frames and filters which the young people in this family draw upon to 'read' this epic. The two versions offer very different interpretations of the text. They employ different aesthetic styles, modes of realism and narrational strategies. They are communicated in different languages and, above all, they are set in very different cultural frameworks. Thus, in 'reading' both versions, the young people in this family mobilise, and in the process develop, distinctive kinds of literacies and sets of competences.

Thirdly, in responding to *The Mahabharata*, two separate perspectives, or ways of perceiving the world, emerge in the discourses of the young people in this Hindu family: the first may be described as a common-sense perspective, in that it emphasises the pragmatic rather than the ideal course of action; while the other is religious and informed by Hinduism as a cultural system, and may transcend as well as contradict the pragmatic world view. Viewing and discussing *The Mahabharata* contributes directly to their religious world view which shapes activity in the pragmatic world. The interaction of these distinctive components in their world views are evidenced in their readings of *The Mahabharata*.

Fourthly, the video-cassette recorder and local cable TV have made popular Hindi TV programmes and films available to families in Southall on an unprecedented scale. The didactic use of religious films and programmes and their integration in acts of religious worship and ritual are contributing to changes in the practices of Hinduism itself. In particular, such uses are facilitating the increasingly central role of domestic as opposed to public worship among Hindus in Southall. TV as a domestic technology is uniquely suited to the purposes of domestic worship. Viewing *The Mahabharata* fuses domestic and religious ritual and through such concrete acts of religious observance, religious beliefs and convictions are articulated within the framework of a general conception of the world, of the self and of the relations between them. As a consequence, the boundaries between public and private, as well as between male and female roles in these domains, are being realigned.

Fifthly, for the young people in this family, and in Southall more generally, there is no easy equation between geography, culture and the media. The new TV delivery systems allow Punjabis in London to keep in touch with Indian and Pakistani popular culture. TV plays a significant role in re-creating and re-presenting 'tradition' among first and second generation Hindus in Southall.[10] But the ideological implications of viewing *The Mahabharata* are a more elusive matter. Already in India the hugely popular TV serialisations of the *The Mahabharata* and *The Ramayana* are criticised for playing into the hands of a growing Hindu fundamentalism. And yet how different are their ideological connotations in the context of Southall, a Punjabi Sikh town where, in certain quarters, Sikh fundamentalism thrives but where Hindus themselves are a minority and where Hindi audio-visual media dominate. The complexities of this situation require further analysis. For the moment suffice it to say that the system of beliefs and values that *The Mahabharata* and *The Ramayana* propagate are to be found reinscribed and reinstated in every contemporary popular Hindi film. So pervasive is their influence that, it is argued, they function as a pan-Indian metadiscourse, an understanding of which is essential to any exploration of contemporary Hindi media.[11]

Finally, while ethnographic methods have long been advocated in media audience research, few studies have taken on board what characterises ethnography as a method, namely long-term participant observation in a selected field. A more fully ethnographic approach to audience research can deliver the kind of data which would take us beyond the sterile dichotomy often erected between approaches which emphasise 'TV doing things to people' and those which consider 'people doing things with TV'. Conversely, anthropologists who have long ignored everyday uses and interpretations of the media in their studies of contemporary cultures and societies may find, as I have done, that audience research offers a beautifully oblique research strategy which can deliver rich ethnographic data.

Notes and references

1 Details in this paragraph were obtained from *The Mahabharata: A Viewer's Guide to Peter Brook's Epic Film* (Channel 4, 1989). However, Vijay Mishra ('The Great Indian Epic and Peter Brook', pp. 201–2 in *Peter Brook and The Mahabharata: Critical Perspectives* (Routledge, 1991)) argues that Peter Brook succumbs to the power of the seductive extension of the Sanskrit words *maha* and *bharat* to mean 'The Great History of Mankind'. Despite this universalistic and humanist interpretation he does, according to Mishra, seem to be conscious of the epic's propensity to destabilise, distort and confuse the basic categories of good and evil, fate and free will.

2 See 'The Ramayana TV serial – and Indian secularism', *Intermedia*, 17: 5 (October/November 1989).

3 M. Gillespie, 'TV Talk in a London Punjabi Peer Culture', Ph.D thesis (Department of Human Sciences, Brunel University, Uxbridge, Middlesex, 1992). To be published by Routledge as *TV, Ethnicity and Cultural Change: An Ethnographic Study of Punjabi Londoners* (forthcoming, 1994).

4 See, for example, Catherine Ballard, 'Conflict, Continuity and Change: Second Generation Asians', in V. Saifullah Khan (ed.), *Minority Families in Britain* (Macmillan, 1979) and Community Relations Commission, *Between Two Cultures:*

A Study in the Relationships Between Generations in the Asian Community in Britain (1978).

5 This summary of the story has drawn upon *The Mahabharata: A Viewer's Guide to Peter Brook's Epic Film* (Channel 4, 1989).

6 For full production details, see Garry O'Connor, *The Mahabharata* (Hodder and Stoughton, 1989).

7 See Victor Turner, 'Colour Classification in Ndembu Ritual', in Michael Banton (ed.), *Anthropological Approaches to the Study of Religion* (Tavistock, 1966).

8 Tapati Guha-Thakurta, *Artisans, Artists and Mass Picture Production in Late 19th and Early 20th Century in Calcutta*, paper presented at the South Asia Research Conference, School of Oriental and African Studies, University of London (summer 1986), p. 11.

9 Rustom Bharucha, 'A View From India' in David Williams (ed.), *Peter Brook and The Mahabharata: Critical Perspectives* (Routledge, 1991).

10 For a fuller account of this issue, see Marie Gillespie, 'Technology and tradition: audio-visual culture among south-Asian families in west London', *Cultural Studies*, 3: 2 (May 1989).

11 Vijay Mishra, 'Toward a theoretical critique of Bombay cinema', *Screen*, 26: 3–4 (May–August 1985).

4

VALERIE WALKERDINE
WITH THE ASSISTANCE OF JUNE MELODY

'Daddy's gonna buy you a dream to cling to
(and mummy's gonna love you just as much as
she can)':
young girls and popular television

Introduction

Six-year-old Eliana plays in front of the video of *Annie* that her father has
given her and her sisters as a present. Her mother talks to them and to
me as a drama unfolds in the living-room that has painful resonances
with the *Annie* story itself. In this chapter I will be concerned to analyse
this case-study as a way of examining the place of popular television and
video in constituting the subjectivity of young, predominantly working-
class girls. I intend to explore how these media enter the lives of young
girls and help to form their sense of themselves.

The approach that I am using here derives from psychoanalytic
and post-structuralist theory. It proposes that subjects are created
through their insertion into practices which are the object of regulation
and that it is in and through their positionings within those practices
that girls' subjectivities are constituted. I propose to address this in two
interrelated ways: by examining the regulation of working-class children's viewing practices and by considering its relation to the positioning of girls within the actual practices of domestic viewing. To do this I
will examine in detail one case-study of a six-year-old girl who watches a
video of the film *Annie* in her home.

It is my proposition that existing accounts of family viewing are
deeply regulative, not only in their voyeurism,[1] but also in their claims to
tell the truth about the families watched. The knowledge such studies
produce needs to be seen as part of the broader regulation of families
and the attempt to guard against the threats to the existing social and
political order presented by the pathological family.

What part does television play in the regulation of working-class
children, in this case, especially girls? To answer this question it is
necessary to examine the place of broadcasting in the regulation of the

masses. David Oswell[2] points out that radio and television initially formed part of strategies of regulation of proletarian families. In the early decades of this century the prime concern was to get women and children off the streets and into the home. Such a strategy was part of the government of the masses, which placed the mother as the relay point in the production of the democratic citizen.[3] The mother was first of all to be taken out of the gin palaces and streets and made responsible for a clean, hygienic and disease-free home and later was to become responsible for the psychic health and emotional and cognitive development of her children as well as their preparation for educational success or failure. The family thus brought off the streets, out of the factories and under the surveillance of the mother had to be watched and monitored. Her fitness to properly mother became the target of technologies of population management in medicine, welfare, law, education and other areas of social policy. The emergence of radio and then television thus provided a way of getting working-class families off the dangerous streets and into the home. As Briggs relates: 'Children's Hour was conceived by Reith as "a happy alternative to the squalor of the streets and backyards".'[4] However, television and radio had to be regulated both at the point of transmission and of consumption. The only way to ensure that the threats posed by the street did not enter the televisual home was to attempt to regulate the amount and type of viewing. For this the parent, usually mother, had to be drafted in to be the relay point in the regulative process. As in other aspects of the regulation of children's development and education, it was the mother who was held responsible for the transition of her children into mentally healthy, upright, democratic citizens. The discourse of normal and natural development had a central part to play this process. Normal family viewing became understood as viewing correctly regulated by the mother, a sign itself of a normal family and therefore one which did not pose a threat to the existing social order.

Regulation entered the home and found working-class viewing practices wanting. Concern in this area centred on the ways in which parents (read mothers) were regulating their children's viewing and, relatedly, the amount of viewing, as well as on children's exposure to sex and violence. Children had been taken off the street, where they could be exposed to violence and to sex, both of which could lead to anti-social uprising, only to be confronted with television programmes which brought sex and violence into the living room.

The classic study in this regard is that by Himmelweit, Oppenheim

and Vince.[5] They expressed considerable concern about parents' regulation of their children's viewing, describing children who they felt viewed
excessively as 'addicts'. 'Addicts' and 'heavy viewers' in their analysis
came mostly from the working class, where they felt that parents were
more likely to be optimistic about the effects of television. This study was
extremely influential and set the scene for the kind of research which
was to follow. Commenting on the Himmelweit study, Oswell argues
that the division of the television audience into normal and pathological
allowed the possibility of a twin strategy. On the one hand, middle-class
parents were to be encouraged in their responsibility to correctly supervise their children's viewing, while on the other broadcasters were to
take responsibility for the viewing habits of children in working-class
homes, where parents appeared less willing to supervise them in the
desired manner. In this way transmission and reception were regulated
in a strategy that joined the art of parenting with 'the art of broadcasting'.
I wish to suggest that this concern was absolutely endemic to the vast
bulk of research on families and television which followed from
Himmelweit, particularly within the field of social psychology.

More recent studies present a number of ways of relating family
viewing to patterns of interaction and communication, using psychological models ranging from social learning theory to family therapy. I want
to suggest that these studies have a number of problems. The first is that
the knowledge that they produce is deeply regulative: it is a descendant
of precisely that concern about the point of reception and the regulation
of children and families I have identified. Secondly, and relatedly, the
approaches all operate on a very superficial level, assuming a direct link
between certain actions or patterns of communication and the learning
of children. This approach is dominant within Anglo-American psychology and has been very important in defining the relation of mother–
child interaction to children's learning development and education.[6]

Not only do such approaches assume that a child is a 'human
animal' to be made social within practices of socialisation, but they
assume that whatever a mother does is related directly and cognitively to
what a child subsequently understands. Where such accounts mention
the emotions, it is to critically examine the emotional attachments and
bonds between mother and child.[7]

The target of regulation, then, is especially the working-class family, the so-called 'socio-oriented' families, who do not critically discuss
programmes and use television to foster family harmony or as a means
of avoidance rather than a tool for advancement by beginning 'viewing

TV more critically'. In all of this research, attitudes, behaviours and patterns of interaction are monitored so that types of normal and pathological families may be classified. Much work also focuses on the way that television may act as a means of escape and avoidance, clearly understood as negative, within a framework that understands health in terms of conflict airing and resolution. Television then is to be used to 'facilitate arguments' and 'convey family values' rather than to avoid conflict or to produce a false sense of harmony.[8]

Any family which has defences, fantasies, or escapes is therefore 'badly adjusted to reality' and by implication, unhealthy. There is no place to consider conscious and unconscious processes, meanings and fantasies within this paradigm except in a model of ill-health.

The framework within which I am operating is critical of the paradigms outlined above both because of their failure to engage with the voyeuristic and regulatory aspects of the research and because of the essential model of the human subject which they employ. Foucault's post-structuralism argues that knowledges contained within technologies of the social, such as knowledge about families watching television, are not only deeply regulative, but also form the discourses and practices within which the human becomes a subject. This is not the same as a socialisation account in that the child is not 'made social': on the contrary, all participants are literally inscribed and created within the specific discursive practices which they inhabit.[9]

In developing this approach in my analysis of one family's viewing, I want to examine the possibility of an alternative approach which subverts the regulative one. In addition, and again in contrast to the work I have outlined, I want to pay close attention to the complex relations between the fantasies of the participants and those in the televisual text itself.

I want to look specifically at a family which is already the object of regulation and which is understood as pathological and unhealthy. I shall concentrate on the way in which the family view and the relation of the film and the viewing to the constitution of the young girl's subjectivity. I am deliberately taking a 'pathological' family as my case in order to question the assumptions made about family viewing and the working-class family within mainstream psychological research. I want to suggest that such research, while it claims to tell the truth about the family, actually regulates that family and elides other aspects of subjectification which cannot be spoken within that discourse.

The family in question

The family which I shall call the Portas consists at the time of the research in a father, who is Maltese, a mother from Yorkshire, who is pregnant with her fourth child, and three daughters, Melissa, who is twelve, Eliana, six and Karen, three. The focus of the research was Eliana. The family was well known to the local social services, as the mother had been abused by the father on several occasions and the police had been called in. The educational welfare officer was also involved and concern was expressed about the mental health of the children, especially Eliana. The mother had been offered a women's group at a family centre, but since getting there involved travelling on two buses and she was agoraphobic, the likelihood of her getting there was remote. Although the family had not been the object of regulation in terms of television viewing, I want to make clear that they were considered by social welfare agencies to be extremely unhealthy. They in no way counted as a family who viewed or interacted in the right kind of way.

On the first sight indeed, Eliana's television viewing could not have been understood as more unhealthy. Her mother or father did not watch with her and there was no discussion at all. Instead, Eliana played with her sisters in front of the television, and, as will be seen, appeared only to watch extremely intermittently. However, as I shall argue, this does not mean that the programme being watched, in this case the video of the musical *Annie*, did not have a profound impact on her and on other members of the family.

Creating Eliana's subjectivity

I am going to discuss one audio recording that I made in Eliana's home one morning during a half-term holiday when she and her sisters had the *Annie* video on the television. I was present in the living-room during the recording and the surveillant effect of this practice is important.[10]

The video *Annie* had been given to the girls by their father. They had clearly watched it several times, as on this occasion when playing in front of it they knew what was going on without really watching at all. *Annie* would seem, in terms of the regulation of children's viewing, a 'suitable' choice for children. It was made as a 'family movie', stars a little girl and is full of happy singing and dancing.

I want to divide my analysis of Eliana's viewing practices into three parts. I want to consider aspects of the film *Annie* itself, go on to examine how Eliana watches and then examine the interrelation of the meanings within the film and those made by Eliana and other members of her family. Finally, I want to set this analysis within the framework of a wider discussion about Eliana and her family.

Annie is a musical premiered in 1982, based on the stage version, which received rave reviews and Toni awards, running from 1977 to 1983 in the USA and 1978 to the mid-1980s in London. It was based on the comic-strip 'Little Orphan Annie', syndicated in the *Chicago Tribune* and elsewhere in the USA. The film had the largest merchandising tie-in to date and was first shown on television in 1986. Two previous versions of *Annie* films had been made, in 1932 and 1938, and a radio show of the same name ran for ten years from 1930. Annie is an orphan in an orphanage run by a drunken woman, Miss Hannigan, clearly presented as a bad mother-substitute. Annie is a little girl with a lot of 'fight' who attempts to run away from the orphanage several times. Her parents are thought to have left her at the orphanage during the Depression because they were too poor to keep her, although it turns out later that they died in an accident, unknown to Annie. One day, the secretary to an armaments millionaire, Daddy Warbucks, arrives at the orphanage to choose an orphan to spend a week at his home as a publicity stunt. The Daddy Warbucks character appears to be a direct reference to a businessman who was hired by Hoover during the Depression to obtain support for a programme of charity (though in the film this is transposed to helping Roosevelt obtain support for the New Deal). A similar character is presented in a number of films starring Shirley Temple.[11]

When Annie is taken to Daddy Warbucks's palatial residence she is greeted by happy, singing and dancing servants. She attempts to start to clean as she had done in the orphanage, but is told that the servants are there to look after her. They bathe her and offer her beautiful new clothes. When the extremely bad-tempered Daddy Warbucks comes on to the scene he wants to send her back to the orphanage, because he says that he ordered a boy. Annie uses all her charm to dissuade him and she stays, much to everyone's pleasure. She has already won the hearts of all she meets and goes on to win the heart of hard-hearted Daddy Warbucks. It is she who charms and softens his hard exterior, who turns him into a father-figure. Not only does he start to have fun as well as make a lot of money, but he begins to notice his secretary Grace and the two get gooey together over Annie. They become a quasi-couple as they become substitute parents. The major charm which Annie works is to take Daddy Warbucks to tea with President Roosevelt and to help the president enlist him in a programme of support and fund-raising for the New Deal. Annie then has a profound political impact. She can soften the hardest hearts and even charm the president and make an arch-millionaire support the New Deal.

But then we learn that Daddy Warbucks grew up poor in Liverpool. He inaugurates a search for Annie's parents and Miss Hannigan's criminal working-class brother and his girlfriend pretend that they are the parents in order to get the reward money. They are overheard plotting by other girls in the orphanage and Annie is rescued after she has been kidnapped by the nasty couple. After this Daddy Warbucks then adopts Annie and is shown clearly to be romantically interested in Grace. Annie has therefore attained a happy and rich family, brought together two parent figures and helped in the economic salvation of a nation gripped by deep economic depression.

On one level, the position Annie takes bears many striking similarities with contemporary comic stories for working-class girls.[12] She is orphaned, poor, subjected to cruelty and by dint of her efforts finds the longed-for happy family. Such themes are ubiquitous in girls' comics. In relation to class, then, the story is very interesting, because it is the poor little girl who has nothing who in fact has something very precious: her charm and capacity to induce love. Not only does this bring her the reward of a family, but it solves the problems of a nation. Similarly Charles Eckert demonstrates how Shirley Temple also takes on the role of being the poor girl whose main function is to charm the rich, persuade them through their love for her to love the poor and the unemployed, and to provide charity in the face of depression: 'her principal functions in virtually all of these films are to soften hard hearts (especially of the wealthy), to intercede on behalf of others, to effect liaisons between members of opposed social classes and occasionally to regenerate'.[13] In this sense then, like Shirley Temple, Annie has a very special place. She is a mythical working-class girl whose function is to induce love in the rich and to promote charity. I use the term mythical because while she is coded as working-class, she actually has no past, no history, no family and no community. The way out for her is not to refind those things, but to strive to enter the bourgeoisie. She has nothing to belong to.[14]

She represents a working-class ripe for transformation, in this case, the case of the female, to be achieved through marriage. Although Annie is a little girl she finds her parents this way: they only fall in love in the course of looking after her. So, within this narrative, being working-class can only be lived as a rootless pain, which can only be cured by finding a haven within the bourgeoisie.

Thus, we are presented with a man whose hard heart is softened only by a girl child: only then can he 'see' and fall in love with a woman. Annie therefore has a special, Oedipal place. In addition, there is the fantasy of the three contrasting mother-figures: the drunken Miss Hannigan, the criminal girlfriend and the pure, good, unnoticed Grace. The former two are clearly coded as working-class, of the streets and unsuitable parents. The little girl, by her charm, can omnipotently avoid these in favour of Grace. I want to suggest that for Annie, as for Shirley, the kind of love that she offers is to be understood as above all innocent and that this covers over and elides issues of sexuality and erotic attraction which enter only as unsavoury.

There are some very powerful fantasies at work here, which provide ample sustenance for a poor young girl living in an abusing family. These fantasies provide both a point of identification for Eliana and a way of reading, and perhaps in fantasy overcoming, the terrible obstacles that confront her in growing up. How then can we explore the role of these fantasies without succumbing to the pathologisation of her family so central to the efforts of those concerned with family viewing, outlined earlier? I think that it is necessary to understand the place of these fantasies precisely in the life histories of the participants concerned, so that the multiple interweaving of fantasies may be understood.

The viewing practices

In this section, I am going to describe and analyse the domestic practices in which *Annie* enters as a relation. From a developmental perspective, we might define Eliana's viewing in terms of her stage of development, which would allow her to make certain meanings in interaction with the semiotics of the television text. While the meanings made are crucial to the analysis I am conducting, I will argue that they are not shaped either in terms of stage of development, nor simply through a process of linguistic meaning-making in interaction with the text. They are produced in the complex family history in which the participants are already inscribed in meanings – the meanings which regulate them, the meanings through which their actions, needs, desires and fantasies are made to signify. There is an emotional and unconscious dimension to meaning-making which is completely absent from developmental accounts. On the other hand, interactional accounts of family viewing appear to ignore the role of the text altogether. Here the television itself is simply a vehicle for the display of family dynamics, which can be classified as either healthy or unhealthy. By contrast, my analysis understands the text as central not in making the family dynamic but in having a place through which certain meanings can be made. I am not interested in the regulative health/unhealth debate, but rather in understanding how the family produces a narrative of their circumstances, their hopes, longings, pain and so forth. That this family is in horrific circumstances is undeniable, but that does not mean that the only reading of their situation is of an inherent pathology to be corrected.

At first sight it would seem as if there were little to say about Eliana and her sisters' viewing of *Annie*, since they play the whole time the video is playing and hardly speak about it at all. The family does not sit round and discuss the film, and so they can easily be located within the pathologisation framework. However, a more careful reading of this transcript and transcripts of interviews with the parents indicates a story which is different from and indeed opposite to that which appears at first sight. I wish to demonstrate that the film forms the relay point in a complex and ongoing discussion within the family about their plight. Far from there being no discussion, there is a great deal of it. The film offers a way of picking up and talking about issues that are very painful and difficult for the family, and also presents a way of understanding and working with those issues.

What I want to do is to piece together the place of the film and its fantasies in the dreams and nightmares that make up the narrative of the life of Eliana and her family and to examine the place of the *Annie* narrative within this.

Eliana's case is a very difficult one. Both her mother and her father came to London with hopes and dreams, dreams which lie shattered in poverty, oppression, abuse and illness. Eliana's mother presents herself as a victim, as does Eliana. It is my contention that Eliana finds solace in a narrative of a little orphan girl, who escapes from her drunken mother-substitute to find true happiness with a wealthy man and thereby ensures that she also obtains a good and beautiful stepmother. Such a narrative provides for her a pleasurable, comforting reading of her situation, both in terms of its poverty and oppression and in terms of the way in which her relations with her father and mother can be told through that story. In other words, her deep pre-Oedipal feelings about her mother can be turned into dislike for a woman who it seems must deserve the beatings she is getting, and who comes between her and the deeply admired father, the father who abuses his wife.

To explain this reading, I want to refer to aspects of the watching of the film, and to related issues that emerge in other recordings in her home as well as school recordings and interviews with her, her parents and her teacher. At the beginning of the recording which I shall consider in detail here, Eliana and her two sisters are playing in the living-room. Their mother is in the kitchen and their father is out. They decide to put on a video and choose *Annie*, which is in fact a video bought by their father, and is a favourite, an issue which is significant in itself, as we shall see.

In fact they do not sit down to watch the video, but continue to play in front of the television. The children play with a bottle of water that has been in the freezer, trying to melt the ice, enjoying seeing that the frozen water keeps its shape even when they have cut the bottle away. The three girls ask me about the microphone and tape-recorder, and then decide to watch a video. They discuss which one to choose and wind back the tape that is already in the machine. Karen, the three-year-old, is given instruction by the others in how to do this. Earlier their mother had asked me if I would like a cup of tea. Eliana had asked for one too, although she never got one. Eliana grumbles 'might as well make myself one. She can't make me one' and makes herself a cup of tea instead. Her mother is upstairs at this point. She fills the kettle and talks to herself as she makes a cup of tea. At one point she cannot find the sugar and asks Melissa, who tells her where to look. She has to distinguish between three 'new jars': 'look in the red and white marble jar then. You know, the three jars, the new ones. The tea and the coffee. Look in that, the sugar one.' As Eliana looks she sings and talks to herself. They continue to play with the ice from the bottle and cut up the bottle. Melissa sits with the ice-shape on her knee until their mother comes into the room. She then appears to tell them off for going near a bottle which has had bleach in it. The bleach makes them think of chlorine and they talk about going swimming in the children's pool at the local park. Eliana also sings the alphabet and they continue to talk about the ice. They discuss who has more ice and how it freezes their hands. Eliana does not want to have her sister's ice which she says has her germs on it. She starts to sing 'five little ducks go swimming one day, over the hills and far away. One little duck says quack, quack, quack and all the four little ducks came back' and so it goes on until there are no ducks left. Eliana tries hiding her ice cubes under a towel and then revealing them to Karen. She calls it 'magic'. They continue to play and argue with each other until their mother calls out for Karen. Melissa then tells Eliana to clean up the mess she has made by dropping all the ice. Mrs Porta and Melissa appear to be having a row, Mrs Porta having told her off, though about what is inaudible. She tells Melissa 'next time, all right? Go and live, go and live with him.' She is referring to Mr Porta, whom she says is having an affair with another woman. She claims when talking to me that Melissa sides with her father and can be bought off by him. At this point Karen hits Eliana with her doll and they put their tongues out at each other. Eliana then tells Karen off: 'Karen, you're not going swimming, you know.'

Eliana now makes her only reference to the video which is still playing in the background. She says to me, referring to Miss Hannigan, the drunken woman in charge of the orphanage, who at that moment is appearing apparently drunk in the screen:

'She's supposed to be drunk, but she ain't.' I ask her why not, to which she replies 'cos it's water'. The children continue to play and thirteen minutes later hear the sounds of what they think is their father coming into the house. Karen tells me excitedly 'It's daddy come back. My daddy's come back', which provokes the response 'Jesus Christ' from her mother. In fact, it is someone else at the door and their father does not come in during this recording. At this point Eliana asks her mother if she may ask me if I want a lager. She asks her mother how to ask me, although of course she knows very well how to formulate a sentence of this type. I take the question to be about how I am to be addressed. I say 'no, thank you very much', and she repeats back to her mother 'she says, no, thank you very much'. Within two minutes Karen says to me 'mummy's drunk', which provokes the reaction to me from her mother 'they say I'm drunk, but I'm not'. At this point Mrs Porta begins a long conversation with me while all the children sit and watch the film. She talks to me about the fact that she does housework all the time and that it is never done, about the possibility of a late abortion and why she does not like the procedures they use and what happened when she had a miscarriage. She tells me that Melissa knows what is going on between her and her husband and that she felt so desperate the previous weekend that she hitched to Yorkshire to see one of her sisters.

During this conversation the film ends. Mrs Porta carries on talking about her hard life with her husband, who has a bath and 'leaves his clothes on the floor and leaves it dirty'. 'I do everything, clean the bath, everything. Well, that's what I do now. I don't think they'd dominate a Maltese woman. I know they wouldn't. A Maltese woman wouldn't stand for it.' She continues talking about an abortion and then about her husband's affair. She reiterates that Melissa sides with her father: 'That's why I get mad with her. She sticks up for him. She knows what's going on, she really knows what's going on. If he gives her a pound to keep quiet, she's all right then'. At the end of this conversation, Eliana announces to me that she found a dead mouse in her garden and that her friend downstairs found a frog while they were having a barbecue. At this point Eliana takes off her microphone and the recording ends.

Analysing the conversations

Although the only reference made to the film *Annie* while it is on is the comment about Miss Hannigan's feigned drunkenness, I want to argue that the film plays a significant part in the domestic practices and the attempts of the participants to understand and cope with their situation.

The video of *Annie* does indeed give the participants a way of dealing with extremely difficult aspects of their lives. While it does not shape an overt discussion of the middle-class kind, sitting round the television, it allows them to dream, understand and face conflicts over what is happening to them. The video is a relay point in producing ways of engaging with what is going on – and so am I, because my presence enables other people to address remarks to me that can be heard by other members of the household and therefore be attended to. In particular, the children discuss their mother's drinking, both by implication in relation to Miss Hannigan and through me; while their mother is able to respond to the threat posed by her being likened to the cruel drunken mother-figure by channelling her refutation through me. The *Annie* narrative thus helps form a way of understanding and judging the circumstances they are in (the dispossessed working-class girl in pain who can only deal with her situation by escape and finding a middle-class family). Thus, escape in this scenario is not the moralistic 'escapism' put forward by many of the interactionist school of research. Escape is the only route presented in this narrative, as in the Shirley Temple narratives discussed by Eckert. In addition, escape to another woman is a route that their mother claims that the father is also using. In this narrative, then, there is also a way of understanding and judging their mother's behaviour. She can be coded as drunken, cruel and weak, the mother who is to be judged and found wanting, the mother whom one would need to leave in order to find safety and happiness.

On the other hand, there is no narrative here for addressing the oppression suffered by the mother, nor of the conflict between the mother and father. There is no model for a father's cruelty that cannot be tamed by an alluring and enticing little girl. The mother does, however, use the film and my presence to provide a counter-argument to the one represented by the film and by the children's reference to her drunkenness. She not only claims that she is not drunk but goes on to talk about the difficulty of her life, her suffering and why she gets angry with Melissa's siding with her father. She thus tries to convince her children and win their support through my presence, which gives her a vehicle through which she can refute the *Annie* version of events. The father is symbolically present during this exchange, his place being metonymically held by the video of *Annie* itself. He is thus symbolically marked as the benefactor, the bearer of the gift and the bearer of the means through which their escape from this oppression might be possible.

Discussion is therefore not absent from this interaction at all. However, it is not a matter of sitting down and rationally debating the content of the programme. It is a deep and heated discussion, a very painful one, which it is surprising that the participants manage to have at all. In this sense then the video is an element which facilitates discussion, while it also shapes the narrative through which that discussion might take place and the moral discourse through which the participants' actions might be judged.

However, the nature and type of discussion engaged in by the Portas reveals the regulatory nature of the discussion discourse. This family discusses, but there is no way that they would be judged to be healthy within the social psychological frameworks outlined earlier. In this sense the regulatory discourse is judgemental while ignoring the complexity of the interactions examined here. It is even the case that what the Portas discuss is sex and violence, since there is certainly a lot in the household. Yet they discuss it not in an abstracted and rationalist way but in terms of the conflicts and pain in their lives. The remark made by the children about the mother's drunkenness joins the film text with other narratives about the situation of their mother, while I play the role of the surveillant Other, through whom remarks can be addressed so that they can be heard and attended to by the other participants. In this way, the *Annie* narrative passes through the children to the mother to me and back to the children.

Conclusion

This analysis has only just begun to examine the issues at stake here.[15]

I do hope however, that I have demonstrated that any analysis of the place of a film text (*Annie* is heavily coded as a family film, a children's and women's picture) as either reactionary or progressive is vastly over-simplistic. The place of *Annie* in the lives of the Portas cannot be reduced to something which either helps or hinders, though it clearly does both. I hope that I have begun to demonstrate the regulative nature of the discourse in which family viewing is understood and presented the basis of another kind of reading, the production of a narrative of subjection and subjectivity. It is a story in which the family in question is neither totally free to transform their own lives, nor totally determined by the factual and fictional narratives and discourses in which they are inscribed. Watching television is a powerful force in shaping their understanding of their lives and may even have a place in transforming them. But it did not constitute their oppression by itself, nor can any adjustments in the way in which they view change their circumstances. Watching television differently cannot solve their problems, the complex psychic effects of dealing with oppression, the complex mixing of conscious and unconscious, psychic and social. While this analysis only touches the surface, I suggest that at least it begins to lead the way towards a line of work which might be of more benefit in understanding this relation, while the academic looks on, as usual, able only to analyse, not to change anything.

Notes and references

1 V. Walkerdine, 'Video replay: families, films and fantasy', in V. Burgin, J. Donald and C. Kaplan (eds), *Formations of Fantasy* (London, Routledge, 1985).

2 D. Oswell, *Watching With Mother, 1946–1960: Democracy, The Domestic And Techniques of Viewing*, paper presented at 'Changing The Subject: Readings In Literature/Culture from Medievalism to Postmodernism', Glasgow University (29 June 1992).

3 V. Walkerdine and H. Lucey, *Democracy in the Kitchen* (London; Virago, 1989); N. Rose, *The Psychological Complex* (London, Routledge, 1985).

4 S. Briggs, *Those Radio Times* (London, Weidenfeld and Nicolson, 1981).

5 H. Himmelweit, A. Oppenheim and P. Vince, *Television and the Child: An Empirical Study Of The Effects of Television On The Young* (London, Oxford University Press, 1958).

6 See Walkerdine and Lucey, *Democracy in the Kitchen*, for a review.

7 These studies are cited in a special volume of *Communication Research Trends*, 5: 3 (1984), on television viewing and family interaction.

8 Working-class families in this scenario are escapists who would not know a concept if they saw one and use television to induce a false sense of harmony in the household. This is particularly well developed in one of the papers, by Goodman, in which she explores the possible use of family systems theory in the study of family interaction with television. While she addresses the dynamics of the family, she, like a number of others, stresses the role of television viewing as a key to healthy family functioning. An unhealthy family can be found on the basis of the way it

watches television. So, television, in this research, is watched well and critically by healthy (middle-class) families and uncritically and in an escapist mode by unhealthy (working-class) families.

9 See J. Henriques et al. Changing the Subject (London, Routledge, 1984) for more detail.

10 See Walkerdine, 'Video replay'.

11 Little Miss Marker, Bright Eyes, Curley Top, Dimples, and Captain January. See C. Eckert, 'Shirley Temple and the House of Rockefeller', in C. Gledhill (ed.), Stardom (London, Routledge, 1991).

12 See V. Walkerdine, Schoolgirl Fictions (London, Verso, 1991).

13 See Eckert, 'Shirley Temple', p. 67.

14 The same kind of working class is shown in Shirley Temple films: 'a non-working proletariat made up of the dispossessed and outcast', Eckert, ibid.

15 I have not discussed other information obtained from the school recordings of Eliana nor the interviews with her, her teacher and her parents. These provide an important source for further analysis. I have also not dealt here with the complex issue of sexuality, seduction and allure, the issue of the young girl as object of a male erotic gaze as it is presented both in Annie and in the relations of the Porta household. Both of the above form the subject of a longer discussion as does the issue of Mrs Porta's domestic work, her lack of leisure and the problem of her pleasure (going to the pub, going out, having a baby) in relation to her husband's social and sexual life. All are highly pertinent but beyond the scope of this paper. They are discussed in V. Walkerdine and J. Melody, Young Girls and Popular Culture (forthcoming).

5

Boys' talk: television and the policing of masculinity

The media, alongside other cultural artefacts such as books and toys, are often seen to play a central role in reinforcing negative gender stereotypes. While the media are routinely condemned for their lack of positive female role models, they are also seen to provide the raw material for boys' fantasies of power and violence. The vast majority of comics, films and television programmes aimed at young boys, it is argued, portray a landscape of war, death and destruction, peopled with impossibly muscular superheroes and bristling with the technology of cars, computers, robots and weapons. In this world, 'real men' are fearless and invulnerable, unburdened by emotion or sensitivity to others. And while these fantasies are seen to be manifested directly in boys' aggressive play, they are also considered to exert a powerful influence on their everyday social behaviour.

Yet if anti-sexist education and child-rearing are essentially about 'empowering' girls, there is much less certainty about what they might involve for boys. Separating what are often seen as the 'negative' aspects of masculine identity – aggression and insensitivity, for example – from those which are seen as more 'positive' – such as assertiveness and physical self-confidence – is far from straightforward. For many parents (myself included), the attempt to police or censor the material which is assumed to influence children's behaviour often proves counter productive. Boys' ability to turn everyday household objects into lethal toy weapons often seems unbounded. Likewise, a great deal of anti-sexist teaching has foundered on boys' ability to take on feminist arguments without necessarily changing their own behaviour, and even to marshal those arguments for their own purposes.[1] There is often a sense in which 'disempowering' boys – forcing them to give up male power and privilege – seems to conflict with the desire not to hold back one's own child, or indeed one's students.[2] What to do about boys remains a difficult, if not intractable, problem.

Gender, sex roles and the media

Conventional approaches to studying children's acquisition of gendered identity have largely been based on the notion of 'sex roles'. According to this approach, children learn to become boys or girls through a process of conditioning. They observe role models of acceptable male or female behaviour, and their attempts to imitate the appropriate model are then positively reinforced through rewards and other forms of social approval.[3]

This behaviourist argument is particularly prevalent in psychological research on the media. Here, the media are regarded as an extremely powerful source of stereotyped role models which children simply absorb and internalise. Children are seen as 'bombarded' by stereotypes, and as effectively helpless in the face of the onslaught. Media messages are typically conceived as uniformly sexist, and thus as inevitably producing sexist attitudes.[4]

However, as Lynne Segal and others[5] have argued, there are a number of significant problems with this approach. Sex roles are seen here as unremittingly coercive, and the acquisition of gendered identity is regarded as a smooth and unproblematic process which is achieved once and for all in childhood. As Segal suggests, this approach ignores the dynamic complexity and the contradictions of actual gender relations in favour of a view of individuals as unitary and wholly conformist. Children, in this account, are regarded merely as passive recipients of adults' attempts at socialisation, rather than having any active part in determining their own social identities. This approach defines the process in individualistic terms, as something that happens inside children's heads, rather than in and through social interaction.

This idea of individuals as helplessly conditioned into rigid sex roles leads in turn to some highly deterministic research methods, which effectively produce the differences they purport to identify. For example, research on pre-school children's use of toys has pointed to consistent gender differences. Yet such studies often begin by choosing toys that would be most likely to produce these differences. In reality, it would seem that children spend most of their time playing with toys which are not gender-differentiated. Furthermore, as Henshall and McGuire argue, the differences demonstrated in this research are relatively small, and seem to be largely dependent upon the characteristics of the group and of the context in which they are observed.[6] Despite the endless search for innate differences between the sexes, the picture that emerges from such work is one of massive psychological similarity.[7]

In the case of media research, this approach to studying sex-role socialisation has much in common with the behaviourist account of the effects of television violence. Children are seen here as little more than 'television zombies', passively absorbing everything they see. As Kevin Durkin[8] has demonstrated, this approach drastically underestimates the diversity of television itself, and of the ways in which children make sense of it. While content analysis may well suggest that television is often sexist, this does not in itself prove that it makes viewers adopt sexist attitudes, let alone that it is a primary source of them. Much of the research that has been used as evidence here is in fact inconclusive, and relates only to short-term effects, which are those most likely to be 'cued' by the research itself. As in the violence research, correlation is often mistaken for causality.[9]

Yet audience researchers within Cultural Studies have not always managed to avoid a deterministic approach. For example, some recent studies have tended to conclude that men and women possess quite different 'cultural competencies' and use television in radically different ways. Yet such research has often failed to provide systematic comparisons between the two groups, and in certain cases has neglected to consider the influence of the context and the methods of the research.[10] Here again, the research ends up supporting an ideology of sexual difference which is in fact written in from the start.

Finally, sex-role theory would also appear to have some problematic implications in terms of education. Anti-sexist teaching materials in this area often appear to subscribe to a notion of media education as a form of 'demystification'.[11] According to this approach, the objective, rational analysis of media stereotypes is seen to offer a means of liberating students from false ideologies. Perhaps paradoxically, this appears to overestimate both the owner of the media and the possibilities for changing students' consciousness. By isolating the media from other social experiences and by oversimplifying the social context of teaching and learning, it offers an account of media education which can only be described as utopian.

The context of research

In this chapter, I want to suggest a rather different approach to these issues. I will be considering a series of extracts taken from small-group interviews with boys aged between eight and twelve, which range widely across different aspects of film and television. Rather than regarding masculinity as something simply fixed or given, I want to suggest that it is, at least to some extent, actively defined and constructed in social interaction and in discourse. In studying boys' talk, we may begin to identify some of the inconsistencies and contradictions which are at stake in this process, and hence some of the possibilities of change.

This material is drawn from a much more extensive research project about children and television, which I have described in detail elsewhere.[12] Among other issues, the research was particularly concerned with the relationships between children's talk about television and the social and interpersonal contexts in which it occurs. Rather than regarding talk as a transparent reflection of what goes on in people's heads, I have attempted to analyse talk as a *social act* which serves specific social functions and purposes.

In developing this approach, the research has sought to move beyond deterministic accounts of the relationship between people's social positions and the ways in which they make sense of television – the implication that people read programmes in a given way *because* they are working-class, or male, or because of some other single demographic fact about them. By contrast, I have argued that social identities are both material *and* discursive. Thus, being male is on one level a straightforward biological fact. Yet what it *means* to be male – or to be 'masculine' – is a matter of social definition and negotiation.

These arguments have several implications in terms of how we present and analyse children's talk. Rather than regarding interview groups as homogeneous, and as straightforwardly 'representative' of broader social categories, we need to pay much closer attention to what goes on *within* the group. In particular, we need to consider the functions of talk in terms of the shifting power-relationships both within the group and between the group and the interviewer. These relationships will in turn reflect broader relationships of social power, for example in terms of age, class and gender – although they will also *in*flect them in particular ways.

This approach is thus part of a broader move within audience research to locate the use of media within the context of social relationships and practices – although it also seeks to go beyond the often

unquestioning use of talk as 'evidence' of individuals' attitudes or beliefs. From this perspective, the construction of meaning from television
is regarded not as a matter of the isolated individual's encounter with the
screen but as a fundamentally social process, in which talk itself plays a
significant part.[13]

Policing masculinity

I would like to illustrate some of these arguments by considering a
couple of brief extracts from discussions recorded during the pilot stage
of the research. These discussions focused primarily on American cartoon series, and included a screening of an episode of *Thundercats* – a
series which had provoked considerable adult criticism for its alleged
violence and sexism. The first extract, taken from the very beginning of
one discussion, features a group of five 7–8-year-old boys. I have started
off by explaining to the group what we will be doing, and that I will also
be talking to some groups of girls.

> *Rodney:* Have they [the girls] got *My Little Pony* cartoons to watch same as
> us, we've got=
> *Interviewer:* =No, they're going to watch *Thundercats* as well.
> *Boys:* Oh .... (...)
> *Richard:* They ain't for girls.
> *Anthony:* Anyone can / they can watch it!
> *Robert:* Yeah, it can be for girls and boys.
> *Rodney:* Yeah, girls can watch it.
> *Gareth:* It's sexist. It can be for girls and boys. Like, a girl / like, girls are in
> it. Like, Cheetara's in it. Cheetara's in *Thundercats*. Cheetara's a girl.
> *Rodney:* She's a woman, you idiot.

For both the boys and the girls in these discussion groups, the issue of
gender was a central preoccupation right from the start. Clearly, the
decision to use single-sex groups was likely to accentuate this, although
the heavy gender stereotyping of the cartoons themselves undoubtedly
played a part.[14] As this brief extract indicates, the question of whether
the programmes themselves were 'for boys' or 'for girls' as well – and
the criteria one might use to establish this – were a major focus of
debate.

Despite Robert's assertion, there was a clear distinction here
between the boys and the girls. While the girls tended to define themselves *against* the cartoons, identifying them as 'for boys' – and, by
extension, as 'babyish' and immature – the younger boys were much
more interested in celebrating their own preferences. Predictably, their

discussion was largely concerned with the display of technology, violence and physical power, and much less with the complexities of the narrative or the relationships between the characters.

This assertion of tastes and preferences is clearly more than a personal matter.[15] On the contrary, statements about what you like or dislike provide a powerful means of defining the 'self' and its relation to others. While this may not always be an explicit or self-conscious process – or even a matter of 'impression management' – the centrality of gender undoubtedly made it so here. In taking up a position on the cartoons, the children were also consciously claiming a particular 'subject position', effectively defining themselves as 'masculine' or 'feminine'.

Thus, what is notable even in the above extract is the boys' use of a 'meta-discourse' which enables them to distance themselves from their own preferences and to reflect upon them in gendered terms. This is implicit, I would suggest, in Rodney's initial reference to *My Little Pony* – a programme none of the girls here were at all interested in, and which was only referred to in the context of these kinds of arguments, as a quintessentially 'girly' programme. In effect, this reference 'cues' a set of more general arguments and understandings – that is, a discourse – about gender differences.

However, this 'meta-discourse' is most apparent in Gareth's use of the term 'sexist' – although it is notable that this is used not as a criticism of the cartoons themselves, but to counter Richard's argument about their gender bias. Here, the main criterion for establishing the gendered address of a text is a numerical one: if there are girls (or women) in it, then it can qualify as being 'for girls'. While they are not yet acknowledging more complex arguments about tokenism, the boys are already beginning to co-opt the anti-sexist arguments to vindicate their own preferences. Interestingly, it was *only* the boys in these discussions who used the word 'sexism', suggesting that they felt on particularly uncertain ground here.

The next extract is taken from a discussion with another group of boys, and addresses these potential criticisms of the cartoons more directly. In this group, Vinh and Daniel are aged nine, Darren and Colin eleven.

Vinh: I think that Three Musketeers [*Dogtanian*] is quite racist.
Darren: Racist, why?
Vinh: Because it's always a boy going on heroes and all that stuff. Why couldn't it be a girl?

Darren: There is a girl. Milady. And Juliet.
Vinh: But why isn't Juliet doing all the adventures?
Int: So what do the girls or women do in *Dogtanian*?
Vinh: All they do is walk away, like, wiggling their bums.
(...)
Vinh: See, I told you it was quite racist. Why can't it be a man going down the street wiggling his bum instead of a woman? *[laughter]*
Daniel: Men do wiggle.
Colin: Let's see you do it, then, Daniel, go on! *[laughter]*
Vinh: See, why couldn't a man be captured and a woman capture him?
Int: Have you ever seen that in a cartoon on TV?
Colin, Darren: Yeah. *She-Ra.* Yeah. Always does. And *Thundercats.*
Colin: But it's only because *He-man* was made and people were saying it was sexist. They made *He-Man* first but I reckon that people were saying that it was sexist and everything so they made *She-Ra.*
Vinh: She-Ra is the opposite of *He-Man.*
Int: So do you watch *She-Ra*? Do you like that?
Vinh: Yeah! *He-Man, She-Ra*, my best programme!
Others: No.
Colin: I watch it, but only because there's nothing on the other side.
Vinh: I don't! *She-Ra's* my best programme!
Int: OK, tell me what you like about *She-Ra.*
Vinh: Me? Because she always goes 'I am She-Ra!' and she hold up her magic power.
Darren: And then her legs look really sexy! *[whistles] [laughter]*

Here again, the boys are broadly familiar with the anti-sexist discourse, although they employ it in more subtle ways. Their criteria are not simply to do with head-counting, as in the previous group: they are also concerned with comparing male and female roles, and (albeit ambiguously) with the emphasis on female sexuality.

However, Vinh's confusion between racism and sexism is revealing. As in the case of the previous extract, it should be emphasised that this issue was introduced 'spontaneously', rather than in response to a question from the interviewer. Nevertheless, as an adult, the interviewer is almost inevitably identified as a kind of teacher, and his presence may well cue responses which in one way or another reflect this. In this case, I would suspect that the anti-sexist discourse derives primarily from the school, where racism and sexism (and other 'isms') are likely to be dealt with together as aspects of 'equal opportunities'. Vinh's eagerness to introduce and pursue these issues may well reflect a desire to 'please teacher'.

At the same time, there are tensions within the group, with the older boys effectively 'policing' the younger ones. Thus, Darren consist-

ently questions Vinh's criticisms, providing counter-examples to undermine his arguments. In his final contribution, Vinh's enthusiastic celebration of She-Ra's power at the moment of her transformation is
undermined by Darren's reassertion of her status as a 'sex object',
produced for the male gaze. In the process, Vinh's identification with (or
at least imitation of) a female superhero is clearly defined as inappropriate and even immature, by contrast with Darren's more 'adult' reading.

Colin's role here is rather more complex. Throughout these discussions, he was concerned to make distinctions between himself and the
younger children (at one point saying 'I'm eleven, I'm big'), and to
appear adult and worldly-wise. During the screening of *Thundercats*, he
kept up a stream of modality judgements, pointing out continuity mis-
takes and questioning the plausibility of the action. The way in which he
disclaims his interest in the cartoon here is also highly indicative, as is
his cynicism about the programme's producers – although neither statement necessarily implies an acceptance of the criticisms of the cartoons
themselves. At the same time, he also undermines Daniel's attempt to
support Vinh's argument, shaming him by calling for a display of
'effeminate' behaviour. Here again potential deviance from the masculine line results in humiliation and laughter.

In analysing these extracts, I have sought to move beyond a deterministic account of the relationship between television and children's
gendered identities. On the one hand, I would certainly wish to refute
the idea that these programmes simply 'produce' sexist attitudes. The
programmes were perceived as strongly gendered by the children themselves, and this undoubtedly led to gendered positions and discourses
being invoked in the discussions. Yet these positions and discourses do
not derive primarily from television, nor is television's role within them
necessarily straightforward: even in these highly-charged exchanges, for
example, it was possible for Vinh to express an enthusiasm for a female
superhero which was clearly seen by the other boys as immature, if not
downright deviant.

Furthermore, there were contradictions within and between these
various discourses: despite the ambiguities here, the children themselves
were capable of some complex – and indeed even cynical – judgements
about the sexism of television. While some of the boys tended to use the
anti-sexist discourse as a means of displaying their own sophistication,
or indeed simply of justifying their own preferences, it also offered them
the possibility of reflecting on their own and others' tastes.

On the other hand, I would also wish to question the idea that gender positions – or indeed sexist attitudes – are fixed and pre-given, and that this in turn determines how the programmes will be read. Even in this comparatively 'extreme' situation – extreme in the sense that gender was so obviously at stake – there were uncertainties and divisions among the groups which cannot easily be reduced to a single gender position.

In the case of the boys' discussions and I would argue more broadly, masculinity is actively produced and sustained through talk. Far from being unitary or fixed, it is subject to negotiation and redefinition as the talk proceeds. Masculinity, we might say, is achieved rather than given. It is something boys *do* rather than something that is simply done to them – although, equally, it is something they can attempt to do to each other. 'Doing masculinity' can therefore take a variety of forms and serve a variety of purposes in different social contexts. While it undoubtedly represents a claim for social power, that claim can be resisted or redefined, with a variety of consequences. It is to some of the contradictions of 'doing masculinity' that my account now turns.

Talking masculinity

While there are undoubtedly some problems in the account I have just outlined – and I shall return to these in my conclusion – the approach does find some support in recent work on masculinity. Lynne Segal[16], in her invaluable overview of research in this field, argues that masculinity should be regarded not as a fixed and singular possession, but on the contrary as insecure and fragile, and in need of constant reassertion. Becoming masculine is not something which is achieved once and for all in childhood: it is part of an ongoing struggle to overcome an underlying sense of contradiction, ambivalence and incompleteness. Learning masculinity is about learning a code – or at least learning to appear to others as though one conforms to a code – rather than simply being slotted into a pre-determined role.[17]

Using psychoanalytic theory, Segal argues that this process depends primarily upon the rejection or repression of the feminine 'other', and that this often takes the form of homophobia – that is, the rejection of the 'effeminate homosexual', or of any form of behaviour which would seem to carry these connotations. Homophobia is thus a primary element in the construction and maintenance of masculinity, and provides the central rationale for men's policing of their own and each other's behaviour.

Likewise, in his 'critical autobiography', David Jackson[18] argues that masculinity is defined as much in relation to other men as it is in relation to women. Establishing masculinity involves exerting power over weaker, more vulnerable men, and entails a ritualistic rejection of deviance, of the 'other' that is feared. Thus, for many men (myself included), adolescence is characterised by a fear of being labelled homosexual by other boys. The attempt to evade this charge has physical dimensions – in terms of controlling one's gestures and postures, for example, and following certain prescriptions in terms of the style and colour of one's clothes. Yet, as Jackson argues, it is particularly manifested in talk, in the kind of 'banter' which goes on between boys:

> In the non-adult public arena, especially from the age of 13 to 17, my language use became much more careful, guarded and defensive. If I didn't watch my back I'd be stabbed with verbal darts before I had time to turn around.... The mocking, teasing, ridiculing of anything slightly out of the ordinary (or a physical defect or weakness) was a powerful pressure towards linguistic conformity in becoming 'one of the lads', or rather one of those marginal boys who hovered, uneasily, at the fringes of the group....
> The penalty for not joining in on the endless repartee, wisecracking and banter was to be made the butt of jokes, or to be labelled 'sissy' or 'queer'.[19]

Jackson argues that banter and teasing, for example in the form of mock insults and fights, is a central means whereby the 'homosexual' is repressed and masculinity sustained – although, as he also suggests, it may often reflect unacknowledged homoerotic desires. While banter is thus part of male bonding – and is undoubtedly pleasurable for this reason – it can also be wounding and self-alienating, even for heterosexual men.

In my own research, the implicit 'educational' framing of the interviews inevitably meant that these characteristics of masculine talk were less apparent than they might have been in the playground, for example. Nevertheless, particularly when it came to single-sex groups, the boys were often much less mutually supportive than the girls. In mixed groups, girls generally spoke more, and boys were often reluctant to volunteer their opinions even when asked. There was often a sense that in talking about certain aspects of television, boys were unavoidably putting themselves on the line, and rendering themselves open to ridicule and possible humiliation from their peers.

On the line: Allan and Chris

In this section and the next, I want to develop these arguments by considering some more extended extracts from the interviews, again with all-boy groups. The first of these features two eight-year-old working-class boys, Allan and Chris, talking to a male interviewer. In this instance, the interview was based around a set of questions about the domestic viewing context, although the discussion ranged much more widely.

Allan and Chris began by talking about some 'scary' films they had watched on video:

> *Allan:* Whenever my mum or my dad are watching something horrible, um, like *Nightmare on Elm Street* and / / and um, [*deleted*] *Ghosts*
> *Int:* So you don't like that sort of stuff, right? Why's that, you just get too frightened?
> *Allan:* Yeah / and um, / / *Terminator*
> *Chris: Terminator* ain't scare, scary /
> *Allan:* I watched it before, but it's a bit scary, so I don't really like it.
> *Int:* So what happens then, you go off to your own room, yeah?
> *Allan:* Yeah / [and /
> *Int:* [What about=
> *Allan:* =And *Commando*, I don't like that, it's too scary.
> *Int:* Is that, it's a war film, isn't it, yeah?
> *Allan:* Yeah, and there was another one, *Applause*, all this army, and there was this lady and she was trying to get away, and then they left her for a while, and then they thought that she was getting away, that was about an hour, I was watching it for about an hour, and then when she got killed, I had, I just went into my bedroom and watched um *Catchphrase*.
> *Int:* So you didn't like it then, when she got killed?
> *Allan:* And I know a really good one, *Mac and Me.*
> *Int: Mac and Me*, what's that then? Is that a cartoon?
> *Allan:* No, it's a film. It's a bit sad.

Throughout this discussion, there was an interesting ambivalence about 'scary' films. For both boys and girls, these films carried a considerable degree of peer group status. Many of the working-class children in particular offered detailed accounts of 18-rated films, both of the violent action genre (as in this case) and of horror films such as *Nightmare on Elm Street.* Yet these were often characterised by an uneasy combination of excitement and disgust. While many were keen to assert that the films were not scary (as Chris does here), this was often disputed.

In an earlier discussion, Allan had in fact offered a very detailed retelling of *Terminator*, focusing directly on the violence. In that discussion he had been the only boy in the company of four girls, and had an increasingly desperate struggle to gain the chance to speak. Choosing to talk about *Terminator* partly seemed to do the trick, although even this was not wholly successful in silencing the girls. Here, he is much more willing to admit that he was scared by the film, and seeks to redirect the discussion to the safer territory of *Mac and Me* (a children's science fiction film in the mould of *ET*). While it would seem from this account that his parents do not prevent him from viewing this kind of material (although this is contradicted later on, as we shall see), Allan effectively seeks to regulate his own viewing by physically removing himself from the room and escaping to his bedroom to watch a game show.

Despite Chris's rejection of the notion that he might be scared by such films, he does in fact admit to this a little later in the discussion. Significantly, however, this comes at a point where Allan has briefly left the room:

> *Chris:* My dad's got a lot of them [videos] and he gave it to me and my mum, and it's a karate one, and it's very deadly and, one of, was very scary, the worsest one, and I started to cry.
> *Int:* Yeah. And what was that, what was that called?
> *Chris:* I don't know.
> *Int:* Don't know. And what made you cry, just cause it was very / there was a lot of fighting in it or something, yeah?
> *Chris:* No, there was this boy right and he was very good at karate and he was Chinese *[Allan returns to the room]* and there was this big, this big man and he was the deadly one at karate, and then in one of the, near the end, there was the boy, he was learning more karate and the big man / didn't um / didn't know so / the big man had to um / had to / can't remember.

Chris's tone of voice becomes much more enthusiastic when Allan returns to the room, although he is eventually unable – or perhaps unwilling – to pursue his retelling.

Significantly, his accounts of this film (which I suspect is *Karate Kid*) and of another karate film he described in more detail focus centrally on the threat posed to the boy by the 'big man', and on the boy's eventual success in defeating him. At least potentially, the films explore and offer fantasy solutions to young boys' anxieties about their own physical weakness: yet by refusing the suggestion that he finds them 'scary', or only admitting to it when Allan is out of the room, Chris effectively disavows this anxiety.

A further contradiction emerges later in the interview around the discussion of parental regulation. In general, the children, and particularly the boys, were keen to assert that they were not restricted by their parents, either in terms of what they watch or in terms of their general behaviour – although these accounts were often contradicted by those of the parents themselves. Throughout this discussion there is an ongoing competition between Allan and Chris about who is the least restricted by parental authority – for example, in terms of when they have to go to bed or whether they have to ask permission to go out to the park. What is clearly at stake here, and seems to infuse much of the discussion as a whole, is the attempt to claim a more 'adult' position, although in general Allan is much less interested in this than Chris, whose resistance to parental authority was carried over into his disruptive behaviour in school. This kind of bravado is also apparent in the discussion of television:

> *Int*: So do you have, are there programmes that your mum says that you can't watch / Chris?
> *Chris*: Nn-nn.
> *Int*: Nothing at all. So you can watch what you like, yeah?
> *Allan*: Except for the ones your dad says you can't watch.
> *Int*: / Yeah.
> *Allan*: I can't watch *Terminator* / I can't watch / I can't watch *Commando*. I've watched it before, when my dad was at work.
> *Int*: Right, but your dad doesn't like you watching those, then. So why? Why does he say that?
> *Allan*: Because um, because he thinks I'm having nightmares about it....
> ...
> *Int*: So have you ever had dreams about stuff you've seen on TV? Chris, what about you?
> *Chris*: Ummm, no.
> *Allan*: I did. *Lion, Witch and the Wardrobe*. I dreamt that all of them were on to me. And Aslan came and he roared at me and he bit me.
> *Int*: Really. 'Cause he doesn't bite people on TV, does he? He doesn't bite people in the programme.
> *Chris*: He's not a real lion anyway.
> *Int*: No.
> *Allan*: I had a dream that he was a real lion.
> *Chris*: Me?
> *Allan*: No, I did. /
> *Chris*: You had, that I was a real lion?
> *Allan*: Yes, you was the lion!

Here again, Allan is much more willing to admit to being distressed or frightened – although the example he discusses in fact relates not to a forbidden 18-rated film, but a children's TV programme which was widely praised for upholding the best BBC traditions of 'quality' drama. As I have argued elsewhere,[20] what children find frightening is often hard to predict, and what they say about this is not necessarily the most accurate guide. Chris's use of modality judgements – 'he's not a real lion anyway' – is typical of the ways in which the children used their knowledge of the production process, and particularly of special effects, to defend themselves from potential distress. Certainly for some of the older boys, learning to watch horror was very much a matter of learning not to display your own fear – a process in which fathers and older brothers appeared to play a key role. Nevertheless, in the hinterland of dreams – or indeed in the moment of viewing itself – such defences may prove less than effective.[21]

As I have noted, the competition over parental regulation is part of a broader battle for 'adult' status between the two boys. Allan admits to a greater degree of parental regulation here – although this account partly conflicts with the kind of self-regulation he describes in the first extract. At the same time, he also undermines Chris's 'adult' position by referring to the fact that his father regulates his viewing.

Yet this battle for status takes a variety of forms. In the final exchanges here, and at a number of other points in the interview, the boys engage in a kind of banter which is based on wilful misinterpretation. Later, there is an extended comparison of their collections of TV toys, which culminates in a competition over the size and prowess of their toy robots: Allan claims that his robot is able to make potato crisps, while Chris caps this by claiming that his had gone out shopping! Finally, asked who he would like to be if he could be on TV, Chris responds by saying that he would be the robot on *Lost in Space* – a metaphor of contemporary masculinity if ever there was one.

The final extract from this discussion returns to material which was rather more problematic, at least from the boys' point of view. The Australian soap opera *Neighbours* was at this time extremely popular with children generally, although the boys were much more guarded in talking about it:

> *Int:* But you quite like *Neighbours*, then, yeah?
> *Allan:* Yeah.
> *Int:* So tell me what you like about *Neighbours*, then? Who / who /
> *Allan:* It's got a pretty girl in it. *[laughter]*
> *Int:* Who's that, then, which pretty girl?
> *Allan:* Kylie Minogue.
> *Int:* Kylie, yeah.
> *Chris:* She's not pretty, she's ugly, I don't like her. I like Daphne.
> *Allan:* Uuuugh!
> *Chris:* No, I don't like Daphne, I don't like any of them, I just like the programme.
> *Int:* Mmm, so who's your best character, then? In *Neighbours*.

Allan: Err, Jason Donovan / Scott.
Int: Yeah. So what do you like about him, then? /
Chris: He's a crap singer.
Allan: No, Mark. Mark. He looks cool.
Int: Uhuh. / All right. What about you, Chris, who's your best character in it?
Chris: Ummm, no one.
Int: No one. / So what things that have happened in *Neighbours* [have you thought have been good?
Allan: [Who is no one anyway?
Chris: [laughter] No one. I don't like any of them.
Int: So what things that have happened in *Neighbours* do you think have been good? Chris.
Chris: What?
Int: What things have happened in *Neighbours* that you think have been good?
Chris: Um / er / I don't know.

What is particularly striking here is the way in which the boys seek to disclaim their preferences. For some reason, the naming of female characters appears too risky: both the characters named earn abuse from the other boy, and Allan progressively retreats to 'safer' male characters. There is further linguistic banter here, as Allan wilfully misinterprets Chris's statement; and Chris eventually retreats altogether, refusing the interviewer's attempts to find another way in to the topic.

Throughout this discussion, then, there is a sense in which the boys are constantly putting themselves at risk – primarily of humiliation or ridicule by each other – and then rapidly withdrawing. Statements are made and then repeatedly contradicted or revised, and there are many inconsistencies in their individual accounts. It is as though they tentatively raise their heads above the parapet, only to be knocked down. In general, Allan is more comfortable with this than Chris, who often refuses to pursue lines of discussion which he perceives to be dangerous. Like the robot in *Lost in Space*, Chris seems to be drawing a protective shell around himself, in his attempts to be self-contained and invulnerable.

Sex talk: Sean, Peter and Petros

For the older boys, this process was less fraught with contradictions, not least because they had a wider repertoire of strategies for avoiding such 'risks'. Nevertheless, there were points at which this broke down, with some interesting consequences.

This was particularly apparent in one of the activities, in which the children were invited to discuss liked and disliked characters in film and television.[22] In this case, the differences between the girls' and boys' groups were particularly striking, not least on a statistical level. While both boys and girls were more likely to say that they liked male characters, this was particularly marked among the boys. Furthermore, while boys nominated as many 'likes' as girls, their tendency to name 'dislikes' increased with age, and was heavily weighted towards female characters. Boys were much less likely than girls to offer positive comments about characters' physical attractiveness, but more likely to offer negative ones. Boys were also more likely to talk about actors rather than characters and to favour comic characters and the comic attributes of otherwise 'serious' characters.

In order to explain the reasons for these differences, however, it is important to consider the interview context. In general, the boys appeared to find this activity comparatively threatening, and often sought to redefine it in such a way as to avoid their own masculinity being put at risk. Thus, while many of the girls were quite comfortable talking about who they 'fancied', the boys found this much more awkward: such statements – or in some cases, *any* positive statement about a female character – often led to ridicule, as they did in the case of Allan and Chris. Likewise, while girls often described female characters as attractive, boys never referred to male characters in this way, except where they identified this as an opinion held by girls (and from which they generally dissented).

What appeared to inform the boys' anxiety was a fear of humiliation at the hands of other boys, although this took a variety of forms. The accusation that one might 'identify' with a female character, or that one might 'fancy' a male character, was clearly to be avoided at all costs. Yet, as in the case of Chris and Allan's discussion of *Neighbours*, even the possibility that one might 'fancy' a female character was somehow problematic.

In this context, talking about comic characters – or redefining serious characters as 'funny' – provided a convenient way of avoiding the issue. Likewise, vilifying characters (and particularly female ones) for being 'ugly' or 'stupid' allowed the boys to occupy a safe position, which merely confirmed their own superiority. Many boys opted to talk about the actor rather than the character, a strategy which enabled them to present themselves as budding film critics, while also again absolving them from the possible accusation that they could 'identify' with the character – or, even worse, that they might 'fancy' him. This adoption of a 'critical' discourse was particularly prevalent among the middle-class children.

Nevertheless, this process was not always easy. The following extracts, which are taken from a discussion with three 12-year-old middle-class boys, illustrate some of the tensions which were at stake. On this occasion, the boys were involved in a discussion about modality in which they were asked to rank programmes as more or less 'realistic'.[23] The interviewer here was female.

The first extract focuses on the US series *Baywatch*, which features the adventures of a group of Californian coastguards. Sean begins by criticising the programme as 'unrealistic' on the grounds that 'it's made to look sunny all the time', although he and Petros quickly move on to complain about the muscular appearance of the male characters. Sean argues that 'it's just sort of a bit over-exaggerated ... the people on it are sort of complete hunks and, you know, all the girls are drooling over them and everything'. Sean's comments are disputed by Peter, who claims superior knowledge of the setting based on a holiday in Florida. These arguments are developed as follows:

> *Sean:* But, but, but I'd say there be like / / they haven't got any sort of middle-size people. All the ladies are immaculate, and all the men are immaculate, there's no sort of middle-size people who aren't so / /
> *Int:* Who aren't so perfect.
> *Sean:* [Yeah.
> *Petros:* [Even, even the boy that's about thirteen years old, he's got //
> *Int:* =He's got [muscles as well?
> *[laughter]*
> *Int:* Is that right? I must check – I've watched it a couple of times. His father's Mitch isn't he?
> *Sean:* Yeah.
> *Int:* The one who's in charge of the life-patrol?
> *Sean:* Even Hobie – that's the kid – a sort of a sex symbol with all the [girls.
> *Petros:* [*[laughs]* yeah [I know.
> *Int:*   [Is that right?
> *Sean:* Yeah, they all have posters of him. It's really=
> *Peter:* =Yeah, even in our class. [(...) they've got posters of him on the desk.
> *Sean:*   [It's really pathetic, to be honest but=
> *Int:* =Why? I mean, because he's not worthy to be fancied or?
> *Sean:* No – but he's, he's / / [all the girls go *mad* over it.
> *Peter:*   [They build it up like that especially for the programme

Int: What – this character?
Petros: Yeah!
Peter: They make him build up his muscles just for the programme, to give him an image in the programme. [They need to build (...)
Sean: He doesn't look like nothing like he is in the programme.
Peter: Yeah!
Sean: You see without all that make-up on, he's probably just the same as – he – probably just the same as someone in school, isn't he?
Int: Mm.
Sean: He's nothing special, just 'cause he's on a film that [makes him
Int: [Well – it adds a certain glamour doesn't it, if [you're on (...)
Sean: [But he's nothing special I wouldn't say, / / [I think he looks ug – ugly to be honest but=
Petros:
Int: =You think he does.   [apart?] from he's rich!
Peter: You would, wouldn't you Sean?
Sean: No, but I don't=
Petros: =It's because he's giving you too much competition!
[laughter]

Here, the boys combine statistical arguments – about the representation of 'middle-size people' as compared with 'hunks' – with assertions about the constructed nature of the programme – the use of body-building and make-up – in what amounts to an attempt to cut the male characters down to their own size. What threatens Sean is not so much the physical power of the characters – which was partly an issue in the younger boys' account of the karate films – as their sexual appeal, the fact that they make the women in the programme and indeed the girls in their own class 'drool'. In arguing that Hobie is 'just the same as someone in school', Sean attempts to allay his anxieties about his own sexual attractiveness – although, as Petros's final comment makes clear, his motivation is perhaps a little too transparent.

While there is certainly some evidence to support Sean's arguments from parallel interviews with the girls in this class, their responses were in fact rather more complex. While the girls who discussed these characters acknowledged that they were indeed 'hunks', they also complained that they had to act 'all macho', and laughed about the way they strutted around with their chests out. Nevertheless, as one girl argued, in *Baywatch* 'you don't really need a great actor, you just need to have hunks walking up and down the beach'. By condemning the girls' responses as merely 'pathetic', the boys fail to acknowledge that they may find these characters as 'unrealistic' as they do themselves.

Interestingly, however, the boys do not comment in any detail on the female characters in the programme whose 'immaculate' bodies are equally on display. As I have noted, the girls were much more interested in discussing the physical attractiveness of male characters than vice-versa, and the gender of the interviewer seemed to make little difference to this. In general, there was a remarkable absence of 'drooling' among the boys – although this is an activity adult men are commonly supposed to engage in all the time. For boys of this age, the discussion of sexuality may well hold more dangers than pleasures, in that their own power and security are so uncertain.

However, this issue was taken up explicitly in the discussion that followed. The boys described a class activity in which they had been asked to name somebody they would like their mothers to choose for them to marry. Again, they expressed contempt for the girls' responses: according to Sean, 'all the girls were going [*mimics*] "Oh! I hope my mum says Tom Cruise!"' in the extract that follows, the interviewer directly questions their account, with some interesting consequences:

Int: And what were the boys saying?
Sean: Nothing.
Int: Why weren't they?
Peter: Oh yeah, well you get Joe who says 'Um I want=
Sean: =Kim Basinger!
Peter: Yeah! Kim Basinger [and Jerry Hall.
Sean: [Yeah, but none of the boys are really bothered about it because it's / just
Peter: Never going to happen!
Sean: Yeah, it's never going to happen – so I mean it's not really practical to think of really.
Int: OK. It's meant to be sort of fantasy question, isn't it?
Sean: Yeah.
Int: It's not likely you are going to be – end up with Tom Cruise unless you're [extremely=
Sean: [Yeah, but all the girls sort of think, imagine that if they say it will – it will. Just sort of=
Petros: [They probably dream about it (?)
Int: [It strikes me that girls are more used to expressing those sorts of things 'cause they're encouraged to, whereas boys aren't in quite that way. Not till they're a bit older.
Petros: [Well, if you fancy someone like that, you keep it a secret.
Sean: [Well, there's all these – there's all these
Int: Yeah, why do you think that is?
Petros: 'Cause all the boys in our class spread it.
Peter: [*laughs*] Yeah! Basically.

Initially, the boys attempt to account for their apparent lack of interest in the activity by rejecting 'fantasy' – and by implication presenting themselves as more 'practical' and mature. However, it is again Petros – who in other discussions was often excluded or ridiculed by the other boys – who provides an alternative reason for this, noting the mockery which could be expected to accompany such statements (although he is obviously supported by the interviewer in doing so). This explanation is certainly illustrated by their disparaging comments about another boy, Joe, at the very start of the extract. The reasons why it should be taboo for boys to admit to 'fancying' female stars – notably in the company of *other boys*, rather than girls or female teachers – may become clearer as the discussion continues:

> *Sean:* 'Cause there's all these sort of [male sex symbols.
> *Int:*   [You got it!
> *Sean:* But there isn't really like a lady superstar like you talk about all the time.
> *Int:* What about Madonna? Isn't she?
> *Petros:* She's not good looking, she can just sing!
> *Int:* Mm.
> *Sean:* And she's sort of a bit, um *[laughs]*
> *Petros:* =The last video's a bit /
> *Int:* Raunchy?
> *Sean:* Yeah!
> *Int:* I think the word is. I haven't exactly seen it, but I've heard about it.
> *Petros:* It's [been banned in the USA.
> *Peter:*   [It's a bit bad!
> *Sean:* No, but I mean you wouldn't exactly want a girl hanging round you, all she was doing was drooling in your ear and stuff. Would you? *[interviewer laughs]*
> *Peter:* She was doing a bit more than drooling in your ear during the video.
> *Sean:* She'll probably die of over- / over-sexing or something she's just / all she – all she=
> *Peter:* =You know the thing that really gets me is that she goes into all this research for AIDS and a lot of money she makes she (Mm) puts into AIDS research and then she goes out and makes a video like that!
> *Sean:* Yeah, making everybody want to 'do it'.
> *Peter:* Exactly!
> *Sean:* See, if people who are sort of obsessed with her sort of made – might be influenced by / what she does.
> *Int:* But I mean do you think – is she not having – is she being serious when she does her videos do you think?
> *Petros:* No – not really but she [did – she did say that she wouldn't mind having a family now 'cause she's getting on a bit.
> *Sean:*   [But to someone who is sort of obsessed

with her, 'cause she (...) there's quite a lot of people who are sort of – obsessed with Madonna and like wherever she goes, they go and they – there was one in America there was this group, um – English band and they had this song and the background vocals were 'do it, do it, do it now!'

The boys' objections to Madonna – and their attempts to avoid the issue of sexuality – take an increasingly moralistic tone as the discussion proceeds. To begin with they attempt to refuse the suggestion that Madonna might be seen in sexual terms – 'she can just sing' – although this clearly cannot be sustained for very long. They go on to describe the video as 'a bit bad', and there is a brief discussion (omitted here) about the fact that it was eventually screened late at night – at a time when (presumably impressionable) young children would be unable to see it. Sean's final comment refers explicitly to discourses about the 'effects' of television – although typically, he displaces these on to 'other people' who are 'obsessed' and therefore seen to be particularly at risk. The mention of AIDS reinforces this moral stance, and leads to accusations of Madonna's hypocrisy.

Yet it is clear that Madonna's overt sexuality represents a considerable threat. This is defined partly in terms of excess – for example, in Sean's concerns about Madonna's 'over-sexing' and in his description of the video (in the section omitted here) as 'a bit too over-expressive for me'. More significantly, however, Sean also briefly imagines himself in the company of Madonna – although her 'hanging round' him and 'drooling' in his ear is somehow too disruptive and messy for him. As in their discussion of the girls' responses to *Baywatch*, irony would appear to be beyond their frame of reference – or perhaps a luxury they can ill afford. Petros, for example, seems to reject the interviewer's suggestion that Madonna might not be entirely serious, and takes refuge in the comforting thought of her settling down and having a family.

Here again, the discussion of television becomes an area in which the boys attempt to stake out and sustain a 'masculine' subject position – albeit in an area where they appear distinctly vulnerable. In this case, the interviewer adopts a more distanced – and at times ironical – perspective. Her contributions often challenge the boys to be more explicit about what is taking place, and her choice of Madonna – rather than, for example, Kim Basinger – clearly raises questions they find hard to accommodate. In this respect, she effectively forces the boys to 'account for themselves' and thus exposes some of the contradictions they might have preferred to avoid.

On the other hand, however, her active pursuit of the topic offers a means of exercising power in the situation. Her enthusiastic comment 'you got it!' at the start of the extract seems to define her as a sexual being or at least as a person who is capable of the kind of sexual fantasies the boys seem concerned to disavow. What is unspoken here, though implicit throughout, is the boys' anxiety about their own lack of sexual experience – experience which would at one level 'confirm' their heterosexual masculinity. As in the classroom, 'sex talk' offers a powerful means for teachers to exert power over their students, by positioning them as less knowledgeable and experienced, and hence unavoidably as 'children'.

Conclusions: gender theory, audience research and education

Research and debate on masculinity has recently become something of an academic growth area – a phenomenon which has been greeted with justified suspicion by many feminists.[24] Certainly, there are significant dangers in the kind of analysis I have presented here. Emphasising the vulnerability and insecurity of masculinity – and even arguing, as some have done, that it is inherently oppressive of men – can easily become an excuse for ignoring the continuing realities of male power. This position is certainly a powerful option for 'non-sexist' men who wish to play feminism at its own game and thereby exempt themselves from blame.

What this position appears to neglect is not simply the social and material dimensions of male power, but also the *emotional* investments which are at stake here. To present masculinity solely as an experience of suffering and self-alienation is to ignore the pleasure it entails, and the reasons why it is so attractive (at least for men) in the first place.

In addition, there are much broader theoretical problems with this view. There is certainly a danger in my own analysis here of lapsing into a 'dramaturgical' model of social interaction – a view of social life as a matter of putting on masks, or adopting roles, which have no necessary relationship with one's true identity.[25] This is of course to presume that there is an authentic self behind the mask, and that we would be able to identify it if we saw it.

Some postmodernist versions of discourse analysis would seem to lead to a similar approach – in effect, to a view of social life as a matter of freely taking on the discourses and subject positions which happen to be available. At its most 'extreme', however, this position appears to reject the notion that here is a reality that exists independently of discourse: far from positing a 'true self' behind or beyond discourse, it suggests that the self is merely a 'point of intersection' of different discourses.[26]

The problem with both approaches is that they would appear to ignore the apparent 'naturalness' and 'spontaneity' of gendered behaviour, and its consequences.[27] If the acquisition of gendered identity cannot be seen simply as a result of the imposition of rigid sex roles, neither is it wholly a matter of free choice and conscious deliberation. Clearly, these roles or discourses are not equally available to all. 'Doing masculinity' is an option for men, but much less so for most women (although Margaret Thatcher does come to mind here); and it is more available for certain types of men than others, for reasons which are to do with biology (physical size and strength, for example) as well as social factors such as class. For children, as I have argued, age differences – and the social perception and construction of the *meaning* of those differences – are unavoidably significant: what it means to be 'male' and what it means to be 'adult' or 'childish' intersect in complex ways.

Furthermore, we need to consider the social and material *consequences* of 'doing masculinity'. Heterosexual male power is not simply a discursive game: the institutional, economic and physical dimensions of that power depend precisely on maintaining these discourses of 'true' masculinity. As Bronwyn Davies[28] succinctly argues, '[p]ositioning oneself as person within the terms made available within a particular social order also creates and sustains that social order'.

In concentrating on the social processes through which the meanings of television are established and negotiated, there is a related risk of losing sight of the role of texts. Texts clearly do set constraints on the ways in which they can be read – and certainly in the case of many of the texts referred to here, may unavoidably raise and define issues of gender difference and sexuality in quite specific ways. Much of the appeal of *Baywatch*, for example, is undoubtedly derived from its explicit display of male *and* female bodies. Likewise, Madonna explicitly and consciously plays with the conventions and boundaries of sexual expression – to the extent that the issue has become one of the most tiresome clichés in academic debate. On the other hand, as I have implied, much of the appeal of 'violent' narratives in film and television, at least for boys, is that they appear to offer solutions – albeit temporary, and at a level which is clearly recognised as fantasy – to very real and permanent insecurities and physical threats.

Furthermore, while the interpersonal dynamics are centrally important, it is vital to remember that we are dealing here with groups of children artificially constructed as *audiences* for particular kinds of *representations*. 'Fancying' Madonna or Mitch in *Baywatch* is different from 'fancying' someone in your class at school – even if the boys here seem rather concerned about the nature of that difference. Likewise, while the violence of karate films may evoke anxieties about your own physical weaknesses, it is qualitatively different from the violence you are likely to encounter in real life. Talking about the media is obviously different from talking about your direct personal experiences, and children rarely lose sight of that difference.

While media education may play an important role in intervening in these processes, therefore, we should be cautious about overestimating its consequences. As I have shown, talking about the media may be an extremely risky process for boys, particularly where they raise issues of sexuality and physical power, as in many of the texts under discussion here. For example, while teaching about Madonna may prove 'empowering' for girls – or at least *some* girls – her significance for boys is much more ambiguous; and in teaching mixed groups in schools, the often heated debates that ensue may be much more awkward and even counter-productive than one might expect from the security of the academic seminar room. Indeed, as I have implied, academic discourse may offer an extremely powerful, socially sanctioned means of *disavowing* these emotional tensions and contradictions in favour of a secure 'critical' position.

Likewise, teaching about 'representations of masculinity' is inevitably a problematic process, whose more profound implications boys – and male teachers – may well attempt to avoid. Certainly in my own experience, it is tempting to take refuge in a superficial irony, satirising the grotesque excesses of an Arnold Schwarzenegger as a means of avoiding questions which are 'closer to home'. Equally, adopting a propagandist anti-sexist stance can easily lead to a form of political self-righteousness, in which the force of one's criticisms serves as a guarantee of one's own ideological correctness. To privilege 'critical analysis' is to run the risk of adopting a rationalistic position, which fails to engage with students' complex subjective investments in the media, and sanctions a dismissive superiority towards the vulgarity of popular culture and those who enjoy it.[29] Such approaches may end up simply reinforcing the power of the teacher and of the male students, with an added gloss of political complacency.

On the other hand, it seems equally problematic to suggest that 'saying how we really feel' is necessarily the path to political change, or to realising our 'true human potential' – as if 'true feelings' could somehow be expressed irrespective of the context and the language in which we might do so. This approach, which is characteristic of a great deal of anti-sexist teaching,[30] offers an individualistic, psychotherapeutic response to what is ultimately a social and political problem. The power-relationships of the classroom – and teachers' complicity in those relationships – cannot be swept aside so easily.

Notes and references

An earlier version of this paper was presented at the Annual Meeting of the American Educational Research Association in San Francisco in April 1992. Some of the research reported here was part of a project on the 'Development of Television Literacy in Middle Childhood and Adolescence', funded by the Economic and Social Research Council, UK (grant no: R000 23 1959).

1 See Judith Williamson, 'How does girl number twenty understand ideology?', *Screen Education*, 40 (1981).

2 See, for example, June Statham, *Daughters and Sons: Experiences of Non-Sexist Childraising* (Oxford, Basil Blackwell, 1986).

3 This approach, which is broadly based on 'social learning theory', was dominant in the 1970s, although it remains part of the 'common-sense' definition of the issue, particularly within education. One reference point here is Jane Chetwynd and Oonagh Hartnett (eds), *The Sex Role System: Psychological and Sociological Perspectives* (London, Routledge and Kegan Paul, 1978).

4 Myriam Miedzian, *Boys Will Be Boys* (London, Virago, 1992) provides a striking example of this argument, in which an apparently 'feminist' approach to the issue of media violence becomes almost indistinguishable from that of the so-called 'moral majority'. For further examples, see Bob Dixon, *Catching Them Young 1: Sex, Race and Class in Children's Fiction* (London, Pluto, 1977); and Sue Askew and Sue Ross, *Boys Don't Cry: Boys and Sexism in Education* (Milton Keynes, Open University Press, 1988).

5 Lynne Segal, *Slow Motion: Changing Masculinities, Changing Men* (London Virago, 1990), pp. 66-9. For a very valuable application of this poststructuralist approach to the role of texts in the acquisition of gendered identity, see Bronwyn Davies, *Frogs and Snails and Feminist Tales* (Sydney, Allen and Unwin, 1989).

6 C. Henshall and J. McGuire, 'Gender development', in M. P. M. Richards and P. Light (eds), *Children of Social Worlds* (Cambridge, Polity, 1988).

7 Segal, *Slow Motion*, p. 63.

8 Kevin Durkin, *Television, Sex Roles and Children* (Milton Keynes, Open University Press, 1985).

9 Durkin, *ibid.*, provides a particularly effective critique of two pieces of research which are often quoted in this context: A. Beuf, 'Doctor, lawyer, household drudge', *Journal of Communication*, 24: 2 (1974) 142-5; and P. E. McGhee and T. Frueh, 'Television viewing and the learning of sex-role stereotypes', *Sex Roles*, 6 (1980), 179-88.

10 This is certainly the case with David Morley's *Family Television: Cultural Power and Domestic Leisure* (London, Comedia, 1986). Here, men and women were interviewed in couples by a male interviewer, resulting almost inevitably in what Morley himself acknowledges are unusually highly stereotyped responses. While Morley's

conclusions are tentative, he tends to neglect the issue of context, and some of the anomalies of the data, in adopting gender as an overriding explanatory framework. As such studies are then quoted as 'evidence', and become part of the 'common sense' of academic Cultural Studies, there is a sense in which gender determinism has increasingly come to replace class determinism; yet such conclusions seem highly premature. This criticism is also made by Sonia Livingstone in *Making Sense of Television* (Oxford, Pergamon, 1990).

11 See David Buckingham, 'Against demystification', *Screen*, 27: 5 (1986) 80-95. For examples of this approach, see J. Whyld, D. Pickersgill and D. Jackson, *Update on Anti-Sexist Work with Boys and Young Men* (Manchester, Whyld Publishing Co-op, 1990).

12 In *Children Talking Television: The Making of Television Literacy* (London, Falmer, 1993).

13 The analytical approach adopted here derives partly from recent work in social psychology (for example, Jonathan Potter and Margaret Wetherell, *Discourse and Social Psychology* (London, Sage, 1987)) and partly from work in 'critical linguistics' (for example, Norman Fairclough, *Language and Power* (London, Longman, 1989)). This issue of the role of language in studying television audiences is discussed in detail by Bob Hodge and David Tripp in *Children and Television: A Semiotic Approach* (Cambridge, Polity, 1986).

14 For a critical account of these 'new wave' US cartoons – albeit one which appears to share many of the assumptions of sex-role socialisation theory – see Tom Engelhardt, 'The shortcake strategy', in T. Gitlin (ed.), *Watching Television* (New York, Pantheon, 1986).

15 See Pierre Bourdieu, *Distinction: A Social Critique of the Judgment of Taste* (London, Routledge and Kegan Paul, 1984), and Chris Richards's Chapter 2 in this volume.

16 Segal, *Slow Motion*, particularly Chapter 3.

17 See David Morgan, *It Will Make a Man of You*, Studies in Sexual Politics 17 (Manchester University, 1987).

18 David Jackson, *Unmasking Masculinity: A Critical Autobiography* (London, Unwin Hyman, 1990).

19 *Ibid.*, p. 156. These issues have also been raised in classroom research – see Askew and Ross, *Boys Don't Cry*.

20 D. Buckingham, 'Television literacy and the regulation of children's viewing', paper presented to the British Board of Film Classification conference on 'Standards in Screen Entertainment' (London, March 1992).

21 See D. Buckingham, *Children Talking Television*, Chapter 9.

22 For more detailed accounts of this research, see *ibid.*, Chapter 8 and Gemma Moss, 'Children and television: gendered readings', *Women: An International Cultural Review*, 2: 1 (1992).

23 For a fuller account, see *Children Talking Television*, Chapter 9.

24 See Jeff Hearn and David Morgan (eds), *Men, Masculinities and Social Theory* (London, Unwin Hyman, 1990); and Alice Jardine and Paul Smith (eds), *Men in Feminism* (London, Methuen, 1985).

25 Cf. Erving Goffman, *The Presentation of Self in Everyday Life* (Harmondsworth, Pelican, 1971).

26 This is apparent, for example, in some of the essays contained in J. Shotter and K. J. Gergen (eds), *Texts of Identity* (London, Sage, 1988).

27 See Wil Coleman, 'Doing masculinity/doing theory', in Hearn and Morgan, *Men, Masculinities*.

28 Davies, *Frogs and Snails*, p. 14.

29 See D. Buckingham, 'Going critical: the limits of media literacy', *Australian Journal of Education*, 37: 2 (1992).

30 See, for example, Askew and Ross, *Boys Don't Cry*, and Whyld *et al.*, *Update on Anti-sexist Work*.

Girls tell the teen romance: four reading histories

Teenage Mags

Much of the discussion about the teenage romance is locked into debates about the ideological effects of texts upon their readers. So, for instance, John Willinsky and Mark Hunniford[1] characterise the teen romance as a 'preparatory literature' for girls. They warn that it plays on the fears of a particularly vulnerable audience by offering girls a vision of a narrow future at a time when they may have few other ideas of what could be in store for them. The teen romance is conceived of as a particularly powerful text because it is seen to speak directly to a highly specific audience. Worries about its effects continue to dominate the agenda, despite the fact that critics do not agree on exactly what the romance might speak about: patriarchal relations between women and men/boys and girls; desire and heterosexuality; or women's place.[2]

In an attempt to resolve some of the contradictions to be found in the critics' accounts, attention has turned away from textual analysis and to the audience for the romance. Girls are increasingly asked to speak about their reading.[3] What they have to say is then used to probe the question of ideological effect. I want to raise some difficulties with this kind of enquiry, and particularly with the way the female adolescent audience is constructed within it. I begin by examining how, unusually, Elizabeth Frazer in 'Teenage girls reading *Jackie*'[4] uses some interview data to oppose the notion of the romance's ideological effect. I then turn to Martin Barker's reply to this in *Comics: Ideology, Power and the Critics*,[5] before presenting the case for a different kind of enquiry into girls' romance reading.

The romance – Who is at risk?

In 'Teenage girls reading *Jackie*' Frazer disputes the usefulness of the concept of ideology, particularly as it is applied to the relationship between text and reader:

> All too often theorists commit the fallacy of reading 'the' meaning of a text and inferring the ideological effect that text 'must' have on the readers (other than the theorists themselves, of course!) We may oppose this strategy at two points. First we may dispute that there is one valid and unitary meaning of a text. Second we may care to check whether ... it does have ... an ideological effect on the reader. (p. 411)

Frazer takes up the question of ideological effects by looking at how seven different groups of girls reacted to a *Jackie* story she gave them to read. In each case the girls show themselves to be well able to dismiss the story as rubbish. They evaluate it as fiction, and find it lacking; they compare it to their own lives and find it unrealistic; they identify its purposes, the hidden messages it contains, and reject them; and they comment explicitly on its role in creating fantasies. Frazer concludes that:

> My preliminary analysis of the transcripts of these discussions ... strongly suggests that a self-conscious and reflexive approach to texts is a natural understanding, not only of fiction, but of the genre of publications for girls of which *Jackie* is an example ... . Ideology is undercut, that is, by these readers, reflexivity and reflectiveness. (p. 419)

She argues persuasively for considering girls as knowing and critical, far from the image of a passive and vulnerable audience more commonly associated with examination of this age-group reading this kind of material. However, Frazer does not suggest that girls are entirely free to imagine life in their own image. On the contrary, for the remainder of the paper she moves on to explore the idea of discourse registers as important factors which limit what can be said in specific contexts. She argues that girls have access to a variety of discourse registers which produce and validate different kinds of knowledge. In this instance they read the *Jackie* text through a variety of different discourse registers which undercut its message. This leads her to look for the constraints which produce girls as gendered individuals, not in the texts they consume, but primarily in the social settings for speech.

In his response to this piece, Barker raises a number of queries about the status of the data Frazer presents. But the main thrust of his argument is to discount the criticisms these girls make by claiming they have no relevance to an enquiry into what *Jackie* means to its readers. He does this first by querying the assumption that to be critical of a text is to be uninfluenced. Secondly, and at greater length, he suggests that Frazer is looking at the wrong group of readers. He argues that the girls she interviewed are not *Jackie*'s '"spontaneous" or "natural" readership':

> This tells us where Frazer goes wrong. Her misunderstanding (along with so many other people) is to suppose that anyone who reads *Jackie* is its 'reader'. Just because certain girls in very widely dispersed social locations will pick up the comic and read it – perhaps even regularly – does not mean that they are the ones we need to be studying. (p. 256)

For Barker, those whom we ought to be studying are the readers who take up a 'contract' with the text:

> A 'contract' involves an agreement that a text will talk to us in ways we recognise. It will enter into a dialogue with us. And that dialogue, with its dependable elements and form, will relate to some aspect of our lives in society. (p. 261)

He goes on to argue:

> (1) that the media are only capable of exerting power over audiences to the extent that there is a 'contract' between texts and audience, which relates to some specifiable aspect(s) of the audience's social lives: and (2) the breadth and direction of the influence is a function of those socially constituted features of the audience's lives, and comes out of the fulfilment of the contract. (p. 261)

'Natural readers' – some problems

In relation to more general arguments about media audiences these points about the kind of contract 'natural readers' enter into with a text sound innocuous enough. Indeed, in relation to a more general debate about ideology they represent a considerable improvement upon the kind of conspiracy theories which see the media industries in some Svengali-like role, keeping the rest of us from true knowledge of the way things are. However, these contentions do not work so well when applied to an adolescent and female readership for *Jackie*. This is partly because no other genre besides the romance is seen to work so comprehensively against the interests of its main readership. In this respect, the relationship of girls to the romance is not interchangeable with that of children to comics such as *The Beano* or *Whoopee* (which Barker analyses at some length): or of boys to comics such as *Battle* or *Action* (again a focus for Barker's analysis). It is highly problematic to assert that somewhere there is a group of girls to whom *Jackie* speaks without locking such a group into the position of hapless victims unable to act in their own best interests, before one has ever heard what they might have to say.[6]

There are other more fundamental objections. For a start, how do we know who the 'natural' readers are? Barker argues that this cannot be judged by the regularity of reading, nor by the presence or absence of critical comment. He points out that in the latter case, criticism may be motivated as much by the failure of the magazine to live up to its side of the contract, as any rejection of its influence. Instead, Barker defines a text's natural readers in terms of the kind of relationship they have with its contents. They are the ones who are spoken to. But he also presupposes that the critic will be able to recognise the form that address will take – the nature of the contract – in advance. S/he must already know what that relationship will be in order to discount what it is not. This seems to me to be a highly questionable research procedure. All too easily it will lead to the dismissal of any data which doesn't fit the critic's existing assumptions about what the natural audience's relationship to the text in question should be. This is exactly what happens when Barker turns his attention to Frazer's data. As a research strategy in relation to the romance it will do little to get critics beyond a view of girl readers as essentially passive and hapless dupes.

I am arguing against the notion of dividing the audience for romance into 'natural' readers whom we will study, and other kinds of readers whom we won't. I suspect this is a pointless exercise which simply creates a mythical group wholly dominated by the romance's agenda, whom we would have great difficulty in actually tracking down.[7] In the meantime it detracts from any full examination of a more varied range of responses.

However, I don't want to lose sight of Barker's reminder that different readers come to texts with very different histories of engagement with a particular form. This should be recognised in any analysis of what they have to say. The weakness of Liz Frazer's piece is that she provides no information about the relationship of the girls she interviewed to the magazine, or indeed any other kind of reading material. This makes it hard to set these girls' comments in context, or indeed, to know quite what weight to give them. This is a lack.

Reading histories – another approach

I am proposing another approach to girls' reading of the romance by starting, not with questions about ideological effects, but with questions about the reading histories which create and sustain girls' interests in particular texts. Starting with reading histories allows us to differentiate between levels of engagement and to build that into any analysis without prejudging the nature of the relationship with the text. It also enables us to focus on reading as a social activity – something which takes place at particular moments in time, in particular social settings, involving particular participants. This is in contrast with much of the work on ideological effects which, for all its concerns with the links between the contents of the text and the way people live their lives, still focuses on reading as primarily a mental phenomenon, something which happens in the interior space of the mind rather than in the social space of everyday transactions.

Examining reading histories allows us to consider the range of interests any one reader may have and the place for a particular genre within that range. This acts as a reminder that texts are not read in a vacuum, each one considered in lonely isolation on the merits of its contents. They are read through and against a social history of encounters with other texts at other times. Any one reading is both specific to the particular location in which it takes place, the particular text involved, and shaped by a much broader past. To concentrate on reading histories is to explore how a particular reading unfolds in time. This seems particularly important in relation to a young audience. Young people's interests differ from adults' in that they are developed during a period of rapid change for them. Different objects come in and out of fashion in rapid succession, old tastes are put to one side, revisited in a new light or superseded by other interests. Young people are not a stable audience whose interests have been sustained over considerable periods of time – in direct contrast, for example, to the adult audience for soap operas who may indeed bring a lengthy history of engagement with a particular text to a research interview (just as they will do to their reading of a particular episode). We need to be able to take such patterns of rapid change into account in any analysis we undertake.

In considering the data presented below, I will be analysing how the teen romance genre is judged alongside other texts, how a place is established for it within particular reading histories, and what is at stake for individuals in declaring themselves to be one of its readers.

One group – different readers

The data I will be considering comes from an interview conducted with four twelve-year-old girls – Ceri, Mitra, Sally and Nicola – during the summer term of their first year in secondary school about a range of books they read outside school. I want to start by saying something about how this group came to be interviewed together, and the general range of their interests.

The girls' class was one of six being used by the Television Literacy Research Project.[8] From this class, a sample had been recruited who would be interviewed on eight separate occasions over the course of eighteen months about their television viewing. I was the researcher working with this group. One of the activities the children undertook was to keep a diary of their TV, computer and video use. In the appendix they had been asked to name any books or magazines they had read in the period the diary covered. I decided to use this information to interview some of the children about other leisure interests besides TV. One of the girls, Ceri, had mentioned her liking for Sweet Valley High books, a popular teenage romance series. This looked like an interesting area to investigate further, so some time after the diary had been completed I asked Ceri to convene a group from among her friends in the class who would come and talk to me about romance reading. At this juncture I was imagining myself tapping into a group of committed readers – my label on the tape from this interview still reads 'Devotees: romances'.

In the event though, the group's relationship to the romance genre was more diverse, their interests in reading more eclectic. Ceri, in agreeing to get the group together, told me that she herself was no longer reading Sweet Valley Highs, she'd moved on to Jackie Collins, and the group she finally assembled had a much more diverse range of interests than simply the romance. Of the four, only Mitra was still regularly reading Sweet Valley Highs. At their broadest the group's interests in reading might best be defined as 'girls' fiction'. But even so, Sally declared on her way over to the interview that her interests were in 'gory books', and expressed a certain amount of contempt for the other girls' interests by labelling them as 'soppy books'. She mainly seemed to be there as Ceri's best friend rather than because of a shared interest in particular kinds of books.

In some senses such divergent histories complicate the interview: these girls clearly did not hold a common view of a common text. But I would also argue that (girls') tastes are often shaped in this way, *against* those of others as much as *for* the intrinsic qualities of a particular object considered on its own.[9] Hand-picking a group of committed readers who will only speak about one genre precludes finding out how that interest fits alongside others. Moreover Ceri's choice of the group may also reflect a more accurate picture of the kind of reading network which individuals find themselves part of, where interests differ as well as converge.

In Barker's terms, these girls do not constitute a group of 'natural readers'. The idea of a 'natural reader' focuses attention exclusively on the relation between one kind of text and one kind of reader. Any admission of other interests is seen to detract from the central point of enquiry. I think this is a mistaken view. Any reader, no matter how committed or obsessional, is unlikely to restrict themselves entirely to one kind of text. Ceri's viewing diary was compiled at a time when she considered herself to be a romance reader, yet her leisure interests considered as a whole were much more diverse. Her TV viewing comprised some programmes from children's TV, including cartoons, magazine programmes and serials; and some programmes from mainstream TV, including chat shows, game shows, serials, soaps and particularly comedies. During the two-week period the diary ran she watched several videos, mainly comedies, and looked at a couple of magazines: *The Beano* and *Girl*. It is precisely for this kind of reason that I would argue that we need to understand the way readers establish relations between different kinds of texts.

Teen romances and Sweet Valley Highs

In the interview the romance genre was most straightforwardly represented by the Sweet Valley High (SVH) series. It is important to be clear about the nature of the particular text under discussion, for this helps shape the ways in which it comes to be read. The debate between Frazer and Barker, for instance, centres on the stories *Jackie* magazine carried as picture strips. These qualify as romances in so far as they centre on 'girl meets boy' scenarios, but as texts they are organised, produced and consumed according to different rules from those governing the production and consumption of teenage romance books such as the SVH series. In any discussion of the romance it is all too easy to lose sight of the very different generic locations in which specific stories appear, and consequently to overlook the different social processes which govern the ways in which such texts will be circulated and read. For example, the SVH series's ambiguous status as books featured prominently during the interview (see below).

The SVH series is packaged and promoted in much the same way as Mills and Boon. The series rather than the individual author is given prominence, and each book relies on a clearly identifiable formula. Unlike Mills and Boon, though, the series gains much of its coherence from the central characters who feature in each story. These are identical twin sisters, Elizabeth and Jessica. The SVH series focuses on their romantic encounters during their teenage years, and is marketed specifically for the young teenage audience. It is now preceded by the Sweet Valley Twins and Sweet Valley Kids series, featuring the same twins at earlier stages in their lives, and clearly aimed at younger readers. Neither of these two earlier series makes reference to girl/boy relationships. In this interview the girls I talked to show themselves to be only too aware of the SVH's role as fiction sandwiched in between other kinds of books, appropriate only at a particular moment in a reading career.

I turn now to the interview transcript itself. There are two issues I want to concentrate on. I begin with the way in which these girls talk about book reading as a quite specific kind of social activity. In part, their romance reading is defined by its place in this wider context. I go on to consider the particular position each one of them constructs for SVH books amongst the other texts they know.

Book reading – a regulated activity

When talking about children's leisure interests it is all too possible to imagine this as a free space where they make their own choices about how to spend their time. This is in contrast to the demands made on them at school, where they are not free agents. However, most of what children do is the subject of some kind of regulation, if only in terms of the amount of time and money they have at their disposal. Girls are particularly likely to live with constraints on how they spend their time at home: they are most likely to be asked to contribute to domestic labour.

Certainly, the account these girls give of their book reading shows *Problem* this activity to be regulated by pressure from both parents and peers. The *pgs.* kinds of choices they make about what to read and when to read become the subject of others' approval or disapproval. Much of this is governed by the need to be seen to be doing well at reading. This may partly reflect the class and educational background this group share. The school is situated in a relatively affluent suburb which is predominantly white and upwardly mobile, though the ethnic mix includes a sizeable Greek Cypriot community, and a Jewish presence. The school itself continues to operate selection procedures and this group will only have gained entry to it via an exam taken at the end of their junior school. In this context it is not surprising that considerable social value is given to being a fluent reader. But I would argue that such notions have a wider social currency. At the same time gender may be at least as important an influence on the regulation of their reading as class and education. In many ways the reading of fiction has historically been associated with women,[10] whilst the marketing of fiction for children and young adults continues to operate quite clearly with notions of gender-distinct tastes. Certainly much of what this group has to say shows them in one way or another to be dealing with a sense of themselves as gendered readers.

How do the kinds of choices they make about what to read and when to read become the subject of others' approval or disapproval? As I've suggested, much of this is governed by the need to be seen to be doing well at reading. At this stage in their school careers the question of how well they can read is always on the agenda. Reading books in one's spare time has educational implications. It suggests making an effort to do something worthwhile. By contrast, other leisure pursuits such as watching TV are not seen to have any bearing on progress at school. Nicola doesn't report any way in which her parents try to regulate what she reads, but she does say she reads because she gets told off for watching too much TV. Watching TV in comparison to reading appears a frivolous distraction.

If book reading itself is important, then the kinds of books that are read become another means for judging competence. These kinds of judgements are also used by the girls against each other. Sally gets taken to task by the group when her version of what she reads is interpreted by the others as too easy:

> *Sally:* I like these books called, I think it's published by Macmillans or something, and they're all different like the *Ghost of Culloden* or something and they're all gory, and they're quite thin so you can read them in [bed at night and they're really good.
> *Ceri:* [Oh I know, you read them in school / [yeah] yeah, they're just really thin with lots of pictures in and so they're [(...) pictures. *[laughter]*
> *Sally:* [NO (...)
> *Mitra:* YEAH, I used to read them when I was three!

Sally uses her interests in gory books as a means of denigrating the other girls' reading. But the description she gives of the books she prefers allows the others to judge her as not yet a competent reader. They get their revenge for the way she has attempted to discount their interests.

These girls come from homes where there is both a positive value put on reading, and some anxiety about how well it is being done. The romance fits uneasily into this space:

> *Mitra:* My Dad's always going 'Ooh reading all these soppy love stories' and everything and I go, 'Ok I won't read at all' and he goes 'Oh, all right then, read them!' *[laughs]*

In this instance Mitra actually uses this kind of educational anxiety over reading to defend the time she spends on reading romances against her father's concerns about the contents of the material. As a book the romance is to be welcomed. It provides a sign of relative fluency, but it is not the best kind of book. This much is clear:

> Mitra: 'Cos my mum, like my mum and I, go to the library with me then she comes over to my bit and picks up like all these like big sort of enormous classics and goes 'Oh yeah, why don't you read this?', 'No thank you it's quite all right', 'cos she picks really like, boring books!

If thin picture books are a sign of relative inexperience as a reader, true adult status is not conferred by reading the romance. I have been drawing attention to the way the place for the romance is shaped by concerns which are not specific to the genre but relate to reading and schooling. How well these children are reading (indicated by the kinds of books they choose and the amount of time they spend on them) and what they are reading for (self-improvement or wasting time), are questions these girls must deal with.

Thus far, concerns about reading and competence have been shared by the group as a whole. But the view they present of themselves as readers, and the place they construct from which to read the romance are very different.

Mitra's story

Mitra was invited to the interview because Ceri knew she owned a great number of the SVH series and regularly read them during form-time. Of all the group, Mitra looks most like a committed romance reader. At the time of the interview she was reading *Double Love*, the first in the SVH series, presumably not for the first time. She also mentions reading other kinds of books, including children's books by Enid Blyton and a great deal of teenage fiction, though the SVH series and another romance series, Sweet Dreams, seem to be her favourites. For Mitra, the appropriate audience for the SVH series is established by the series' place on the library shelves:

> Mitra: 'Cos like in my library it's got a whole teenage bit ... and then like ... at the top there are all these Sweet Valley High books and Sweet Dreams and all that, then at the bottom there's all these really boring books and in the middle there's all these books you've never heard of before.

Mitra makes frequent references to her mother's reading in the course of the interview, often contrasting it with her own preferences:

> *Gemma:* Does she read, wha – does she read romances, does she read?
> *Mitra:* Well, I don't know, 'cos, like, I always see her coming out of the library with books about that thick, with really boring covers, and they're normally about, I don't know what they're about really. ...

Later in the interview Mitra characterises this kind of adult reaction by the way in which it is written:

> *Mitra:* I started reading one of my mum's books and they were so boring, right the first was something like this man and he was driving and they like describe everything, right, they wouldn't say like, in the books that I read (...). there was like, say something like a brown table, and in their books right, there was an oak, I dunno, [(...) a varnished round oak...
> *Nicola:*   [yeah, which, which had a little scratch on it...
> *Mitra:* Yeah, and then I got through the first, the first one and a bit pages=
> *Ceri:* =page and it was still describing the table!

The other girls know exactly what she is talking about and join in the parody. Adult books are incomprehensible, too long-winded, and too full of description to be worth following.

For the moment Mitra stays in the teenage section, rejecting her mother's invitation to read 'boring books'. In the teenage section she has no hesitation about choosing the romance:

> *Mitra:* I like soppy books 'cos everything goes perfect, and I don't know, and at the, like, you always know wh – , like if you read the back of the book you always know what's going to happen and I like it when I know what's going to happen, 'cos I know what's going to happen *[laughter]* ... like, I dunno, she's madly in love with this boy but then he won't talk to her and you know in the end, that they're going to, right in the end then they're going to get together.

What she stresses about the SVH series is the formulaic quality which makes them predictable, and also pleasurable. Whilst Ceri's foray into best sellers has led her to stop reading SVHs, Mitra's first encounter with more adult material has led her back to them:

> *Mitra:* You know what Ceri was saying about like them being really boring and all that, they're not boring, they're just stupid. [What are?] They're really stupid, but I still like them.
> *Gemma:* So it doesn't matter that they're stupid.
> *Mitra:* No, I like them 'cos they're stupid, 'cos I read *Flowers in the Attic* and that's like really, sort of, one of the, like they're really growing up people, and then I started reading them again and they seem really stupid but I still like them.

For Mitra the teenage section is a half-way house between childhood and adulthood in her history as a reader. It is a temporary stopping-off place.

Behind her are children's books such as those by Enid Blyton and the Sweet Valley Twins series, ahead of her the kind of books her mother prefers.

Ceri's story

Ceri's reading includes adult best sellers, some of the teen romances, and a variety of children's books. At the time of the interview she had just finished *The Ballet Family*. Most of what she reads could be described as girls' fiction, except for the best sellers, which are clearly targeted at an older female readership.

Like Mitra, the way in which Ceri talked about her reading indicated a clear sense of its future, as well as its past. Because they deal with girl/boy relationships, SVHs qualify as teenage books. As such they have a certain status for both Ceri and Mitra. They are clearly to be preferred to the Sweet Valley Twins series, which they both reject pretty comprehensively:

> *Ceri:* [I read Sweet Valley Twins first of all and they're so boring, Sweet Valley Twins, I hate them.
> ...
> *Mitra:* have you seen the dresses they wear, you know in the front of I don't know, forgotten what it's called, and then she's wearing like a pinafore, I wouldn't be SEEN DEAD in a pinafore!
> *Ceri:* I mean they wear dresses, yeah I mean they wear DRESSES, I mean no one wears, they wear dresses to picnics and things!

Yet there were differences here too. In contrasting the SVH series with the very different kinds of books her mother reads, Mitra mainly talks about the way the books are written. Ceri, in looking ahead from SVHs to other kinds of adult fiction, is more concerned with differences in content:

> *Ceri:* Yeah, 'cos I like Sweet Valley High and then I read *Lace* and um, what's it, *Lace* and um things like that, and they're the same, right the beginning of *Lace*, it's about the same thing, the girl's about the same age and what they're, as um Sweet Valley High, what they're doing is like, it's just, it's really pathetic it seems in Sweet Valley High what they do, because they're much more/
> *Gemma:* Keep going, Ceri.
> *Ceri:* advanced in the oth – , in *Lace* and things, in Sweet Valley High they just, if you just kiss with a boy, you know, you're just, you know, shock, and everyone hates you, but in *Lace* it goes much further /
> *Gemma:* ['Cos they actually ...
> *Others:* [OOOOOOOOOOHH. ...

For Ceri, SVHs are increasingly being superseded by best sellers. The romance is losing its place to more sexually explicit fiction. Ceri is very definite about why she reads the latter:

> *Gemma:* On Jackie Collins, Ceri, is that because it happened to be around at home, is that how come you got to read it, because it?
> *Ceri:* Yeah, because I thought it would be dirty / [*laughter*] and it was. I read *Lace* first, which was really boring.

At first glance, her curiosity seems to be about what books will tell you about sex. In the case of the SVH romance the answer is not a lot, so Ceri turns elsewhere. But this is not just a quest for the facts of life. After all, there are always 'body books' in every school library which will tell you that part of the story. In turning to the best sellers, Ceri also seems to be curious about what such books say to an adult audience. The books she reads are her mother's and she describes at some length how she first came across them:

> *Ceri:* My mum changed the furniture round and like, we found all these books which my mum's been hiding behind the settee 'cos she doesn't want anyone to know she's reading, yeah, 'cos they found out there were these three best, *Lace* and *Lace 2* and this other one, I've forgotten what it was called, it was a Jackie Collins, oh yeah, *Gamblers and Lovers*, that's it, and they're really boring actually but I like the dirty bits! [*loud laughter*]

What she makes of the rest of the book or even how much of it she reads, is uncertain, as she consistently dismisses the plot lines:

> *Ceri:* ... they're really good, the story though is crap and it's a bit, it's a bit ...
> *Sally:* It's a bit crap!
> *Ceri:* No, it's crap really, but the dirty bits are good. [*laughter*]

Each time Ceri talks about the dirty bits in the best sellers one or more of the other girls joins in to tell about dirty bits they know, though their reference points are different. Nicola and Mitra both talk about *Forever*, a Judy Blume book which contains one notoriously explicit love scene, whose exact location seems to be common knowledge:

> *Nicola:* If you want to read *Forever*, but you can't be bothered ... with the boring bit, chapter nine and thirteen are what to read.

In each case the stories they tell are of adults interrupting this kind of reading:

> *Nicola:* I read it and everyone else in my school wanted to borrow it, so I lent it to Lisa, this girl, and she read it and she went out into the playground, and all the fourth-years were, were, it was a massive circle because they were, because she was reading them out all the dirty bits / [oh really] Yeah, and then all these first years were going and suddenly the Head-

master came so we were going 'LA la la' and sort of hiding the book and everything.

The story Mitra tells is very similar, only in this case the teacher interrupts a group of boys reading the same pages in class; Sally tells a story of a dinner-lady almost confiscating a magazine a boy had brought into school and was passing around at lunchtime. Making 'dirty bits' public in this way obviously involves breaking adult rules about who should know what. In following up Ceri's account of reading best sellers with these kinds of stories, the other girls reinterpret what she has to say in that light. Nevertheless, it seems to me there is a difference here between their accounts and Ceri's. The other girls' stories focus on the possibilities of being found out, how this is avoided or what the adults actually do (Nicola tells another story about a friend's father throwing away a dirty book he found her reading). In Ceri's case, the roles are reversed: she had found her mother out. Moreover, Ceri is therefore able to link these 'dirty books' directly to a known audience. In the case of the others I suspect it is much less clear precisely who these kinds of texts are intended for. Even *Forever*, which as a teenage book is readily available in that section in bookshops or libraries, isn't treated as intended for them. Rather, they seem to regard it as information they have come across by mistake and which adults would do something about if they realised it was there. Consequently, talking about these kinds of dirty bits doesn't seem to have any impact on the rest of their reading. By contrast, for Ceri the best sellers are both replacements for and extensions of the romance. She sees them as treating similar themes in a more adult way. The best seller recontextualises the romance.

For all their differences, in some respects Mitra and Ceri share a common view of their reading career. They see the teen romance as holding a particular place between children's and adults' fiction. They are neither of them bothered by the romance's connection with a female readership. Indeed their own place as female readers seems pretty secure: neither of them is put off talking about their own interests by gibes about 'soppy' books. Ceri mainly ignores the word. She never uses it herself about her own or others' reading. Anything she doesn't like, from *The Ballet Family* to *Gamblers and Lovers*, she refers to as 'crap'. Mitra doesn't bother to deny that SVHs are soppy books, but uses this label as a way of identifying the teen romance as a specific genre. By contrast, what can be labelled as 'soppy' becomes a bone of contention between Sally and Nicola.

Sally's story

Sally seemed less interested in reading fiction than the other girls. Almost all of Sally's books seemed to come from the school library and were chosen entirely by topic, the gorier the better. The last book she said she'd read was *The Black Death*. Sally consistently referred to her own reading as 'gory books'. For her, 'gory' and 'soppy' act as mutually exclusive categories. In her view, someone who is interested in 'gory' books (herself) wouldn't possibly be interested in 'soppy' books. 'Soppy books' seem to be anything that could be associated with a specifically female readership, including of course books about girl/boy relationships. By contrast, her 'gory books' are generally to be found amongst the children's fiction, and tend to be those books which attract as many boy as girl readers:

> *Gemma:* Do you read all different sorts of books?
> *Sally:* Mostly Roald Dahl, 'cos he's a combination of gory kind of / but if I see like, I go round the library and I see Roald Dahls, but I've got Roald Dahl, I've got a whole lot of Roald Dahl books, but I just go round the library, I see like, *The Black Death* or um, *Murder on the Nile* or something, I just pick it up and then take it out and read it.

By dismissing what the other girls read as 'soppy' books, Sally highlights the relative low status of fiction associated with girls. Yet her declared lack of interest didn't stop her coming to an interview where this kind of literature would be discussed. Indeed, part of Sally's assertive confidence in her right to be present seems to be tied up with the relative weight she gives to the official topic of conversation. She clearly thinks that the position she speaks from is a more powerful one. The other girls dispute this:

> *Sally:* ... it's good when you see someone's head getting chopped off or you're listening, you're reading: 'the guts fell on the wall'.
> *Mitra:* Yeah, what's so good about that? It's disgusting.
> *Nicola:* She should watch *The Fly*!
> *Mitra:* Oh god, that's disgusting!
> *Nicola:* *The Fly*, the fly's head, that is evil.
> *Mitra:* At Maria's party in the middle of the night whenever a scary bit came on, she was in her sleeping bag, she was having a fit, going like this. *[laughter]*

Sally's description fails to impress Mitra, although it also reminds her and Nicola of a 'gory' video they've seen. Yet their relationship to this kind of material seems quite different. Whilst Nicola remembers a disgusting bit to match Sally's, Mitra remembers Nicola as the terrified girl viewer. Watching 'gore' doesn't necessarily offer the kind of escape into a genderless space which Sally seems to look for.

Sally's division of the territory into 'soppy books' versus 'gory books' both signals the extent to which romances are seen as gendered texts, and stresses the ambiguous position of the romance's female audience. To be a romance reader is not to speak from a position of power. Yet there is no consensus in this group as to what kinds of texts carry what kinds of prestige for girl readers. This contrasts sharply with a group of boys from the same class whom I interviewed about computer magazines. The boys spent more or less the whole interview vigorously arguing about who had the better computer and using the magazine to show up each other's lack of real knowledge. But they were all agreed on the central point, that computer knowledge was worth having.

Nicola's story

Nicola came to the interview because she was known to like Judy Blume books. Judy Blume has written a lot (though not exclusively) for the teenage girl market. Much of her work is concerned with the problems of growing up, whether that be to do with issues like divorce in the family, friendships or girl/boy relationships. Most of the other books Nicola mentions reading were more obviously girls' teenage fiction than the kind of books Sally talked about. But unlike Ceri and Mitra, Nicola eschews formulaic teen romances.

I've already pointed out that neither Mitra nor Ceri react particularly strongly to the use of the word 'soppy' to label their interests. Nicola is much more concerned. I think a great deal of this is to do with her assessment of the implications of being identified with a specifically female readership. Unlike Ceri and Mitra, Nicola vigorously denies that she reads soppy books:

> Nicola: The last book I read was um, Lonely Hearts, [a Stevie Day book
> Sally: [See, I told you you
> like soppy things
> Nicola: IT IS NOT SOPPY!

Despite the fact that the title suggests the romance genre, the book in question features a young girl detective called Stevie Day who goes round solving people's problems. There are another three books in the series. Later on, Nicola sums them up as follows:

> Nicola: It's really good because they've all got fun bits, they've all got really scary bits, it's a good mixture ... because she was going to stab her and the police break in and you're sort of going 'Oooh!'

The gender-ambiguous name and the role the key character plays push these books towards at least a gender neutral readership, if not quite into the area of boys' interests. The gory details Nicola provides in this instance also fit with Sally's interests. In this sense, Nicola redefines the book as suitable for a genderless reader, rather than being marked out for girls' consumption. Rather than challenging the appropriateness of using the word 'soppy' to label girls' interests, Nicola simply tries to line herself up on Sally's side of the divide.

But actually doing this isn't always so straightforward. It proves particularly difficult in relation to Judy Blume, who, as Sally reminds Nicola, provides the main reason for her presence at the interview:

> *Sally:* Judy Blume's soppy.
> *Nicola:* What's soppy?
> *Sally:* [Judy Blume.
> *Ceri:* (... god!) *[possibly quoting a Blume title]*
> *Gemma:* Judy Blume is soppy books?
> *Nicola:* I don't read them any more.
> *Sally:* Yeah, well you're talking about them, she, she got you because Judy Blume.
> *Nicola:* Yeah, but they're all right / they're not that soppy, they're not like 'Ooh, love me *[laughs]* ... (help me, promise) me tonight! Promise me to go out with me tonight' *[spoken in a little girl voice]*. They're not all like that.

Having failed to deny any association with Judy Blume books, Nicola's strategy is to try to confine the term 'soppy' to a particular kind of romantic fiction (SVHs) and to deny this has anything to do with the kinds of books she reads. In the process, what she mocks is not just this other kind of book, but also its readers. Throughout the interview she consistently puts on the tone of voice of a credulous little girl when talking about what she considers to be soppy books. In distancing herself from the fiction she also distances herself from those whom she imagines to be its readers:

> *Gemma:* Sweet Valley Highs, do you read any of them?
> *Nicola:* I read about three of them when I was about nine 'cos I used to 'Ooh' *[in soppy voice]* like that, but now I don't read them.
> *Mitra:* On the front it says for, for people of eleven and upwards actually, so...

Whereas Mitra justifies her choice by quoting the recommended age on the blurb, Nicola dismisses the series by conjuring up a vision of herself as a once young and impressionable reader. She insists she is no longer that kind of girl:

> *Gemma:* What put you off them, Nicola?

Nicola: They were just boring like all 'Ooh, hello, Herby' and then I've changed because I used to be really la-di-da, and 'Ooh' but, and then I sort of changed and became, weird ...
Ceri: Loud, loud and noisy
Nicola: (...) and now I don't like those books, they're too soppy.

There is something defensive about Nicola's reaction. At the same time as she is busily defending herself from the change, she actually uses the word 'soppy' more frequently than any of the others during the interview, most often to label the books Ceri and Mitra read in a derogatory manner. In many ways Nicola's view is closest to that of the romance's critics. Like many of them, in rejecting the teen romance she also rejects its readers.[11] Yet the kinds of assumptions she makes about who the romance speaks to are not borne out by the kinds of comments Ceri and Mitra make.

Four different histories

In deciding how the genre will be read, critics have imagined a homogeneous interpretive community, defined according to the social position they occupy. I am seeking a more divergent account, capable of dealing with change as well as stasis. This has led me to focus on the place the romance holds amongst other interests. I have sought to show how the romance is always contextualised in relation to specific reading histories, which may differ. These reading histories are constructed in relation to knowledge of specific social practices, in particular the ways books are shared out amongst their audience. Whilst broadly united in terms of class and educational background, these girls' reading histories are far from homogeneous and the places they construct for the romance very different. Concern over girls' romance reading fails to take this kind of contextualisation into account.

The romance does not speak about a single thing. It speaks differently to the girls in this group, but those differences can only be understood in relation to other kinds of texts which it is not, other kinds of reading from which it differs. The trouble with much of the debate over the romance is that it treats the romance as if it contained an abstract philosophical proposition with which readers either agree or disagree. Instead, we need to understand the genre in relation to the range of social practices which constitute reading and which mediate the text.

Notes and references

1 J. Willinsky and R. M. Hunniford, 'Reading the romance younger. The mirrors and fears of a preparatory literature', in *Reading-Canada-Lecture*, 4: 1 (1986), 16–30.

2 G. Moss, *Un/Popular Fictions* (London, Virago 1989); J. Batsleer, 'Pulp in the pink', in *Spare Rib*, 109 (1981). A. Light, '"Returning to Manderley": romance fiction, female sexuality and class', in *Feminist Review*, 16 (1984); A. McRobbie, 'Jackie: an ideology of adolescent femininity', in B. Waites, T. Bennett and G. Martin (eds), *Popular Culture: Past and Present* (London, Croom Helm and Open University, 1982); P. Gilbert and S. Taylor, *Fashioning the Feminine. Girls, Popular Culture and Schooling* (Sydney, Allen and Unwin, 1991).

3 L. Christian-Smith, *Texts of Desire* (London, Falmer, 1993); Gilbert and Taylor, *Fashioning the Feminine*.

4 E. Frazer, 'Teenage girls reading *Jackie*', in *Media, Culture and Society*, 9: 4 (1987), 407-25.

5 M. Barker, *Comics: Ideology, Power and the Critics*, (Manchester University Press, 1989).

6 To be fair to Barker, he does try to suggest that there might be more to *Jackie* than a simplistic set of negative effects. And he is able to defend the magazine against the charges brought against it by Angela McRobbie in her early analysis of *Jackie* (McRobbie, 'Jackie'). His own analysis of *Jackie* shows that the magazine in several ways supports female friendship, whilst the stories are much more ambivalent about the place for boys in girls' lives than McRobbie allowed for. None the less he displays none of the same sense of ready sympathy with the magazine that he brings to his analysis of other comics.

7 Barker himself even seems to suggest at times that *Jackie's* 'natural' readers no longer exist (so who keeps buying the magazine one wonders?). He explains this decline in terms of changes in the magazine's production history and the consequent mix of articles it carries, but then curiously admits in a footnote that the story Frazer's groups were reading (and rejecting) was recycled from that earlier, more potent, era.

8 This project was funded by the ESRC from 1989/91 and was based in the Institute of Education, University of London. The other project members were David Buckingham and Valerie Hey.

9 See Chris Richards, Chapter 2 in this volume.

10 T. Lovell, *Consuming Fiction* (London, Verso, 1987).

11 See, for example, P. Hoggart, 'Comics and magazines for schoolchildren', in J. Miller (ed.), *Eccentric Propositions* (London, Routledge and Kegan Paul, 1984); D. Margolies, 'Mills and Boon – guilt without sex', in *Red Letters*, 14 (1982).

Untidy, depressing and violent:
a boy's own story

he shot but Zartan bloked it with the sword. Zartan gave him a double
kick, he went down zartan picked up the swore and droke it through Dark
storms head Dark storm try to get up but he fell he was dead zartan was
relifed but frostbite got up and shot a freeze at Zartan.[1]

'*Action packed, although I find all the battles a little difficult to follow –
spelling and punctuation – we must have a talk. I prefer knowing more
about character and scene than just the action, it adds to the overall effect.*'
What else could be said? *Ninjas of the Night, the Quest for Power* or
fourteen pages of *frostbite's Revenge* (from which the above extract is
taken), just seemed obsessive, repetitive and 'unsound'. Like many English teachers I found teenage boys' writing alienated and alienating.
Focusing on surface errors was a neutral way of circumventing the kinds
of literary competencies that I didn't know how to deal with. These
stories just seemed inferior and somehow outside models of pupils'
good writing.

Yet the frequency and commitment of this kind of writing made
me realise that, however much it was unrewarded by me, it was deeply
meaningful to the boys who spent time and thought on these productions. When I found five twelve-year-olds actually sharing *frostbite's Revenge* as a group reading I realised that there was more at stake than just
producing stories for 'English'. This chapter began simply as my attempt
to find out why there might be such a strong investment in certain kinds
of stories and to identify what kind of masculine culture they reveal. In
effect, I want to investigate the totality of what I called above a 'literary
competency'. The substance of this chapter is an analysis of one particular boy's story, *Plaz Investigations*, which involves detailed study of the
author's reading and use of film and comics.

This research is clearly shaped by my position as a teacher and
hence my relation both to the object of study (my pupils) and to its

cultural and political purpose (boys' consumption of masculine genres) is heavily compromised. This fact has several implications. First of all, my role needs to be set against the positions the other writers in this book have adopted, from parent to visiting academic. I began this research as an active player in my classes' production of stories and could almost be seen as the commissioning agent for *Plaz Investigations*. However, as I moved from being an English teacher to a Media Studies teacher over the period of this research, and perhaps towards a different evaluation of cultural products, my attitude changed. And as I became more receptive to the writer's outlook, this must have influenced the way he chose to confide in me.

As my marking of *frostbite's Revenge* indicates, my initial response to boys' writing was to perceive it as a weakness and a problem. Institutionally, as a probationary teacher, I was encouraged in this view. Much research into boys and education has constructed boys as a problem in terms of their attention-seeking and disruptive behaviour or their control of a scientific and work-oriented curriculum. The culture of the subject 'English' has also been heavily inflected by gender; English is perceived as a feminine subject and many values in literary appreciation are again associated with the feminine.[2] Thus my criticisms about 'character and scene' above, or other comments about motivation or feeling, belong to a repertoire of cultural values that have historically developed out of a specific class and gendered reading of literature, and in particular the novel. It is also common currency amongst most English teachers that boys read less than girls and if they do read, it is unlikely to be anything worthwhile: scientific manuals, violent science fiction action stories or comics.

If my position as an English teacher negatively predisposed me towards boys and their culture, my position as a teacher–researcher also inflected my enquiry in two distinct ways. In my interviews with 'Ponyboy', the author of *Plaz Investigations*, the particular power relations entailed in a pupil giving up his lunch-break to talk to a grown up about his leisure interests set up a variety of contradictions, some of which surface in my account of the interviews. Secondly, and without wishing to be sanctimonious, this kind of research clearly has a point to it beyond the production of knowledge for the groves of academe. The unequal power relations between the cultural theorist and the object of study have often resulted in considerable anxiety.[3] Not only do teachers actually seem to enjoy this dilemma on a daily basis; there is also a political investment in mobilising the inequality as an opportunity for change. What I attempt to do in this chapter is intended as that kind of intervention; not that the present educational climate is at all receptive to this kind of change.

Michael, the author of *Plaz Investigations* and *frostbite's Revenge*, had adopted the character Ponyboy Curtis from *The Outsiders*, the novel by S. E. Hinton, at the age of twelve. He had obstinately refused to be called anything else and wouldn't even answer the register unless called 'Ponyboy'. In the novel which I discuss however, he is called Plaz, and when he returns from the future at one stage, his former friend Raymond recognises him as Pony – his real identity, before he became a time-travelling bounty-hunter. In fact Michael isn't even Michael. He is Michaelis (and if he reads this he'll kill me for revealing that) and is a boy of Greek Cypriot origin living in Tottenham, north London. His specific identity, family and ethnic origin are relevant to this study and the adoption of several fantasy identities, signalled by his various name-changes, indicates a serious investment in imaginary fictions which is crucial to an adult understanding of the meaning of masculine genres. It also raises the spectre of psychological disturbance and the way we pathologise boys as psychotic. (I will return later to the ways in which it might be productive to use psychoanalytical theories as a way of under-standing both 'Ponyboy' and masculine power.) From 1986 onwards 'Pony' produced endless epics along the lines of *frostbite's Revenge*. But after the school summer holidays in 1990 he turned up with a 6,000-word novel, *Plaz Investigations*.

I want to offer a detailed reading of *Plaz Investigations* as a form of audience research. As with all qualitative research, one can be sceptical about the generality of findings deduced from such a small-scale piece of 'evidence'. However, I would want to assert first of all, that *Plaz* is typical of a large amount of writing produced daily by male teenagers across the country. Secondly, although the specific history of 'Pony' and the production of 'Plaz' is obviously central to its meaning, it is the process by which 'Pony' reads and re-reads elements of male adolescent culture that I want to bring out: and I would argue that this process can only be identified by a detailed study. Thirdly, this study is different from traditional ethnographic research in that I am using a fictional construct as a means of finding out about the reading process (furthermore, that construct is, as I have already indicated, implicated within the culture of school and the school subject 'English' and therefore already predetermined in so many ways).

This is not an original approach: Phil Cohen[4] has used children's drawings to gather insights into young children's understanding of racist codes and conventions, and Greg Philo used group simulations to analyse the putative effects of the news, whereby groups formed by class interest were asked to 'write' news programmes for different TV channels.[5] Nevertheless, there are relatively few academic studies that use the audience literally as 'active' producers of meaning within the process of research itself. I would suggest, however, that this remains a potentially rich arena for future research.

The other area of study which does look at cultural productions as a form of audience research is the study of fans and fandom.[6] The work of Henry Jenkins and John Fiske has brought to our attention a remarkable profusion of fan productions.[7] These might be songs, novels, scratch videos, fanzines or virtually any other imaginable format produced by fans for consumption at specialist gatherings, for circulation amongst fan groups or even in personal homage. There is a sense in which it is productive to view *Plaz* as a fan production in as much as it explicitly refers to certain Marvel comic heroes and film narratives. 'Pony' also fits the model of an enthusiast. However, the novel also situates itself within other genres, for example the 'English' story, and isn't quite like the Madonna videos or *Star Trek* novels described by Henry Jenkins or John Fiske. The claims made for fan production are, however, pertinent to this study. Fiske writes of the videos produced by Madonna fans that 'a textual analysis .... does indeed reveal features that accord well with ethnographic investigations into the way that people make popular culture out of mass-cultural products, and that support theorisations of this process'.[8] He argues that the fan differs from the 'normal' audience member in degree rather than in kind and that the excessive nature of fan production offers a particularly clear insight into the normal process by which we use and make sense of popular culture. This is what I am suggesting is the case with *Plaz*.[9]

Like most first novels, *Plaz* is unfinished. It is in three sections and is a third-person narrative, although at times the narrator explicitly ascribes authorial insight to the protagonist. The first chapter is entitled ~~The Choice~~ and describes how the Tottenham schoolboy Plaz ends up protecting an 'attractive brewnet' Sam from kidnapping thugs who turn out to be the FBI. Reluctantly, Plaz rescues Sam and her friend Danual and escapes with them back to the future (AD 8963) where he becomes 'a freelance peace keeping agent' or 'bounty hunter'. The second and third parts, entitled 'The wrong case', deal with an adventure where Plaz is hired by an image-conscious and impotent police force to kill various gang leaders. His adventures take him through time and space, including a visit to 'his ex-home town tottenham' and he gains a mechanical or robotic arm in the process. A couple of pages before the manuscript breaks off he is employed on a third adventure to capture a gang who have escaped from a high security prison. He is, needless to say, successful in his mission and has many battles along the way where he kills the major evil characters of that time as well as various cyborgs and mutants.

Not only is the novel generically derivative, it also explicitly references and borrows from a number of other texts. Thus 'Pony' was motivated to write the novel in the first place because: 'I was watching *Escape from New York*, yeh, um, and I thought the guy, yeh, that was in there [ ] Kurt Russell yeh, I thought he was a very good character.' He then goes on to list the other major influences behind the story:

> There's, er, *Death's Head, Dragon's Claw*, um, *Blade Runner*, all the *Star Wars* trilogy, um, *Terminator* sometimes. I didn't use that much of *Terminator* just about the war and the computers taking over and all that and er, what else? All those futuristic films. (...) Suppose I'd better mention *Robocop*, uh, I got *Action Force*, some of the comic *Action Force*, like some of the ninja stuff.

Some of the references are just borrowing names: for example Plaz visits the 'dagerba system' (from *The Empire Strikes Back*) but doesn't use any of the borrowed qualities from *The Star Wars* context. Other references are direct quotes, like the mechanised/electronic arm from *Robocop* or the phrase 'freelance peace keeping agent' (from the Marvel comic *Death's Head*), and are significant adoptions of ideological value. Thirdly, there are the borrowings of narrative structures and character types, such as the hero being used by a corrupt police force to carry out 'real' law enforcement.

What this wealth of references indicates is an intense involvement in certain kinds of fantasy. By choosing to identify with particular heroes and by selecting key moments and actions from his favourite films and comics, indeed by joining in as it were with *Plaz Investigations*, 'Pony' is revealing the salient structures and pleasures of his media use and consumption.

These can primarily be described in terms of gender and age, as adolescent boys' culture. This needs to be differentiated from generalisations about forms of adult masculinity, although there are obvious points of continuity. In fact there has been a remarkable absence of research in this area. The best known study of boys' culture in contemporary Britain is Paul Willis's *Learning to Labour*[10] which examines the ways boys 'resist' their schooling through 'laddish' behaviour, which also serves as a way of preparing for work on the shop floor. However neither this study or others[11] really looks at the *affective* or *aesthetic* aspects of boys' culture: even Willis's later study of the 'symbolic creativity in everyday life' in *Common Culture* tends to emphasise the subcultural activities of style or street rather than boys' feelings and pleasures.[12] This is in striking contrast to feminist studies of women's culture[13] which have focused on the gendered pleasures soaps or romance have afforded the female reader and viewer, and the relationship between enjoying popular culture and theories of identity.[14] Analyses of masculine genres have been very broad, such as studies of detective stories or empire fiction,[15] and have tended to ignore the question of audience readings.[16] In this respect, the study of the particularly *male* pleasures in the kinds of texts described by 'Pony' does not seem to have been carried out with any degree of specificity.

In the analysis of *Plaz Investigations* which follows I have tried to trace 'Pony's' use of the texts he identified as well as other texts like the 'new' Batman stories *The Killing Joke* or *Wolverine* which 'Pony' lent me to further my study.

'Ready to take them on'

One of the first tensions in the narrative is that between description and action. Indeed, compared to the almost continuous battles of 'Pony's' earlier work, *Plaz* is a model of restraint. As in the case of its 'sources', *Action Force*, *Wolverine* and *The Sleeze Brothers*, a large proportion of the narrative is dedicated towards establishing the parameters of the fantasy world rather than describing the actual events of the fantasy. More of the narrative is devoted to getting ready than actually acting out the investigations or fights. This skewing of the narrative seems to have two distinct functions.

First, the story takes the way in which we enter fantasy extremely seriously. There is lot of pleasure in setting up situations, such as the mechanisms of time travel:

> 'listen, me and my friend Danual came here from the future 7026 yrs in the future, wait let me finnish, In our time we that is earth found this crystal which opens doors through time when you pas an electrial current through it,'

and an enormous amount of sheer descriptive detail:

> It has been one year since Plaz Hunter came to this time. (8963 ad) Plaz

has become a private investigator and he owns a craft a set of guns which consist of an normal handgun which never leaves Plaz's side two daggers which are always atthe sides of his boots a fusion canon and one puls rifal with an under carage pump at ction grenade luncher and he's only 15years old., Plaz is also a 8th level black belt at 12 differerent martial arts such as karate, Te quan do, Ninjitsoo and tichee. Plaz has to deal with the most dangerous peo kind of people like police don't have to deal with like gangs such as the mafear but in this time the mafear does not exist but we do have gangs much r more dangerous like THE KOO – VAKS MOB, The NOMEAGO and The Empire Force

Finding the right names for the right enemies and listing the various elements in his arsenal all seem to contribute to the credibility of the story. What this second extract also demonstrates is that this preparedness is a form of empowerment, that the 'skilling' in martial arts and the detail of the weaponry enables the hero to be ready for anything. As 'Pony' writes later in the story after Plaz has lost his arm in a fight:

> At the hospital they replaced Plaz's arm with a robot arm which has a built in ardour cuff a compter, weapons system and also anything Plaz could ever need and more.

The phrase 'anything Plaz could ever need and more' is revealing. First it indicates an underlying anxiety that however prepared Plaz might be, 'Pony' might not be able to predict the kinds of eventualities he might have to face. This exposes a kind of paranoia at the heart of the adventurer or warrior, that however invincible he might be, there remains the possibility that somewhere, somehow there might be a greater power. This possibility is even more likely in a futuristic world where the human imagination, by definition, can't know probable outcomes.[17] Yet it is certainly more likely in an adolescent or boy's world where the fantasy power of the child has an in-built recognition of his (or her) powerlessness compared to the power wielded by adults. Plaz reveals his fears in the same moment he purports to be all-powerful, thus bearing out Fiske's argument that 'Masculinity becomes almost a definition of the superhuman, so that it becomes that which can never be achieved.'[18]

This is 'Ponyboy's' rationale for Plaz's eclectic martial arts training: 'Plaz is also a 8th level black belt at 12 differerent martial arts such as karate, Te quan do, Ninjitsoo and tichee.' The enormous popularity of 'Eastern' fighting skills with their associated magical and mystical powers has a long tradition within male genres, and they exercise an extraordinary hold over the adolescent imagination. (For those in the know, the inclusion of 'tichee' or 'tai Chi' may seem bizarre, but it adds narrative colour and, as 'Pony' explained, it's what his maths teacher does in an evening class.) A quick look at *Action Force, Bad Company* or *Wolverine* show similar periods of preparation and the advertisements and 'profile' pages often carry information about such putative skills. For example, in *Snake Eyes* we learn that 'the young master could hit what was the mark'. What 'Pony' stresses is the mental control such skills confer, to the extent of compensating for physical weakness. It indicates the reassuring capacity of external forces, in this case training rather than military hardware, to supplement and redress material and historical power relations. As Plaz explains to the obtuse and ignorant police officer Browning towards the end of the novel:

> He's a' browning stopped to think, he started to clik his fingers 'Nineja or Nin something away' 'Ninja' ~~Plaz correctedg~~ said Plaz correting browning. 'Yeh thats it Ninja, anyway he's a ninja warrier, I think its one of those ~~unarm~~ unarmed combat things' 'Its an ancient Martal art, it gives you the abilaty to defend yours self agenst almost any weapon' Plaz said.

The idea that being a ninja can make one more powerful than weapons reveals its psychological attraction. The ninja way of life initiates the powerless into a position of 'superpowerfulness' or 'hypermasculinity' through a ritualistic transformation of almost transcendent power.[19]

'His little gadget thing'

The other traditional form of empowerment is of course weaponry. Fiske refers to guns and vehicles as 'penile extenders' within a Lacanian analysis of power and the phallus.[20] The obsession with vehicles and weaponry is interpreted as a way of closing the gap between the imaginary (the phallus) and the real (the penis). Thus, guns, forms of transport and robotic arms all function as a way of extending Plaz's control of his environment. And, as we have already seen, *Plaz* has its fair share of weapon fetishism and gadget adoration.[21]

Yet if we end up merely satirising *Plaz* for its explosive arsenal and 'willy-waving' technology, we run the risk of ignoring the ways that boys construct themselves as masculine. 'Pony's' own explanation for his interest in gadgets does in fact move the emphasis away from the phallic to the social, as he explains why he likes James Bond:

> *'PB'*: he had a suitcase and it had a plane inside it, have you seen that? (...) It's good that.
> *JSG:* Why is it good?
> *'PB'*: (...) 'cos what his stuff is like disguised into normal day things like a pen and all stuff and he has a wristwatch and things like that.
> *JSG:* So would you like to have a wristwatch that was really a laser?

'PB': Wouldn't mind really 'cos that way yeh, say you get captured by people right and they search you for guns and all that stuff right and they take them offa you, right, but if you've got it disguised like a watch, yeh, then they won't take the watch off you will they?

JSG: True, how often have you been stopped and searched?

'PB': I have been stopped a few times by the Old Bill [the police].

JSG: But is that what you meant by being stopped and searched?

'PB': No I meant the hero, being captured by the enemy.

JSG: Like you being stopped by the Old Bill?

'PB': No, like say James Bond yeh, he's got his little gadget thing yeh, he always seems to get captured, taken prisoner and they take away his gun and all that stuff right but they always seem to leave his little gadgety thing (...) and then he just escapes and saves the world.

The idea of powerful weapons being disguised into 'normal day things' is intriguing, not so much because of 'Pony's' professed explanation that it will help him get past the police but because it reveals a desire to endow the mundane and everyday with the abnormal and heroic. Similarly at the beginning of the novel, the schoolboy Plaz is just trying to get to a class registration on time whilst being distracted by having to save the damsel in distress. There is a great willingness to transform the normal into the exciting, and although the ironic tone at the end of this extract shows that 'Pony' is aware of the unlikelihood of 'saving the world' through using guns and gadgets, he can't help fantasising about such possible transformations. He also recognises that he isn't James Bond and that being stopped by the Old Bill is not the same as being a superhero. For all these reasons, therefore, the level of explanation he initially offers about the usefulness of concealed weapons can't be taken at face-value.

Gadgets offer a way of escaping the regulation of authority and seem to allow a way for fantasy to evade external reality. Rather than interpreting gadgets merely as forms of phallic power, it makes more sense to interpret them within the contexts 'Pony' proposes: as a way of overcoming his fears about those who are more powerful than himself, i.e., the Old Bill and other forms of authority. This would be supported by Lynne Segal's neat summation of the contradictory nature of masculinity: 'the more it asserts itself, the more it calls itself into question'.[22] Thus we can see them more as an articulation of possible vulnerabilities and weaknesses, rather than the simple desire to impose power.

'Some sort of trouble with a form of othoroty'

'Pony's' expression of anxiety about being stopped and searched brings us close to his concerns about his position in relation to authority and, more broadly, about the relation of the individual to society at large. In this section I want to explore some of these contradictions and anxieties in more detail. As we have seen, 'Pony' has to create an 'other' to articulate his own sense of identity: 'say you get captured by people right and they search you for guns and all that stuff right and they take them offa you, right.' Yet why is one likely to get captured in the first place, and who would be the 'they' constricting and imprisoning the protagonist? The emphasis falls on secret and hidden powers, as the external forces control and restrict. This is most evident in his attitude towards the police. Indeed, part of his motivation for writing the story in the first place stemmed from his enjoyment of *Escape from New York* (dir. John Carpenter, 1981) and the attitude of its hero Snake Plisskin, played by Kurt Russell, towards the police and criminality: 'Well maybe I just like the character, the way he doesn't like the police and, um, he was a soldier and he was the best and then he turned criminal and all that'. Likewise in *Plaz* the hero is employed by an impotent and corrupt police force to carry out *real* law enforcement.

Significantly, the first group of 'baddies' that Plaz has to deal with are the FBI. They are after Sam to get her 'to open a door way to our time so they can come through'. The FBI are nameless and unindividuated. They seem simply to shoot indiscriminately, so much so that Plaz has to escape back with Sam to the future. Just before departing he asks her:

What's it like where you come from?
'Well, theres more crime than ever and there's police agencys as well as the normal police you can now hire a cop, we don't have cars just hovers crafts but with these you can fly realy high, almost everyone has one of those energy cuts for pretetion'

The choice of policing, crime and transport as the salient characteristics of the future are ideologically revealing, although they also serve a narrative function, directing the reader towards the immediate concerns of Plaz's impending career. When he gets to the future, he sets up as a detective and in the major case he solves he is employed by the 'l. E.A. (law Enforcement Agents (new F.B.I))' to 'go after and kill the leader of the [ ] Nomeago gang'. The following conversation takes place:

'Why? Why don't you do it youself?'
'Think about it Plaz'
'Oh yeh your the athoritis aren't you and because its murder it would

make you lot look bad'

'No. No. Not murder, Questor has comited a lot of crimeshe. murdered more inocent people then you could ever imagin, so you see you'll be doing everyone a favour'

Towards the end of the story Plaz is hired by another cop who is described as 'the kind of cop who hides behind a desk taking credit for other peoples work'. He is asked to capture a gang who have broken out of a high security prison: the police have already lost an army in the pursuit of these criminals. However, Plaz is 'different from everyone', he is 'the best' and therefore more likely to succeed. This is directly borrowed from the plot line of *Escape from New York*, except that in the film the protagonist is ideologically compromised by already being a war hero turned criminal. In *Death's Head*, *The Sleeze Brothers*, *Batman* and virtually all 'Pony's' sources, the forces of law and authority are effectively impotent and their functions are carried out by independent individuals.

There are several contradictions implicit in 'Pony's' borrowing and adaptation of this theme. First, there is the notion of institutional corruption and weakness, set against the pure embodiment of justice in the shape of Plaz. Plaz is, of course, individualised, as opposed to the FBI organisations. Again, there is a tension between the weak forces of society opposed to the strength of the one man. The authorities are constrained by being accountable to public scrutiny, whilst the hero is only answerable to himself. There is an ambiguous tension between the values of pro-social behaviour and violent anti-social activity, and an ironic sense of the torn fabric of society being sustained by those forces which that society appears to marginalise: the violent, the individual, the independent and the free.

Yet the key question here is why 'Pony' adopts the role of justice in a society that appears to devalue it. Whatever kind of psychological purpose might be fulfilled by acting as an agent of murder and physical force, or whatever the thrill might be in having a robotic arm, Plaz's actions are moral. This partly stems from the ideological framework which equates masculinity with the individualistic. Thus, as Fiske argues, the striving for achievement which characterises male genres is part of the way capitalist patriarchy motivates men to work in order to prove themselves.[23] To prove oneself, one must necessarily oppose the mass; rebelling against authority becomes a way of defining oneself. Thus, it is required that the symbols of authority are emasculated and that the virility of the various police forces Plaz encounters is open to question. Their weakness defines him. However, why then does Plaz support the social *implicitly* through his actions?

This seems to be yet another contradiction in the role of the hero of these genres. Society is left vulnerable and comes under threat from anti-social elements; yet those elements can only be defeated by a more powerful force, and that force is similar in kind to the anti-social. In other words, masculinity is torn between asserting itself in relation to the larger whole, and in doing so, destroying it. However, society can only be protected by a privileged version of its anti-social impulses: the hero. This is why Plaz is outside the law. He becomes, in 'Pony's' favourite phrase borrowed from *Death's Head*, 'a free lance peace keeping agent' or 'bounty hunter' as the uninitiated would describe it. The heavy irony in this phrase embodies the ideological contradictions caught up in this role and gives some insight into the ways the person of the hero is fraught with anxiety, doubt and multiple identity.

'At least I'll die Knowing I tryed to be someone o.k.'

'Trying to be someone' underpins the whole story: but the salient question to ask, given the fraught uncertainties surrounding the person of the hero, is who that someone might be. In the previous section, I looked at how 'Pony' defined himself in relationship to the social body. But he also defines himself internally, in relation to the contradictory tensions within the masculine *persona*. In his analysis of *The A Team* Fiske describes the four characters in terms of the separate elements that combine to form the contradictory whole of the masculine identity.[24] The relationships between Mr T, Face, Murdock and Hannibal thus bring into play 'a structure of masculinity' that gives the programme its ideological meanings. There is an absence of other characters in *Plaz Investigations* to allow us to discern an equivalent 'structure'. However, Plaz does define himself in relation to his enemies and allies and equally importantly, in relation to his previous incarnations as 'Pony'.

In virtually all the sources of *Plaz*, a common feature emerges: that of an opposition either between the different aspects of the split personality or between the protagonist and his enemy. In *Wolverine*, the hero Logan is transformed into a beast with an adamantium skeleton through the intervention of either 'Lady Deathstrike', the daughter of a Japanese scientist, or the Canadian government. Either way, the hero leads a schizophrenic life as a 'super-soldier', combating his bestial impulses in order to serve as part of a superhero team, many of whose members, like 'the Hulk' (in reality Paul Cartier, victim of a supernatural curse) also embody this dual identity. In discussion, 'Pony' talked about the berserker (a Marvel modification of the Anglo-Saxon personality category for an adventure game book), and how he can't be controlled when 'nutty': and he also described himself as possessing a similar uncontrollable essence which often breaks out of his disciplined social identity.

In the new *Batman* stories, in particular *Batman: The Killing Joke*, Batman becomes increasingly aware that the Joker isn't so much an independent criminal force as his alter ego. As the story progresses, the similarities between Batman and the Joker become more and more obvious: they are both mutated (through dress, self-discipline and, in the Joker's case, acid) and outside society; both contain anti-social impulses, that Batman is forced to repress for the social good, and so on. Batman seems to decline into a kind of existentialist introspection, as he realises that what appears to be a moral struggle is more a question of rationalising a transcendent meaning in a postmodern world.[25]

There are various manifestations of this narrative structure as Plaz proceeds through the course of the novel. Primarily, masculine difference is established in relation to the feminine and in particular the traditional absence of women from male stories. However there are two female characters in *Plaz*: Sam, 'the brewnet' whom Plaz rescues at the beginning of the story, and Kim, a girl 'he use to like a lot', who is kidnapped as a hostage to trap Plaz on his return to Tottenham and who rescues him at a vital moment, before he has to leave her in tears as he returns to the future.

Both fulfil obvious passive roles, both have to be rescued and both are described in terms of physical attributes. However, although Sam may begin the novel as an irritatingly needy female, she changes as the novel progresses. Perhaps having an ungendered name gives the game away, as she becomes Plaz's assistant in his adventures. She becomes the person he asks advice from as he embarks on his adventures and she alternates between maternal rebuke and giving him the choice in these matters – although he tends to walk out on her as his way of ending debate. She also plays a physical role in some of the adventures and as long as she is subordinated to his prowess, she can also kill and fight. In a sense she is necessary as a measure of his ability: a male assistant would be threatening. Her most vociferous attempt to dissuade Plaz from taking on dangerous work is when she says "'Why are you always trying to be that stupide comic book charter Deaths head, You'll never be him you will always be Plaz Hunter no one els'". I feel her commonsensical plea to 'grow up' and stop pretending you live in a fantasy world allies qualities of adultness to the feminine, and again the fact that he proves her wrong by succeeding in his fantasy role seems to point to the fiction acting as a form of transformation, showing that 'Pony' can assert himself against a common-sense female viewpoint and thus define himself. By choosing Sam as the embodiment of those qualities 'Pony' despises and allowing the narrative to recuperate her, 'Pony' uses Plaz as a way of proving grown-ups (is it too fanciful to say 'Mum' here?) wrong and thus confirm his own status.

Kim, the other woman in the story, is far more unproblematic. She is introduced as 'a girl Plaz use to like a lot' and she was upset at his disappearance into the future. She is used as a conventional romantic heroine. When she rescues Plaz at a crucial moment, she breaks down in tears and has to be held in his arms. She even blows him a kiss as he departs and Plaz realises that 'she must really like him'. She functions as a fictional way for 'Pony' to live out what I suspect is a specific fantasy. What is noticeable about his identity in relation to her is that he can infer her interest in him without exposing any vulnerability on his part: he can disappear back to the future having solved the romantic conundrum but without having to commit himself. He is the better for having saved her and the fact that she breaks down because she has to kill in order to save him only serves to intensify his invulnerability.

In *Batman* and *Escape from New York* the hero is measured against the villain, respectively the Joker and 'the Duke': similarly in *Plaz* the main adventure involves the destruction of a gang, 'flaming fist' whose main leaders, Questor and Kelgor, are not described in any detail. (At the end of the novel, where Plaz is employed to catch a gang of escapees, these villains are endowed with a variety of specific characteristics, such as ninja skills, physical strength and so on, more in keeping with the classic 'Manichaean' binary opposition of the genre.) However, the actual moment of victory in the deaths of both Questor and Kelgor is notable for the roles played by the cyborgs and troopers that guard their leaders. This is perhaps a surprising shift in 'Pony's' reading of his primary material and a curious re-working of the binary opposition between hero and villain. First of all, the actual description of Questor is balanced by his bodyguard:

> A great big guy said obveusly the leader Questor he had a scare on the right side of his face and a silver glove with spikes on the left hand ond his left stood a great big 6ft s cyborg who had muccel on his mucsel and sword on his back and two miny rockets on his left cuf. and a double barrol lazer gun on the right other.

It is the cyborg who blows Plaz's arm off, leading to its mechanised replacement; and when Plaz kills Questor it is, according to the conventions of the genre, an impersonal act (blowing up his spaceship). However, this leads into a duel with the cyborg, because although Plaz expected the cyborg to stop serving Questor when Questor is killed, Questor's legacy was to endow the cyborg with a mind of its own after killing whoever killed its master. (This is symmetrically balanced by the troopers' response after Kelgor's death, who feel they are no longer bound to serve him after he has been killed.)

The cyborg's independence is pertinent for two reasons. First, it implies that a relatively democratic status is bestowed on master and servant (in terms of narrative importance, at least), which may reflect 'Pony's' awareness that battles between lesser social actors are more relevant to his future. Secondly, and more importantly, there is the narrative function of the unstoppable and literally 'mindless' opponent. By contrast, it's important to the hero's self-esteem that he is self-motivated and existentially responsible for his actions. Similarly, on at least two occasions Death's Head is caught up in duels with either mechanical or animal opposites: Plaguedog and Iron Man. In both cases, he wins out due to the application of human cunning, often ironically expressed, referring at one stage to 'behaviour that gets us mechanoids a bad name'. Clearly, the greater drama and fear implied by the unstoppable and impersonal destructive force makes it central to the masculine narrative. This is partly explained by 'Pony's' earlier references to 'berserkers' and the immutable forces within the male psyche. It also articulates a contradiction, that Death's Head and Plaz are themselves partly de-humanised and machine-like, yet they possess enough significant human qualities to overcome such weaknesses. In this sense, strength and vulnerability are almost confused: physical power is only really powerful when allied to human weakness, which may explain the structural significance of overcoming the indestructible. Plaz is thus defeating the cyborg within himself as much as outside his character. The focus on subservient characters elevated to the position of opposites thus indicates an attempt to dramatise conflicting desires within the male identity 'Pony' is creating for himself.

The final 'other' identity that I want to discuss is the persona of Plaz himself, and the fictional characters of Death's Head and Snake Plisskin (the hero of Escape from New York). There are several points in the novel where Plaz reflects upon who he is in relation to his heroic role models. These moments offer an insight into the author's conflicts over modality status as well as a sense of what 'Pony' takes from his heroes.[26]

We have already encountered Plaz's first reflexive moment when he is criticised by Sam:

> "Why are you always trying to be that stupide comic book charter Deaths head, Youll never be him you will always be Plaz Hunter no one els"

It is significant that this threat to his self-image brings forth an explicit acknowledgement of the weakness of fantasy identity and an avowal of its strength.

> "look maybe I'm not lik you, I need something to keep me going o.k. I know I'll probobly never be Deaths head but if I die tomorrow then at least I'll die Knowing I tryed to be someone o.k."

Later in the story Sam again accuses Plaz over behaving like a star-struck child:

> "look I know you like Deaths head alot but you will never be him, he's a comic book charter this the real world you can't take on both of them at the same time".
>
> "I'm going to and if you want you can help"

There is a level of irony and wit at play here which it is well not to ignore. We can't seriously believe that Plaz thinks he is living in the real world, if only because Plaz is not a real character. Yet the novel persists in this fiction. It often refers to Plaz's reputation and character as if he were a real person and, even more confusingly, Plaz also refers to 'Pony' as if *he* were real:

> "Hi who are ... wait a minute Pony (Plaz's name which he used fr from the book the outsiders)
> "Yep you remember"
> "of course I remember my best friend, come in" Ray said dragging Plaz in.
> "I've changed my name again its Plaz Hunter now"

In theory, if 'Pony' is real, Plaz is too. But despite the episode which follows with Kim and the more naturalistic setting of school in Tottenham, which is obviously modelled on a specific fantasy, it is difficult to take the story at face-value. If anything, the more the novel appears to claim to be 'realistic' rather than fantasy, the more it offers itself as something in between. According to the extracts above, Plaz is real because he was once 'Pony' (who we know is real because he is named as the author), yet Plaz's grip on reality is insecure because he is always trying to pretend he can measure up to comic book characters. On the one hand, we have an attempt to build a fictional and fantasy world and on the other, the undermining of that fantasy even as 'Pony' builds it.

Who, then, is Plaz, and what might it mean to ask and answer such a question? I want to suggest that Plaz is an amalgam of social and psychological contradictions that make up the *persona* of the male super-hero: he makes choices, he is in control, he is in a position of power over women. Plaz is the mode through which 'Pony' reconciles the contradic-tions and tensions of his fantasy with his real-life situation and experi-ences – that is, the relative powerlessness of 'Pony's' material situation as an adolescent schoolboy carrying the expectations of being a man. He is also a dramatisation of what I can only call 'the reading self': that is the part of 'Pony' who responds (using the term in its widest sense),[27] to an immersion in generic fiction. Plaz reveals the affective and emotional investment 'Pony' has made in his reading and the ways that his reading is a mixture of personal, biographical response, and intertextual connec-tions. It also reveals an attempt to locate himself within a narrow range of masculine subject positions. On the one hand, he is a fantasy figure re-enacting 'Pony's' readings of male genres and on the other, he em-bodies the rationale for that fantasy by exposing the fraught ambiguities that led 'Pony' towards fantasy in the first place.

'If you like killing, imagine how that would be like in a war?'

Throughout my discussions with 'Pony', there was a thread of 'violence' which would only seem to confirm the deeply psychotic readings he is making out of these fictions and which would seem to bear out the destructive effects of fantasy on his tenuous notions of reality:

> *JSG:* Do you enjoy fighting?
> *'PB':* Um ... It's an enjoyable sport.
> *JSG:* What do you enjoy about it?
> *'PB':* Inflicting pain on others ... the thrill of winning.

However, there are numerous reasons why we should be cautious about these avowals of pleasure and how we interpret the significance of the violent action of *Plaz*. Not the least of these is 'Pony's' use of irony and excess. As 'violence' is probably one of the least useful common-sense categories to be interminably misused in discussion of young people and the media, we need to be precise in how we might interpret the 'violence' in *Plaz*. I want to show how the concept of 'violence' is mediated by the ways that the fantasy worlds of 'Pony's' fictions and *Plaz* construct themselves as real. Indeed I shall argue that 'Pony's' excursions into violence represent a crucial stage in the way he negotiates his reading in the context of the real world.

Comics, and in particular the Marvel comics favoured by 'Pony' appear to adopt a specific approach to representing violent moments. Thus, Pony refers to the ways a comic 'freeze-frames' action, allowing for a particular kind of concentration on selected highlights within what is inevitably a stylised and fragmented mode of representation. When 'Pony' and I looked at a comic together, he explained this as follows.

> *JSG:* (...) what do you like about this picture?
> *'PB':* I like the fact he's pulled a man through a windscreen.
> *JSG:* So it's the actual kind of action bit?
> *'PB':* Yeh, I just look at the pictures yeh, right, then say I see a good bit yeh, like that where the man is crawling up the stairs (...), when Death's head is crawling up the stairs. I'd probably start reading it there, (and grief) and flick to that page where Death's head is crawling up (...) 'cos it's like the same innit, 'cos Death's head is doing the hunting here right, and later on he's crawling up the stairs being hunted by some other guy, and then I'd just basically read the whole thing from beginning to the end.

First of all, I am sceptical about statements like 'I like the fact he's pulled a man through a windscreen', or comments above to the effect that 'Pony' enjoys inflicting pain on others. What I believe such comments do signify is not so much psychological insights into the male psyche but discursive markers of masculinity. (The difference is important because it allows for the way individuals can position themselves within a discourse of gender, as opposed to being produced by that discourse.) Clearly the propriety of making such comments to an adult (and a teacher at that) raises the question of how much it is appropriate to offend and to deliberately adopt anti-social positions in order to assert oneself.

Furthermore, there is the element of sharing such pleasures as a group, as 'Pony' made clear from his description of going to specialist comic shops and circulating comics with his peers. Choosing one's favourite moments or boasting about the pleasures one derives from witnessing the destruction of others can offer a way of asserting one's identification with a larger group identity.[28]

The main reason I'm inclined to this interpretation is my sense throughout our discussions of 'Pony' trying to push me towards condemning his pleasures – which of course, would only go towards asserting his masculine identity, through exclusion from the social mass. There were numerous occasions when he purported to enjoy sadism, disembowelling, and so on. Yet what is also revealing about the pleasure he appeared to find in the image of the man crawling up the stairs is that he immediately saw that image in the context of a larger narrative pattern, in that it is balanced against the later picture of Death's Head crawling up the stairs. So the apparent sadistic pleasures he wants to acknowledge in order to appear 'hard' are in fact mediated by other more 'innocent' pleasures like his interest in reading the whole story. His skill in grasping this narrative structure is, it seems to me, part of the game he is playing with the producers of *Death's Head*.

Plaz does contain its fair share of deaths and gory violence. There is one moment where Plaz shoots off the limbs of an opponent before 'blowing him away', and 'Pony' proudly recalled this moment in our discussions. 'Pony' himself is all too aware that the graphic element of comics and films cannot be reproduced in his text and this absence suggests yet another reason why the text is so interesting: it's clearly already a substitute in its own terms, and more likely to reveal its motives because of this. Indeed, there is a superfluity of such violent action within the text. In contrast to the necessary paucity and detailed microscopic focus on action sequences in *Death's Head*, *Plaz* overflows:

> Plaz didn't know what to do fight of run, so he done both, he pulled out hand gun and shot ~~s~~ five guards he couldn't shoot Questor because the cyborg stepped in the way. Plaz then picked up his fusion canon and blew a hole ~~along~~ in the wall along with a few guards. Plaz then began to run but the cyborg shot one of his rockets at ~~p~~ Plaz and blew Plaz's left arm up to the shoulder off.

Nevertheless, the absence of detailed description, which would help create an atmosphere of sadism or violence, is not just attributable to the author's lack of literary skill. It shows that the moments of violent action fulfil different narrative functions. The sequence quoted subordinates an interest in action to the narrative of Plaz's achievements: to be heroic, he has to kill so many guards and cyborgs, and this is meaningful in terms of the narrative tropes that I have analysed above. The sheer lack of impact losing his arm has on Plaz (other than having to go to a hospital which he doesn't particularly like) shows a curious lack of engagement with the story. While this could be read as evidence of male desensitisation to violence, I would argue that, deep down, 'Pony' himself doesn't take the story that seriously. He knows it's following the requisite generic conventions and that these do not necessarily reflect real social situations. Thus, fictional violence might be seen as significant because it allows men a safe way of expressing an anti-social identity, by being offensive and appearing to enjoy forbidden pleasures. It does not necessarily reveal an enjoyment of the emotional or psychological aspects of *real* 'violence'.

This sense of not taking the violence that seriously is also borne out by 'Pony's' use of humour and the comic pleasures afforded by his reading of the source material, particularly the comic *Death's Head*, which he quoted several times in our discussions. This is emphasised in *Plaz* where, as we have seen, Plaz himself wants to be like Death's Head. The opening episode of *Death's Head* is riddled with this irony. The protagonist uses a heavily underscored official discourse to rationalise his shady and semi-criminal activities. Yet the laugh is on polite society for believing the value of keeping up pretences. (One only has to think of the grim irony in official war discourse, like 'friendly fire', to find a pertinent parallel.) Thus 'a freelance peace keeping agent' is preferred to 'bounty hunter'. Time after time, we see Death's Head dupe unsuspecting victims and he is consistently motivated by self-interest; 'A fellow bounty hunter, er, freelance peace keeping agent once gave me some valuable advice "Always remember you're a **businessman**" he said ... "never kill for free, and never turn down the contract – **whoever** the target is!" I thanked him for his advice and put a bullet through his forehead'.

'Pony' couldn't quite manage this level of wit in *Plaz* although many of the exchanges in our discussions were conducted in a similar spirit. 'Pony' said of the above extract from *Death's Head* that he liked it because it shows 'he really doesn't care, he hasn't got that much emotions, he's got a job to do and he does it right'. On the surface this is a worrying comment – indeed, it's like a parody of what's wrong with men – but again I would be sceptical about taking this comment at face-value. Like the way Death's Head is trying to stand outside human and social norms and use his wit to criticise those values, 'Pony's' preference for doing a job, suppressing one's emotions and not caring contain within them an ironic acknowledgement of the opposite. What *Death's Head* offers is the opportunity to mock, rather heavy-handedly, those values 'Pony' is anxious about and keen to suppress.

Thus in the generic use of 'violence' (whatever that might mean), excess and humour act as a way of inflecting the modality status of the story. Detailed study of 'the violent moments' or the constant cynicism and irony undercut the story's pretence to be taken at face-value. 'Pony's' sources and indeed most male genres undercut themselves in this way. What this means is that, far from being escapist dreams or ideological wish-fulfilment fantasies, these narratives constantly play on the tensions between fantasy and real life. They are powerful in as much as they offer ritualised ways of negotiating a gendered identity under pressure. Above all, they illustrate how the adolescent masculine self perceives itself to be at variance with the dominant discourses of adult responsibility and social purpose. The ironic play with those values only articulates the unused and excessive 'advantages' of being a man.

Masculinity and the critic: a conclusion

Following Segal and Morgan,[29] I have implicitly defined masculinity as a non-essential, non-biological 'discourse'.[30] As Morgan argues, 'masculinity is not a quality attached to individuals but a kind of cultural resource ... a set of potentialities which may be realised and shaped in particular contexts'.[31] The implication throughout has been that masculinity is a social construct and that 'Pony' has adopted positions and images within the range of constructs available to him. His reading and writing have enabled him to find the pleasures of identifying with certain positions in the discourse of masculinity.

I have also adopted a notion of masculinity that focuses on underlying tensions and anxieties, as if masculinity is a sort of burden. This is partly because this model of masculinity 'in crisis' applies to adolescence, which by definition, subjects young people to an examination of fears and expectations far more explicitly than most adults allow.[32] In addition, as a male critic, I tend to feel that this model offers opportunities for intervention and change.

However, we need to ask whether we can reduce issues of gender, which are fundamentally issues of power, to a politics of choice and position – even if, as I have shown 'Pony' is positioned as a victim himself. The answer to that question will inevitably depend on the politics of the reader.

There is a sense with *Plaz*, as Morgan argues, that studying men whose masculinity becomes problematic has the effect of 'denaturalising' masculinity. But for whom does that 'denaturalisation' occur and in whose interests does it take place? Inevitably my interpretation of 'Pony's' masculine dilemmas is related to my own concerns. As a teacher I need to be able to prove that men are 'redeemable' and as a man I am using the muscles of my intellect and power over language to pin 'Pony' down. To an extent I feel as if I am using cultural theory as a way of competing with 'Pony' in an arena of my choosing in order to emasculate him and empower myself. By reading *Plaz* and 'Pony' as a natural other and privileging the intellectual status of my analysis, I can assert my own authority over the boys I teach and the kinds of masculine pleasures middle-class academics find so problematic. So am I not 'doing' to his text what I have argued he is 'doing' with his?

This may be an unduly negative note on which to end. In another context, I have investigated the implications for 'Pony' the writer and examined what *Plaz* does for him by positioning him in a position of authority over his consumption of popular culture. The ways his power as a writer interacts with the other discourses of power and weakness in the story have significant implications for the teaching of popular culture.[33] For the purposes of this study, however, my reading of *Plaz* only seems to support Ang's thesis that audience research says more about the anxieties of the researcher than it does about the pleasures of the researched.[34]

This epistemological scepticism should not detract us from the ways *Plaz* does offer a privileged insight into the construction of cultural meanings and adolescent boys' culture. By researching cultural production, we can gain different and important insights into the reading process. By taking masculine pleasures seriously, we can see the meaning of those pleasures for what they are. It's not enough to justify research by saying that something is more complicated than it seems and riddled with contradictions. But at the least, I hope I have shown *Plaz, Death's Head* and the rest, for what they try to do for their readers and not what grown-ups want them to be.

Notes and references

1 All transcriptions of interviews follow the conventions outlined in Jonathan Potter and Margaret Wetherell, *Discourse and Social Psychology* (London, Sage, 1987). I have reproduced the extracts from written pieces as faithfully as possible.

2 See Brian Doyle, *English and Englishness* (London, Routledge, 1989) or Janet Batsleer *et al.*, *Rewriting English: Cultural Politics of Gender and Class* (London, Methuen, 1985) for an extended analysis of this history.

3 This is well exemplified in Valerie Walkerdine's 'Video replay: families, films and fantasy', in *Formations of Fantasy*, ed. V. Burgin, J. Donald and C. Kaplan (London, Methuen, 1986).

4 See Phil Cohen, 'The Perversions of Inheritance: Studies in the Making of Multi-Racist Britain', in *Multi-Racist Britain*, ed. P. Cohen and H. Bains (London, Macmillan, 1988).

5 See Greg Philo, *Seeing and Believing, The Influence of Television* (London, Routledge, 1990). Interestingly enough, in his eagerness to demonstrate the penetration of dominant news values, Philo seems to ignore the ways in which the generic conventions of 'news' programmes or the social and discursive nature of the group production may have influenced the 'programmes' produced by his sample groups.

6 See for example Lisa Lewis, *The Adoring Audience: Fan Culture and Popular Media* (London, Routledge, 1992).

7 Henry Jenkins, '"Strangers no more we sing": Filking and the Social Construction of the Science Fiction Fan Community' and John Fiske, 'The Cultural Economy of

Fandom: The Adoring Audience, Fan Culture and Popular Media', both in Lewis, *Adoring Audience*. See also John Fiske, *Reading the Popular* (Boston, Unwin Hyman, 1989) and Henry Jenkins, *Textual Poachers, Television Fans and Participatory Culture* (New York and London, Routledge, 1992).

8 Fiske, 'Cultural Economy of Fandom'.

9 Stephen Hinerman's essay, '"I'll be here with you": Fans Fantasy and the Figure of Elvis', in Lewis, *Adoring Audience*, on the use of Elvis fantasies offers an alternative explanation: that the fans' fantasy can provide a form of psycho-therapeutic help for distressed or disturbed individuals. There may be a sense in which this is also a valid explanation for 'Pony', particularly if one finds his use of alternative identities significant.

10 Paul Willis, *Learning to Labour* (Aldershot, Saxon House, 1977).

11 For example, Twitchell's *Preposterous Violence: Fables of Aggression in Modern Culture* (New York, Oxford University Press, 1989). This takes a vast historical sweep at 'violent' entertainment from Ancient Greek initiation rites to slasher videos and concludes that such cultural forms provide an articulation of the adolescent male's rites of passage. However, the historical range of this kind of social anthropology precludes any focus on the way individuals might construct *themselves* as masculine; and generalising about 'violent entertainment' loses any sense of the specific historical differences between forms of cultural consumption.

12 Paul Willis, *Common Culture: Symbolic Work at Play in the Everyday Cultures of the Young* (Milton Keynes, Open University Press, 1990).

13 See, for example, Ien Ang's study, *Watching 'Dallas': Soap Opera and the Melodramatic Imagination* (London, Methuen, 1985); Dorothy Hobson's *Crossroads: The Drama of a Soap Opera* (London, Methuen, 1982): Janice Radway's *Reading the Romance: Women, Patriarchy and Popular Literature* (London, Verso, 1984): Angela McRobbie, *Feminism and Youth Culture From Jackie to Just Seventeen* (London, Macmillan, 1991).

14 It is worthwhile pointing out that the political or theoretical concept of gender does not always equal the empirical: at least 40 per cent of soap viewers are male, for example, which may undermine generalised statements about the 'gendering' of particular genres. (This point would be of course be as true for this study, given the fact that many girls also enjoy the kinds of texts I have described as male, but it would need a further investigation to examine in detail.)

15 See for example D. Longhurst (ed.) *Gender, Genre and Narrative Pleasure* (London, Unwin Hyman, 1989) or Joseph Bristow, *Empire Boys: Adventures in a Man's World* (London, HarperCollins, 1991). However, more unusual books like David Jackson's *Unmasking Masculinity: A Critical Autobiography* (London, Unwin Hyman, 1990) offer a more detailed analysis of reader responses.

16 The excellent analysis by John Fiske (*Television Culture* (London, Routledge, 1987)) of *The A Team* is a textual study looking at binary oppositions in the text, although it doesn't look at the meanings that viewers might actually make from the series.

17 This may be one explanation for the preference for this kind of setting: that it articulates masculine paranoia.

18 Fiske, *Television Culture*.

19 See Lynne Segal, *Slow Motion* (London, Virago, 1990) for a discussion of the concept of hypermasculinity. Marsha Kinder's *Playing with Power in Movies, Television and Video Games from Muppet Babies to Teenage Mutant Ninja Turtles* (Berkeley, University of California Press, 1991) compares this act of transformation to the cultural construction of masculinity in her discussion of the ways young spectators read *Teenage Mutant Ninja Turtles* as a psychological quest for empowerment.

20 Fiske, *Television Culture*.

21 Popular discourses about masculinity use the language of 'phallic power' as comprehensively as academic writing and the links between the military industrial complex and male violence have been the subject of recent studies of masculinity; an obsession with guns is often linked to male power in popular debate. See Myriam Miedzian, *Boys will be Boys: Breaking the Link between Masculinity and Violence* (London, Virago, 1992) I think this level of analysis is self explanatory: but as Segal (*Slow Motion*) points out, reducing male power to the phallic does run the risk of essentialising masculinity.

22 Segal, *Slow Motion*.

23 Fiske, *Television Culture*.

24 *ibid.*

25 See various contributions in R. E. Pearson and W. Uricchio (eds), *The Many Lives of the Batman: Critical Approaches to a Superhero and his Media* (New York, Routledge and British Film Institute, 1991).

26 There are arguments against privileging such moments. In the sources, there are many moments where the characters are wittily aware of their status as characters in a story. Jim Collins, 'Batman: The Movie, Narrative: The Hyperconscious', in Pearson and Uricchio *Many Lives*, has argued that this reflexivity is a postmodernist feature of the angst-ridden modern comic and graphic novel.

27 See Charles Sarland, *Young People Reading: Culture and Response* (Milton Keynes, Open University Press, 1991).

28 See David Buckingham's Chapter 5 in this volume for an analysis of the ways boys 'do' masculinity in groups to support their sense of themselves.

29 Segal, *Slow Motion*, and David Morgan, *Discovering Men* (London, Routledge, 1992).

30 See Dorothy Smith, *Femininity as Discourse*, in *Becoming Feminine: the Politics of Popular Culture*, ed. L. Roman *et al.* (Lewes, Falmer, 1988) for an analysis of the way femininity is produced as a form of socially mediated discourse.

31 Morgan, *Discovering Men*.

32 See Gemma Moss's study of another adolescent boy's story for further examination of this theme, in *Un/Popular Fictions* (London, Virago, 1989).

33 See David Buckingham and Julian Sefton-Green, *Cultural Studies goes to School* (Falmer, forthcoming).

34 Ien Ang, 'Wanted: Audiences. On the politics of empirical audience studies', in *Remote Control: Television, Audiences and Cultural Power*, ed. E. Seiter *et al.* (London, Routledge, 1989).

Seeing how far you can see: on being a 'fan' of 2000 AD

> I'd hate to bring kids into the world where they couldn't look at a flower, or a blue sky. That's not my thing for the future. You try and do the best you can. You do CND and the World Fund for Nature, stuff like that. I hate to think this is the future. It seems a bit grim if this is people's depiction of the future. If it is we are in a pretty black state, if this is their vision. Visions should be a better state: a cleaner world, no wars, no fighting. I'm not religious. All the problems of the world come from religion and money. I'd hate the world to be like it is in these comics. I don't know – they bring it home to you, I think that's the reason why I read them.
>
> Mary, 2000 AD fan

The day I began to write this essay was the third day of the anti-police riots in Hartcliffe, on the other side of Bristol. It was also the day I chose (no connection) to get out the video of *Robocop*, that curious morality tale that links themes of cyborgs and the breaking of body-boundaries with justice and the problems of policing in a world where crime and the establishment are linked, and with masculinity and the maintenance of 'cool'. *Robocop* is exactly the kind of film most popular with the (mainly) young men who rioted, despite its central character being a policeman who thinks nothing of blowing away 'young punks'. And as one of my interviewees put it: 'Any 2000 AD reader who has seen this film will know how closely related it is to Judge Dredd. Its mix of sly humour, violence and thinly disguised social comments on American society is pure 2000 AD, as is Robocop himself.'

This chapter is a report on the findings of my research about readers of 2000 AD and, in particular, of its central character Judge Dredd. It arises from an ongoing research project into all aspects of the history of 2000 AD, from its production history, the development of new modes of 'fan'-organisation, the narrative forms and reader-relations in the comic, and the intertextual connections which have parallelled that (in particular with pop). There is no way to understand 2000 AD's readers without returning repeatedly to the other facets of the comic's history – as indeed my results and conclusions indicate.

In one sense, this research is simply a continuation of research I have been doing on comics for fifteen years, including a study of 2000 AD's immediate predecessor, Action.[1] A roundabout approach led to me being invited by 2000 AD's publishers to work on a history of the comic, to which I agreed, provided I had freedom to research and write as I felt necessary, and that I had access to all the information and people I needed.

In a broader sense, it is relevant that I find myself unhappy with the main current practices and theories of audience research within Cultural Studies. The history of this research has been often told: the move from investigations of texts on assumption of their power, to a greater interest in audience resistance to, or negotiation of, textual meanings; the rising interest in contexts of reading and viewing, with particular emphasis on the gendered character of audiences; and the growing popularity of ethnographic work. Some of my unease has been well expressed by others, in particular the concern with the hollow notions of 'audience resistance'.[2] Here, I will only add something else that bothers me considerably. This is the effective validation of female pleasures, and contrasting invalidation of male pleasures, in much current research. There has been a wholesale interest in certain genres with largely female audiences, and often seen as textually 'female' in particular senses. The shift from theories of textual power has been made largely on the back of a rising desire to justify the reading or viewing of romances, soap operas and the like by girls and women. Their pleasure in these, this research repeatedly argues, cannot be read simply as evidence of some textual subordination or ideological construction. Rather, it reveals the ways in which women have to negotiate with dominant constructions of femininity, and through fantasy cope with the stresses and demands of living out those constructions.

I don't wish to disagree, thus far. But I am interested in the *absence of any equivalent for men and boys*. It is curious to ask why it is nigh on impossible to imagine a parallel study of, say, soft porn, violent adventure or sports stories, arguing that men's pleasure in these genres is not evidence of their textual subordination or ideological construction; rather it reveals the ways in which men have to negotiate with dominant constructions of masculinity – or even of femininity – and through fantasy cope with the stresses and demands of living out those constructions.

I believe that audience research is being cramped by being set predominantly within a feminist framework. My argument will be that the return to a *class* perspective is crucial; that is, returning to issues of the organisation and control of production, and of our own lives, within the framework of capitalism; and the understanding of cultural forms – including those of gender – as partial responses to those structures. For my own research on *2000 AD*, this has meant paying close attention to the reorganisations of the production and distribution of comics in the last two decades, and the shifting patterns of intellectual property relations within the comics industry – arguably, now one of the central processes through which capitalism determines the forms and contents of cultural production.[3] As regards audiences, it means an exploration of the role of future-fantasy in thinking about increasingly disempowered readers. It is certainly true that more than 80 per cent of the readers of *2000 AD* are male. Elsewhere I have argued that at key periods there was a deliberate strategy by comics publishers to separate and stratify gendered production of comics and magazines for boys and girls.[4] But what is remarkable about *2000 AD* is the emergence of a strong minority of passionately committed female readers – whose pleasures in the texts cannot be understood as some kind of textual cross-dressing.[5]

What is 2000 AD?

2000 AD was first published in February 1977 by International Publishing Corporation (now Fleetway, after a sell-off). Intended to catch on to the success of IPC's 1976 launch *Action*, *2000 AD* in fact got caught up in the backwash of the controversies over 'violent content' that first squeezed, then soon killed, the earlier comic. But *2000 AD* survived, and eventually flourished, to play a major part in the transformation of the British comics scene in the 1980s.

A few markers of this transformation. In 1977 there were at most five specialist comics shops in the country, the most important of which was *Dark They Were And Golden Eyed*, a surviving headshop from the hippie glad days of the late 1960s; today, there are well over 200 such shops. In 1977, there was no national system for distributing comics, other than W. H. Smith and Menzies. Today, there are two national comics distributors, the larger of which – Titan Distributors – is also linked to the major comics publishing concern, Titan Publications, and to the *Forbidden Planet* chain of comics shops. By 1977, there was beginning to be a small number of comics marts and conventions, but they were few and small. Today, there are nearly 100 major marts annually, and the conventions (of which there are now, to my knowledge, some ten per year) attract thousands of fans. Alongside these are major changes in the kinds of comics published, the age range and social spread of readers, the number of publishers, and the interconnections between comics and other culture industries – perhaps most notable of which is the re-emergence of the comic-film tie.

2000 AD was deeply implicated in these changes in Britain. From the start, it was a science fiction comic. But the meaning of that has changed over time. In the early days, it took Action-style violent stories, and projected them into the near future (for example, 'Harlem Heroes', about a team of future-sport players, who risked death in every episode; and 'Invasion', a near-future scenario of a 'Volgan' invasion of Britain, heroising the resistance). Within a few years, however, a stable of characters emerged which gave 2000 AD its particular flavour: Johnny Alpha, the 'Strontium Dog', a sad-faced intergalactic bounty-hunter forced to live at the margins of all societies because of violent prejudices against mutants; RoboHunter, a quizzical tracker-down of rogue robots who is himself plagued by two sidekick robots who continually put him at risk; 'Nemesis the Warlock' – a story with a total reversal, in which the alien, looking like a devil (horns, cloven feet) is in fact the good guy leading interplanetary resistance to the bad guy, Torquemada, representing repressive, ultra-orthodox Christianity. These, and others, were joined at key moments by shorter-lived stories such as 'Halo Jones', the moving story of a woman mercenary. Written by Alan Moore, this story was crucial to 2000 AD attracting women fans.

At the heart of 2000 AD, from Prog. 2 onwards, was Judge Dredd.[6] Dredd is the key character in a complex post-nuclear world, in which unemployment and crime rates have reached 98 per cent, and law and order are (just about) maintained by an organisation of judges who are police, courts and executioners rolled into one. Centred in MegaCity One, a miles-high jungle of fantastic buildings with a population of 800 million, Judge Dredd has virtually been the lead story of 2000 AD throughout its history.[7] Dredd himself is a complex character. His *powers* are totalitarian, his *manner* is Clint Eastwood, but his *thoughts* at various times have been troubled – as has the spare narration.[8]

From around 1981, the publishers became aware that they had two distinct kinds of reader.[9] One kind, boys aged 10–15, liked the comic for its violent action and fast-moving storylines. The second kind was older, 17–25; still mainly male, this group had a strong student base, and liked different things about the comic – its black humour, its SF-orientation, the art-styles, the implicit social comment, and its popular cultural resonances (2000 AD was a cult item with a number of rock and pop bands, for example *Madness*, in the early 1980s, and the comic increasingly played on these connections).

More recently, the comic has changed. A number of writers and artists stopped working for IPC in the mid-1980s, partly because of conflicts over rights. What had been very much a 'participant' style of production[10] became more company-controlled. The readership also shifted. The original readers had stayed loyal to a surprising extent, and were demanding more sophistication, and a continuation of what had won their (very deep) commitment. The renewing younger readership, however, was changing its cultural reference-points. Computer- and role-playing games grew in importance, and the comic also tried to keep pace with mid-1980s emphases on 'style'. This led to friction, and a fall-away in sales in recent years. From a steady 100,000 for ten years, sales have recently declined steeply.

Yet the comic is very important to its publishers, now Fleetway Publications, because it heads up a group of publications, and because of the potential locked up in its key characters. Fleetway are working hard at merchandising their 'properties', in particular, of course, Judge Dredd. Rumours of a forthcoming film have been legion, and it will surely come. For this reason, it is almost inconceivable that the comic should be allowed to die. Or if it did, then its companion publication, *Judge Dredd: the Megazine* would inherit the properties which the company must keep alive.[11]

This much is largely public knowledge. These tendencies and tensions are the topic of repeated arguments at the annual UK Comic Arts Conventions and elsewhere. But beyond this point, knowledge of the readers of 2000 AD is clouded. The term 'fan' is surrounded by problematic meanings. To the company (and its various spokespeople), 'fans' are a highly troublesome group who lambast them regularly at Conventions like UKCAC, demanding that their sectional criteria be met – yet who only constitute possibly 10 per cent of the sales.[12] To the writers and artists, 'fans' are a breed of often irritating young obsessives who make endless demands on them (for example, for anything from a signature on twenty comics (thus raising their resale value) to a full-scale drawing, with captions, of their favourite character). The meaning of being a committed member of the audience for a comic like 2000 AD is surrounded, in other words, with competing definitions – which the actual readers themselves, we shall see, have to negotiate.

In the mid-1980s the comic itself took on a series of public meanings, in particular in connection with some Heavy Metal bands who sported 2000 AD T-shirts, especially those bearing some of the comic's more bizarre creations such as Judge Death. These public appropriations set up markers that readers have to respond to, be it to accept or reject.

Finally, the public definition of comics themselves is shifting. From being seen as a 'children's' medium, with safe and jolly fantasies to be outgrown as soon as is reasonable, comics are moving into a more complicated arena, inhabited by strange beasts such as graphic novels, sold by publishers like Penguin and Gollancz through major booksellers.[13] For a time *everyone* was into comics, yet to be *seriously* into comics was a curious aberration. This again produces tensions, even antagonisms, among those in love with the particular characteristics of this medium.

Research strategy and methodology

My research began with the design and delivery of a questionnaire. The questionnaire was intended to tap into a wide range of aspects of readers' relations to the comic, and how these fitted with their own involvement in comic culture, and in other forms of popular culture. Over a year, I gathered (exactly) 250 completed questionnaires.[14] These were entered into the Polytechnic's computer.[15] Various subsets and segmentations were run, to see whether there were any evident groupings of factors. I then selected individuals whose questionnaires contained a high number of the grouped indices, and wrote to them, asking if they would be willing to help me further. This first involved sending a blank audio cassette, with a schedule of questions, asking that they talk their answers on to the tape; the final (not yet completed) stage will be to visit each of these people, and talk over the results of both questionnaire and taped responses.

These research procedures in themselves have raised some interesting methodological and practical issues. For a start, it is clear to me that my 250 questionnaires do not constitute a reliable 'sample' of the readers of 2000 AD. But then, I am not sure that I would know what such a sample could look like. The population is not a given entity, which could be reliably sampled in that sense. First, I am interested in readers over the whole history of the comic, not just current readers. Second, it is not clear whether a person who reads the comic casually over a short (or even a long) period is a 'reader' in the same sense as a long-term committed collector of the comic, its associated merchandise, its spin-offs, etc.[16]

What did become clear to me, though, is that only in rare cases did respondents see themselves as *simply* filling in a questionnaire. A high proportion of them added comments to that effect: they were glad to be helping with writing the history of the 'galaxy's greatest comic' (2000 AD's joking self-description); they were glad to have a chance to state their gripes about where the comic was going; it was good to have a chance to be taken seriously as fans, rather than treated with contempt; and they were glad to help me with my research, since they liked other things I had written or said about the history of comics. In other words, in perhaps a majority of cases, even with the anonymity of a question-naire, there was a *perceived social relationship* between us.

I used the device of sending a schedule of questions and blank cassette for pragmatic reasons. Simply, I did not have the time or money to travel to many of the places. But I would now recommend it as a procedure for others – provided that they have established some kind of contract with their respondents first. From the evidence of the tapes, each person, trying to respond to my questions without my presence, constructed a fictional persona of me and talked to that. Because this was not interfered with by what I am actually like, or by my interrupting to ask additional questions, or by making non-verbal responses of any kind, this fictional persona had the effect of enabling people to respond to questions more fully than they themselves expected.[17] In a majority of tapes, the respondent begins by mentioning the oddity of talking to an empty room, yet by the end each is saying that s/he has talked much longer than expected. Answers come with increasing fluidity as time passes. In a number of cases, because I was not there to 'rush' the process, they felt able to turn off the tape, think about their answers, and start again; but again, this tends to decrease as they become more comfortable with the situation and with their version of 'me'.

My approach to interpreting data and responses I have gathered is much influenced by the directions being taken by discourse analysis, particularly by the work of social psychologists working within the new 'rhetorical' approach.[18] I find the approaches helpful, in that they invite open-ended attention to gaps in speech, to suppressed premises which make sense of arguments, to shared purposes and tasks in talk, to discovering the working oppositions around which people's sense of their world is structured. My procedure has therefore been to elicit as much information, and talk about information, as possible, with stages where it is possible to review past responses, to see what puzzles or emergent emphases might be elucidated. In this sense, I do not think that accounts can ever be 'complete'. Talk is not only situational, or context-determined, it is also determined by the degree to which a person has elaborated, or is able or willing to elaborate, her/his own beliefs and attitudes.

The questionnaire

Of my 250 respondents, 226 were male, 20 female (4 giving no indication).[19] The questionnaire was designed to elicit a wide range of information and responses. It ranged from asking when they became readers, to whether they would classify themselves as 'fans', 'regular' or 'casual' readers. A number of questions sought information on their attitude to characters, artwork and storylines (including a detailed Semantic Differential Test on Judge Dredd and its authors), on other leisure activities, on their self-ascribed political position, and on the meanings they would associate with 'being a fan' of comics generally. The statistics are too lengthy to include here, but there were some interesting indications in the gross figures. Particularly striking are the occasions when the diversity of response disappears, and something approaching unanimity appears. A very high proportion of responses indicate the following: commitment to, and keeping copies of, the comic; enjoyment of cinema, TV and reading (with music trailing surprisingly a little behind); at least occasionally visiting specialist shops; and thinking of themselves as comics fans in general.

Regarding Dredd, a large number were prepared to have a go at thinking of someone like Dredd in our world – though since many fewer were sure that Dredd could exist in our world, that may just be imaginativeness on their part! Within the SDT, large majorities think of Dredd as moral in his own world, certain of his beliefs, right-wing, and successful; while they think of the authors as more clearly political than Dredd, fairly moral, successful, left-wing and humourful. Furthermore, they would quite like to know the authors, but are more equivocal about Dredd! What was slightly surprising was the evident preference for storylines over character and artwork.

The results became markedly more interesting when the results were segmented according to a number of different factors: gender, kind of reader, politics, and other comics read. Picking out only the most striking of these, a host of puzzles and possible hypotheses are suggested by the following.

Female vs male readers

Perhaps the only dramatic difference occurs over politics. Here we find a large difference in political self-ascriptions (with 70 per cent of female readers describing themselves as left-wing, as against only 42 per cent of the males). What is interesting is to see that the next largest difference is in tendency to visit comics marts and conventions. Even though girls had a slightly larger tendency to mark themselves as regular/casual readers rather than fans, compared with the boys, there is a distinct upward trend in attendance at these very public events.

My hypothesis is that girls tend to participate in the comics world from some more oppositional political sense. They participate *despite* gender. And the manner of their participation may also be different – in their case, there may be something of an all-or-nothing choice. Either they participate fully, or not at all. The choice to skim the surface may not so easily be theirs. This would then connect with males giving slightly greater weight to comics being a world of secret knowledge, and collecting comics and fanzines, whereas females emphasised subversiveness, sharing an enthusiasm and getting inside an artform.

Kind of reader[20]

There are some interesting swings in other leisure activities, with Committed readers indicating a stronger interest in music, and in role-playing games; while the Casual and Regular readers make double or more the number of references to cinema and TV, to reading, and (curiously) to comic-related activities. What I suspect this indicates is that for a number of these readers at least, while their reading of 2000 AD may not involve commitment, their reading of *other* comics does.

Committed readers differ in their assessment of what it means to be a fan, in some respects: they value more highly collecting comics, following a writer or artist, and following storylines. But the trend is reversed for reading books about comics, learning about the history of comics, and following fanzines. The Committeds also favour entering a world of secret knowledge, and a subversive world; while the remainder value more getting inside an art form.

Which other comics are read

Factoring by this produced some very interesting and indicative results. Hardly surprisingly, those reading both American and British comics (BE) were markedly more likely to have collected their copies (100 per cent in fact). In terms of other activities enjoyed, the rank ordering of preferences did alter quite interestingly, with fans of American comics (MUS) valuing cinema and TV almost twice as much as those who read only 2000 AD, whilst those who read mainly other British comics (MOB) had a much stronger artistic/creative orientation.

Within the SDT, I found it most helpful to note where one category's results veered markedly away from the others. So, those not reading any other comics particularly (NOS) were out of line in: finding Dredd more moral in his own world, and moral generally; declining to rate him as Right-wing; and rating him successful. MOBs were out of line in only one respect: in being least sure about whether they would like to know Judge Dredd. MUSs were out of line in most clearly finding Dredd political, and Right-wing, and doubting his general morality. BEs were out of line in finding the author moral in both respects (a lone result which I simply can't give any determinate meaning to).

In stating the meanings of being a fan, generally both BEs and MUSs make far more indications than the others, with one curious exception: collecting merchandise is the only characteristic on which MOBs take over, with NOSs coming up behind.

Political self-designation[21]

Although there were no differences in having collected their own copies, curiously, more Right readers have tried to add back issues. This surely links with the fact that more of these also reported themselves as Committed readers.

Some curious differences show up in the rank order of other leisure activities. While the *range* of each is broadly similar, different emphases appear – perhaps the most interesting being the higher importance given to role-playing games by those on the Right (whereas for the Left it does not make the Top Ten).

In relation to Dredd, the Left are slightly more sure he is Right-wing; but the biggest differentiation is that the Non-politicals are least able to say. But in assessing his morality generally, the Right and Non-politicals are much more positive.

On the authors, the Left and Centre are markedly surer that they are political, while the Left stand ahead in seeing them as moral, and as certain of their beliefs. The Left also rate the authors as clearly Left-wing, whereas all the others indicate greater uncertainty. The Right and Non-politicals are markedly less interested in the history of comics, but much more interested in merchandising, than the Left or Centre. The Right also avoid involvement with fanzines, and definitely rate comics as a World of Secret Knowledge, over being a Subversive World. The Centre, meanwhile, are the most interested in the artwork.

Interpretation

It seems to me that the use of questionnaires is justified provided researchers are aware that in using them they are necessarily fragmenting the meanings of responses. A questionnaire allows, potentially, the identification of 'typical' readers or viewers in the sense that I have given above. Following Sennett and Cobb,[22] I would argue that we can use individuals' social biographies to show the ways in which they weave lives out of the social and cultural possibilities which are available to them.

My procedure therefore was to try to identify recurrent patterns, indicating an association of some kind between a number of characteristics. For example – puzzlingly – an interest in merchandising seems to be linked in some way to being a fan of British comics, and to being Right-wing. Being Right-wing seems to associate interestingly with viewing comics as a Secret World. Aware that this was all that the complexity of the data would allow, I developed the second phase to my research. I was looking for, in sum, 'typical' individuals who fitted closely to the patterns in the data, and who did not give idiosyncratic answers to key questions. In what follows, I report on just three of these, two men and one woman, whose responses help to draw out and make concrete the meanings implicit in some of the patterns noted above.

In listening to the three 'typical' respondents, I found a number of key issues coming to the surface, partly as a result of the earlier question-naires, partly despite them. These were: the meanings of intoxication with the medium; a recognition of 'layers' in their reading of the comic; ambiguities of heroes and villains; concepts of 'justice'; the meanings of 'political'; suspicions of being classed as a 'fan'; and, organising responses overall, orientations to the 'future'. Each respondent represents a different 'orientation' to the comic.

Three readers[23]

ALAN is 16, and has lived in a small mining town with his mum and sister for six years. He hasn't seen his father since he was small. In his own words, he has a 'funny relationship' with his home town, with few friends – and his comic reading fits that, because 'I could sit in my room and feel I was different to everyone else.'

Aged 7, he saw *Star Wars* for the first time, and was overwhelmed by 'the sheer epicness of it'. The spin-off comic helped him continue his passion for it until on a visit a cousin introduced him to *2000 AD*. He was quickly hooked: '*Star Wars* was 2 hours long, but *2000 AD* already had 300 issues and loads of characters.' (The sheer variety in *2000 AD* has been mentioned to me as important by many fans.)

In understanding Alan's relation to the comic, two words stand out: 'epic', and 'individual'. 'Epic' (a word he uses repeatedly) refers not just to the scope of plot or setting, but also to the depth of meanings and range of implications. For instance, retelling an episode of Dredd, in which a woman makes a citizen's arrest to assist Dredd, but then is herself arrested – because citizens' arrests are illegal in MegaCity One – Alan comments: 'Everyone's really hideous, and there's so much badness – it's got so much edge to it. It's so realistic and unrealistic, terrifying and hideous.' The complexities in this are part of the arena which operates very much *within* Alan's head. He is a very private person, enjoying solipsistic pleasures. Hence his love for Alan Moore's writing, because he's so 'introspective'.

These connect with his reactions to fandom. Although he admits to being 'obsessive', even 'trainspotterish' in wanting to know even what the 'creative team had for breakfast', he would hate to be thought a 'typical fan'. In fact, it's almost that he doesn't like the idea of there being other readers of *2000 AD*: 'when I was reading *2000 AD*[24], I didn't like really like the idea that there were that many other people around who were reading it because I enjoyed the feeling of being different. I would lose the individuality factor of it.'

In fact, 'individuality' and 'epicness' are closely bound together for him. *2000 AD* generally he called 'reckless, against the grain, violent, wild, black humour, unconventional'. There are ways in which *2000 AD* allows him to explore social rebellion in his head, aware that that just isn't possible for him in the world. Alan is a left-wing loner, and *2000 AD* captures but also offers shape to the ambiguities in his political orientation. Of Dredd himself, he admits his fascistic tendencies, but adds that 'maybe' some of those tendencies are necessary in a world as dangerous as his and ours –

and Alan is one who sees Dredd's world as very close to our own, indeed essentially a 'satire' on ours. It may not be going too far to say that in Alan, personal and political responses combine: his personal unease at mass situations, and his political radicalism which incorporates a fear of massification find more than echoes in Dredd's world.

What provides the linkage, it seems, is Alan's view of 'the future', and *2000 AD*'s ability to synthesise and reflect his combination of hopes and fears.

> I believe Dredd is a satire on our present society (especially American society). It is only set in the future and exaggerated so much so that it can be read on two levels: 1) as an adventure: action, cops/robbers story; 2) as an indictment of our society and means of getting ideas across without being total left-wing propaganda.

There is no gap here between present and future. The 'future' has become a mirror of the present. But if the world is difficult and Alan is alone, what solutions does he have? The beauty of *2000 AD* for him is that it also incorporates a solution for him. Alan plans to become a writer/artist of comics, with the ambition of eventually producing comics like *2000 AD* himself. This is not an idle dream. Already he writes and draws comics for many hours every week. The comic at the level of *art* allows him an escape-route, in which he can resolve his fears through creativity. In all these senses, Alan is happy to acknowledge that he has already been 'moulded' by his comic-reading.

MICHAEL is now 18, and lives with his parents, sister and cat in a middle-class enclave on the edge of a large city. Mum is a managerial secretary, Dad an area manager for a large company, so they are very comfortably off.

From his questionnaire, you would have to judge Michael a 'typical fan'. Rating *2000 AD* as his most important leisure activity, he links it with role-playing games and war-gaming, and listening to bands like the Doors. He's always in the local comics shop, and goes to marts as well. What did 'being a fan' mean to him? Collecting comics, obviously, and following particular creators and storylines; but also 'knowing everything about the title/character you like best' (Michael was one of the few to propose additions to my list of meanings of 'being a fan'). And along with ticking 'entering a world of secret knowledge', and 'getting inside an artform', he writes 'stepping into any one of infinite dimensions by reading a comic' and 'escaping reality'.[25] Add to these that in a typical week Michael reckons he spends about an hour of every day thinking about his comics, and 3–4 hours of every weekend reading old and new issues. 'I've got a massive catalogue of what's in 2000 AD, a complete list of all the stories in all the issues ... what artists drew which issues of "Judge Dredd" and so on. It might seem very boring, but I get a lot of pleasure out of it.' In fact, he adds: 'I've now got just about everything that's ever been produced by 2000 AD. It's become a sort of cult – I've got a shrine to it in my cupboard.'

What is fascinating about him, then, is his sharp refusal of any notion that he is a 'typical' fan. Responding to my query about what else I should have asked him, he said:

> 'I think an important question you haven't asked about the 'average comics fan' is mental state. I wouldn't class myself as being in the peak of physical fitness. I smoke, I eat lots of foreign foods, I drink a lot of alcohol – but I don't class myself as below average intelligence. I'm predicted 3 Bs at A-levels, and I've had offers of University places. I don't know if that fits with the idea of the average comics fan, but I think it's important.

In fact Michael reserves his greatest scorn for American comics: 'They are puerile and just insult your intelligence – besides which superheroes are just passé. No one is interested in them any more.' At least, no one whom Michael would count as a significant person, no one 'intelligent'.

Consider further the possible meaning of 'intelligence' by linking it with what Michael says next about the *fans* of US comics[26]: 'younger, shallower, real townies'. 'Townies' – a curiously Oxford-undergraduate word for something that in Michael's meaning is anything but old-fashioned. He invests a great deal in being intelligent, in having a career via University, and placing his comic-reading within that frame. In fact 'townies' seems to represent 'class' viewed through the lens of 'intelligence'. By contrast, he claims, readers of 2000 AD that he knows are 'all 18 or over, all pretty intelligent, going to University, all pretty much like me really!'

Michael was introduced to 2000 AD in 1977 by his father, with whom he has a strong sense of continuity. From 1982 it became more important to him, and he sought out the editions he hadn't kept. His orientation within the comic is to the 'anti-heroes' and to the Future War stories (Kano in 'Bad Company', Dredd, and 'Rogue Trooper' for instance). Dredd he rates particularly highly: 'one of the most developed characters ever produced for a comic'. His relation to the character is itself complex. He doesn't view Dredd as a fascist except perhaps in the earliest days, basically because in his world the punishments do fit the crimes ('though I do think he's a bit over-judicious [sic] at times'). But lest this be read simply as an expression of some identification with right-wing positions, contrast that with a comment in the questionnaire, on whether Dredd's world reminds him of ours:

> Even in the 22nd century drugs are still a problem, only now they're sugar, caffeine and youth preservation. The millions of mutants trying to scrape a living in the Cursed Earth remind me of the starving millions in Africa, also the Judges not allowing them into the city is a definite form of racism.

But Dredd himself is not tainted by this because 'deep down' he is 'emotional and merciful'.[27]

It seems to me that Bourdieu would have a lot to say about a reader like Michael.[28] Even though 2000 AD is evidently a part of popular culture, his orientation to it is essentially like a 'high culture' one, or (perhaps better) is protected by 'high culture' aspirations. And it is certainly worth noting that, at the very end of his tape, Michael remarks that 'I am not sure if being a comics fan is going to play an important part in my future – it doesn't play an important part now, apart from getting enjoyment. I don't think being a comics fan has got anything to do with the kind of person you are.' Clearly, a commitment to 'intelligence' involves a sharp demarcation of comics-reading from the sphere of work, and the future.

MARY is 25, living alone with her cat in a northern town after a difficult split from a boyfriend. Weekdays, she works in a funeral parlour, Saturdays in a hairdresser's. Her dad – 'always a villain, but lovely' – is a window-cleaner of eccentric radical views ('in approved school, he had a tattoo of Castro, spelt wrong'). Mum has a long history of health problems, Mary's manner of talking about herself is important. She confides her uncertainties ('I don't like to see anyone being victimised, but then I let other people shit on me'), but also her hopes and ambitions – as we will see.

Mary rates reading 2000 AD highly – second only to going to parapsychology lectures. She is clear how she came to be a comics fan:

> My uncle Dave used to live with us when I was little, and he was so different and I always used to admire him. He always used to have the DC and Marvel comics, like the Spiderman and Iceman. He was as black as the ace of spades and we were an all-white family. I think this is where all the music thing came from as well. He used to have a hard time, because there were only about three black people in our town. And I just admire him. And I think he was the one who got me on to the comics – not consciously.

2000 AD particularly fitted because it connected with her 'wicked' sense of humour, which embraces things like Red Dwarf, The Young Ones, Robin Williams films and even Viz. Mary 'typifies' female readers in being left-wing, in being slightly older, and in having started reading 2000 AD in the early 1980s. But like most other females, she now feels let down by the comic – she is acutely aware of its shifts in orientation (for example, towards computerish interests) and can't follow. But she is also one of the women readers who feel able to use comics shops and go to marts occasionally.

But her pleasures in the comic go further than its black humour. Some sample quotes from her illustrate this: 'I especially used to like Kano in 'Bad Company'. I really did like that because it was so anti-war. ... It really got to me, that did. It was blood and gore, but it had ethics in it.' She immediately followed that with an appallingly pessimistic statement: 'I think there's two options for us – we either die in the year 2000 from an atom bomb, or we go on to this really futuristic world.' I take this pessimistic structure of feeling seriously, as one enabling context for the comic's success.

Her view of Dredd is complicated. At first:

> I like Dreddy. I liked 'The Long Walk' where it dawned on him that maybe ... he had total faith in his judgement, and then a young boy wrote to him and said his father had got hit on the head on a march and was never the same since and it made him doubt himself and that's when he went on the Long Walk. [a phrase signifying to Dredd readers the voluntary resignation of Judges, who have to leave MegaCity One to live outside in the Cursed Earth]

Later, however, she wonders whether a Dredd without conscience ('a brick shithouse with a hat on') might not be necessary in a world where 'people seem to care more about the villains than the victims'. Lest this be read, again, as some simple tabloid-style conservatism, it is worth hearing her subsequent list of 'the victims': 'our invalids, the Asians in this country, the blacks, the people who just don't fit in'. This connects with her most passionate feelings about the comic, towards Johnny Alpha ('Strontium Dog'): 'I wish Johnny hadn't died. He was my ultimate all-time hero. It was so sad. He always meant well.' Johnny of course is a mutant, forced out of his society by violent prejudices. Mary directly compares him with her list of victims, all (she feels) treated like mutants. Her reasons become clearer when we add that her strongest perceived parallel between Dredd and our world is 'general corruption of government'.

A key term in both questionnaire and tape is 'imagination'. Mary talks of herself as having an 'active imagination', and liking 'imaginative programmes'. She adds several glosses on this. 'For the time I'm reading

2000 AD, I can put myself into the stories. It just appeals to my sense of fun, but it often has a serious side.' One of the attractions, precisely, is that the comic's politics *are* wrapped up in humour, and absurdity. On the tape, at one point, Mary in fact draws out of one worry-filled answer with the remark that 'all the fun's gone out of the conversation'. And she dismisses *Crisis*, a short-lived stable-mate of 2000 AD which wore its politics openly, as 'just like *Militant* in colour'. 'It was nasty – I know there are nasty things in the world, but it pressed its politics too far. It wasn't entertainment, and there was no learning value any more.'

But we shouldn't conclude from this that for Mary 'imagination' is some restricted domain, reserved for fun and play. On the contrary: in a remarkable reprise, Mary summed up her overall feelings about comics, reading, politics, and the world:

> A lot of people are disillusioned, but as long as you're alive, as long as you're free to think, you can make an opinion, you can read what you want, say what you want, as long as you've got your family around you – or if you haven't got your family, your friends – I think those are all the most important aspects of life. If you can read what you want, you can read your comics, there's no one trying to stop you. This country's got a lot to answer for, but it's got a lot to be grateful for. We've got the homeless, we've got child abuse cases, a lot of ugliness, a lot of bitterness, a lot of bigotry; but we've got our freedom. Maybe people disagree with me. Being without money is a lack of freedom, being without choice is a lack of freedom, being without rights is a lack of freedom, being without proper health care, being an invalid, being blind, or deaf, or dumb is a lack of freedom. But I think if you've got a spirit, and you can read things, you can open your mind. I think stupidity, ignorance is a lack of freedom. And that's one thing people can get out of, can open their minds a bit. ... If people could open their minds up, just to read a comic, they'd realise there's something beyond their box they're in, they'd see how far they can see, how far they can touch. It's probably my way of escaping, reading those things, but it's my way of using my imagination. If you lose your imagination, you've got no sparkle in your life, no vision. I think if I hadn't got my sense of humour and imagination, I'd be a slug.

I found this encomium to imagination both moving, and power-fully explanatory. When Mary says 'my comics *are* important to me, like my books, because they enable me to believe in the future', we can see that her ambivalence about the *kind* of future is itself partly overwritten by the sheer power of imagining. Culture and living through the imagi-nation are being invested with the hopes of survival. All the strands of pleasure in the comic are therefore themselves minor acts of subversion and hope: 'The reason I like a lot of 2000 AD is the artwork – it's absolutely spell-binding. "Slaine" – honest to God, it's like jumping into the page, it's so vivid and coloured. I'd love to be able to draw like that.'

For Mary, we might say that the very act of reading, the very submersion in the text, is an act of personal empowerment – literally, she feels stronger. And when the comic in which she submerges gives her contact with this deeply pessimistic structure of feeling, far from defeating her, the imaginative impulse becomes a resource for hope, for being human.

Listening to the readers

What should we say about these three case-studies? There is far more to be said than I can cover in this chapter. First, I am intrigued by the extent of the commonality of the responses to key questions. For all the differences between them, all three see 2000 AD as much the same cultural item, and find their sources of pleasure within recognisably the same textual formation: the variety of stories, the ambiguities of heroes and villains, the problematic relations with our own time, and so on. I pick this out first because it seems to me to throw doubt on one of the key terms of a great deal of recent audience work. Having apparently shed the notion of determinant 'encodings', audience understanding of texts is still often posed in terms of 'decodings', only now these are seen as multiple, contextually-determined and potentially infinite (though sometimes with an inoperable caveat that 'of course' the text ultimately constrains the range of possible readings ...).

I would want to question this both on empirical and on epistemological grounds. The notion of decoding suggests one level of activity – the production of meaning from a text. I want to decompose that into at least three layers:

reading: that is, making literal sense of texts through understanding and using the systems of conventions which comics use for story-telling;

textually-demanded interpretation: a comic such as 2000 AD, through its overt strands of intertextuality which place the comic in an area of our social lives, asks readers to make connections and to think through relations with our own world;

intercalation into the reader's social career: it is not so much that readers read things differently, but that having read them they evaluate and value the results differently, and want to, or are able to, make variable uses of what they have read.

What this suggests is that the differences which show up through the questionnaires are mainly *consequent upon* the reading, not determinants of the reading. Indeed, it cautions that we should be more nervous of terms like 'reading', which squash together a number of processes which we need actively to distinguish.[29]

Second, I am struck by the sheer *intoxication with the medium*. This has a number of aspects to it. There is no doubt that among the pleasures that readers derive from 2000 AD is a sense of the exploration of the possibilities of an unfolding medium. They feel that they are discovering the possibilities of the medium together with the creators. This readily links with the sense that comics are a relatively democratic medium, in that anyone can sit down with a piece of paper and pencil/pens, and have a go at producing their own.[30]

Third, clearly part of the pleasure of reading 2000 AD is the opportunity to 'go deeper', that is, to join with the creators in searching for meanings in the depths of the stories. Indeed, more than one respondent (not among the three I have featured) spoke of the importance of 2000 AD's ability to *surprise* them (one even saying that while she hated the death of favourite characters, she thought it was right that the comic did this to her – it would be 'wimpish' if it didn't). The idea of being 'surprised' by a story warrants closer investigation, since it would, I suspect, result in some renewed complexity in our understanding of the two sides of the text/reader relationship which a term such as 'negotiated' reading does not adequately capture.[31]

Fourth – and here we move decisively into the interpretive levels of 'reading ' – there are clearly significant connections with the ambitions, fears and hopes of individual readers. These are complexly constructed. What is signally so important about 2000 AD to its readers is its address to, and play with, 'futures'. There has been a considerable amount of academic work on images of the future, in work on utopias.[32] There has been less on the dynamics of everyday ideas about futures. As Adrian Mellor and Donna Harraway have pointed up quite differently,[33] science fiction has long provided an arena for particular social groups to formulate their anxieties about social developments. But 2000 AD, I would argue, has done this in a particular way. A useful if unlikely analogy might be the enthusiasm for Charles Lindbergh, as brilliantly evoked and analysed by Modris Eksteins.[34] Eksteins shows how Lindbergh's transatlantic flight, which prompted wild enthusiasms across Europe, was so powerful precisely because it bound together two opposite tendencies: a return to traditional values of 'manners' and aristocratic presence, along with a future-oriented democratic and machine-led populism. In parallel fashion, if with quite different materials, I would argue that to readers 2000 AD, and 'Judge Dredd' in particular, balance between several incompatible orientations to the future: a conservative critique of change, fearful of mobs, crime and lawlessness; a heroic, Clint Eastwood vision of male rescuers overcoming, or at least stemming the tide of, destruction which is endemic in the State as much as in society; and a radical suspicion of the police as enforcers. My readers accurately perceive the ambivalences in the comic, and opt for that relation to them which co-ordinates with their own images of their own futures. What is perhaps common to all is a suspicion of public opinion as bigotry, and easily linked with this, a willingness to delight in their own marginality – though that can be differently conceived.

On being a 'fan'

Do you remember Godley East, one of the world's more unusual railway halts? The Diary put it on the map by discovering that it was the station you might depart – but to which you could never return. ... And now? Bring out your anorak, your sandwiches and your NHS specs held together with sticking plaster. From May 11 ...

Guardian Diary, 1 May 1992

We all 'get' the reference, don't we? The stereotype of the trainspotter neatly evoked. It is one to which, as early quotes will have shown, many of my respondents refer – as something to be avoided, in 'fandom'. It would be tempting to follow Joli Jensen[35] in seeing this as simply representing a gulf between (false) representations of 'fans' as pathologically incapable, and real enthusiasts protecting their self-image. Yet I think this seriously misses the point – and here I come back to my beginning, that it is impossible to understand the fans adequately without a proper knowledge of the context of their reading: the shifting systems of ownership, production and distribution within which comics like 2000 AD are operating.

It would be possible to quote from just about every single tape I have received, to illustrate fans' hostility to the perceived implications of the word 'fan'. Let me take just one not already cited:

I hate the word 'fan'. You have Kylie fans, you have Jason fans. 'Fan' implies it's a fad, a phase, whereas for me it's been so long that I've been reading them that I can definitely say it's not a phase. So I would define myself as ... a comics reader, and collector. ... I like sitting in the middle of them. I don't really like the standard comics fan – they have a very bad image, in my opinion. They all seem to be into role-playing games and they are the kind of people, I imagine, who get a kick out of going paint-balling at weekends. Not that I've anything against going paint-balling. It's just this idea of little boys getting a buzz out of guns and splat and kerpow. Probably I'm stereotyping them, but I don't want to meet the fans – I think of them as grubby little people.

There are a number of very striking features about quotations such as these. First is their honest admission that the image is formed *at a distance* – they really don't know, don't want to know, these people. Second, they seem very 'cut-and-paste'. The image of the comics fan seems to borrow from a repertoire of other images – such as (in this case) from a 'big-macho-boys' stereotype, or (as in references such as the *Guardian* Diary) to trainspotter stereotypes. Third, there is a real ambivalence about whether fans are actually like this, or whether the image is a gross distortion.

From all my interviews, I would hypothesise that there is an actual connection between depth of involvement with the comics medium, and strength of resistance to the designation 'fan'. Those who are most involved are the ones who most strongly resist the term. To the more casual readers, it retains a slight honorific sense. Where, then, does this image – albeit cut-and-pasted – originate? Truth is, not in the main-stream press, whose primary interests in recent years have been either in the continuation of the old nostalgia = old comics/danger = new comics duet; or in an exaggerated celebration of the new, linking it with issues of Style and Postmodern Culture.[36]

I want to propose instead that my readers are responding to a complex of two presences. The first is the 'fan' as projected by the comic itself (and other comics, and the surrounds of comic paraphernalia themselves, such as fanzines, marts and conventions). In many ways this is textually inscribed, from (in the case of 2000 AD) the inanities of Tharg's page of insulting replies to readers' letters (and of course only certain kinds of letters accepted), to the address to the readers through merchandising, fringe activities (such as signings), and the hyping of certain writers and artists. Secondly, there are the kinds of engagement with the medium that the comics industry itself currently encourages.[37] In other words, the image of the 'fan' is not some social/mental 'stereotype'[38] which actual fans feel insulted by. Rather, it is a *real site* which the conditions of the comics industry has created and encouraged. Go to a convention – or just read about going – and experience the careful management of the possible encounters between readers and creators. Watch the comics press news, and see the magnification of new hero-authors to Homeric heights. The image of the 'fan', I would argue, is a cartoon drawn from the *actual* social relationships allowed by the dominant production forms in the present-day comics industry.

The last few years have seen an upsurge in studies of fans and fandom.[39] One common feature of much of this work is an almost uncritical celebration of fans as 'resisters'. Indeed, they have almost taken the place of subcultures in current cultural research, as the site *par excellence* of resistance. At the very least, my research must hope to unsettle this emergent consensus.

Notes and references

1 See my *Action: The Story of a Violent Comic* (Titan Books, 1990).

2 Others are expressed in the introduction (jointly written with Anne Beezer) to a recently edited collection. See Martin Barker and Anne Beezer, Introduction to *Reading into Cultural Studies* (Routledge, 1992).

3 On this, see in particular Jane Gaines, *Contested Culture: The Image, The Voice and the Law* (British Film Institute, 1991).

4 See my *Comics; Ideology, Power and the Critics* (Manchester University Press, 1989), especially chapters 1 and 6.

5 On the opposite view, that female readers of 'male' texts are effectively committing acts of self-subordination, see for example Christine Gledhill, 'Developments in feminist film criticism', in Mary Ann Doane *et al.* (eds), *Re-Vision: Essays in Feminist Film Criticism* (University Publications of America, 1984), pp. 18–48; and Mary Ann Doane, 'The "woman's film": possession and address', same volume, pp. 67–82.

6 'Prog.' means edition. *2000 AD* has consciously sought to establish its own mock language, and mock characters, to the rising irritation of many older readers. The prime object of many readers' loathing is Tharg, the 'galactic editor' who fronts the comic, continuously deriding letter-writers. His presence, his eternal 'Borag Thungg' greeting, and the associated language of 'ArtRobots' and the like have been an important source of tension.

7 For the record: *2000 AD*'s producers and readers will rightly say that it was not the most popular at the beginning, only taking the lead when the first long story ('The Robot Wars') was published; and it has on occasion lost the lead to other key stories such as 'Slaine', a story based on Celtic myth.

8 For a useful introductory analysis of Judge Dredd, see John Newsinger, 'The Dredd Phenomenon', *Foundation*, 52 (1988).

9 The knowledge came as a result of the first ever piece of market research on the comic, combined with evidence gleaned from early fandom (which was represented in a small way inside the company), and the evidence of readers' letters.

10 According to Kevin O'Neill, Art Assistant on *2000 AD* in the early days, the comic was virtually edited 'from outside' in the first year or so (even in spite of boardroom fears about a repeat of an *Action* crisis) – because of the strength of a network of writers and artists that emerged. 'It struck me as having the flavour of the old EC comics, or Marvel Comics when they were starting – that kind of camaraderie, a sense of fun and playfulness' (interview, March 1992).

11 This parallels what Simon Frith has pointed up in the music business: namely, the increasing treatment of musicians and music as 'packages of rights', which can potentially be deployed in films, in advertisements, and so on. See Simon Frith, *Facing the Music* (Mandarin, 1990).

12 Richard Burton, current editor of *2000 AD*, in response to a query about whether he worries that the fans wouldn't be willing to cut up their copies of the comic, to send in 'voting' slips indicating popularity of stories: 'It doesn't worry me at all, because we don't produce *2000 AD* for the comic fans. The last big survey we had done showed that 80 per cent of our readers are non-fans. If we had to survive on fans, we couldn't' (interview, January 1991).

13 On this whole process, see Roger Sabin, *Adult Comics: An Introduction* (Routledge, 1993).

14 This was done by a combination of a leaflet at UKCAC '90, an advertisement in *2000 AD* itself, and some small acts of blackmail. On more than one occasion, when invited to give a talk to another college, I agreed on condition that they could find me at least six people to complete my questionnaire!

15 I'd like to record my thanks to Jan Major for her assistance in producing the programme (a modified version of SPSS), in helping with its operation and in producing the results to my specifications.

16 I was able to run a small cross-check on my questionnaire sample. Fleetway agreed to let me have a copy of all the letters which were written to *2000 AD* in one (randomly chosen) week. Of 40 letters sent, I was able to write to 36, since four lacked addresses. Of those, 24 eventually completed and returned questionnaires to me. These revealed some interesting differences – the letter-writers were, perhaps not surprisingly, slightly more younger readers – in hope no doubt of winning a *2000 AD* Cap. They also, curiously, contained a higher proportion of Regular and Casual readers than my main group.

17 From the middle of one of the tapes, a not untypical quotation: 'Are you getting bored yet? I don't know whether to stop yet. You know, when you are talking to someone face-to-face, you know when you've said enough because you get a come-back, don't you, when they start going to sleep or start getting out of the room.' This respondent carried on with her answers for another twenty minutes.

18 See the extensive work of the group now associated with Loughborough University. For example Michael Billig *et al.*, *Ideological Dilemmas* (Sage, 1988); Michael Billig, *Ideology and Opinions* (Sage, 1990); and Jonathan Potter and Margaret Wetherell, *Discourse and Social Psychology* (Sage, 1987). I do have some worries about the particular direction of the theorisation of this work. Rhetorical psychology places heavy emphasis on the contextual production of talk – how people produce talk appropriately to the social situation in which they are discoursing, and how (differently, in each case) they make it relevant to that situation.

My worry is that this underestimates two important things. First, it understates the degree to which people will carry into any situation different degrees of commitment to organised bodies of beliefs and ideas – which they may then seek appropriate modes to express, or withhold. Indeed, their very entering of those situations will often be a function of those committed beliefs. Second, it underestimates the degree to which there may be *publicly agreed languages* which are working to structure those very situations in which people enter. This means that people entering any social situation may feel themselves to be 'samples' of a certain kind of discourse-predisposition – a situation to which they can react in various ways.

19 For reasons of space, I am not able to include either the questionnaire, or the schedule of questions for taped interviews, here. The questionnaire was long, and I

have to say that I was pleased not only with the general care with which it had evidently been completed, but also with the number of people who appended notes saying that they had found the process of completing it enjoyable, and even stimulating in making them think through their own relationship to the comic. The same was true, but even more so, with the taped interviews.

I have become convinced that questionnaires have two primary functions in audience research. The first is to give the researcher a feeling of confidence that her/his results have some general reliability. This is often given by the achieving of *obvious* results. So, for instance, I would have been worried if my questionnaires had *not* shown that the less committed a reader was, the less likely s/he is to have collected back copies, and the lower s/he ranks the importance of reading 2000 AD. Second, however, is the discovery of puzzles *which the questionnaires cannot explain*. For example, when female readers appear to contradict that 'obvious' result, there is something worthy of further investigation.

On the other hand, researchers, I feel, should be more honest about one thing – and that is the extent to which research such as this throws up useless knowledge – that is, information or results which one does not know what to do with. I hereby confess that both in this sketch, and in the subsequent factored results, a *majority* of the information I derived seems to tell me nothing. I have been highly selective in finding some parts very significant, but I feel that my selectiveness has a defensible rationale behind it.

20 For practical purposes, I combined the categories Regular and Casual, in computing the results, to give a largish group in opposition to the Committeds. I feel this is reasonable on other than statistical grounds, since commitment declares an *attitude* to reading that regularity does not. To decline to call oneself a committed reader, whilst saying one reads it regularly, therefore signals a kind of refusal.

21 For reasons of sample size, I combined these into four categories: Left (-1 & 2), Middle-of-the-road (-3), Right (-4 & 5), Non-political (-6).

22 R. Sennett and R. Cobb, *The Hidden Injuries of Class* (Cambridge University Press, 1972).

23 In retelling their stories, I have followed the standard practice of disguising identities by changing names, and by altering any obviously identifying references.

24 Between questionnaire and taped interview, Alan in fact gave up reading the comic, both disappointed by the way it was changing, and himself moving on to an equivalent passion for music.

25 Note the contrast with Alan, for whom comics were a *social* escape, in letting him live his life in his bedroom; but for him 2000 AD in particular was always a commentary on the world outside the door.

26 'Michael' was picked from among those whom the computer indicated as fitting a 'chain' encompassing (among other things) being Right-wing, reading mainly other British comics, but also being a committed reader.

27 These were dimensions added to my SDT by Michael.

28 See for example Pierre Bourdieu, *Distinction: A Social Critique of the Judgement of Taste* (Routledge and Kegan Paul, 1986).

29 On this, see also the recent essay by John Corner, 'Meaning, genre and context: the problematics of "public knowledge" in the new audience studies', in James Curran and Michael Gurevitch, *Mass Media and Society* (Edward Arnold, 1991).

30 The obvious first resource for thinking about this has to be Walter Benjamin's classic essay, 'The work of art in the age of mechanical reproduction' (reprinted in many places, including James Curran and Michael Gurevitch, *Mass Communication*

and Society (Edward Arnold, 1977), pp. 384–408). Benjamin looks at media such as film, and the mass copying of pictures and photographs. What I am suggesting here is that comics' appeal rests in part on the possibilities of *active participation in production*, and the possibility of the *wholeness* of such participation. Comics can empower, because it is possible in theory to control the whole process, from conception to final product.

One critic who has moved in this direction, in a parallel field, is Dave Kenyon, whose *Inside Amateur Photography* (Batsford, 1992) explores the empowering possibilities of that medium most interestingly.

31 On 'negotiation' as a term to describe active reading, see the intelligent but problematic essay by Christine Gledhill, 'Pleasurable negotiations', in E. Deidre Priband, *Female Spectators: Looking at Film and Television* (Verso, 1988, pp. 64–89). Speaking as a NATFHE Negotiating Secretary, I am very doubtful that any of those who use the term have ever been involved in actual negotiations – or they wouldn't see it so confidently as a term to describe *escape* from (textual) power!

32 See the following representative examples: Frank and Fritzie Manuel, *Utopian Thought in the Western World* (Basil Blackwell, 1979); Barbara Goodwin and Keith Taylor, *The Politics of Utopia: a Study in Theory and Practice* (Hutchinson, 1982); Tom Moylan, *Demand the Impossible: Science Fiction and the Utopian Imagination* (Methuen, 1986); Ruth Levitas, *The Concept of Utopia* (Philip Allan, 1990), also her 'New Right utopias', *Radical Philosophy*, 35 (1985). Particularly useful for my purpose is Raymond Williams's 'Utopia and science fiction', in Patrick Parrinder (ed.), *Science Fiction: Critical Perspectives* (Longman, 1979), pp. 52–66.

33 Adrian Mellor, 'Science fiction and the crisis of the educated middle class', in Christopher Pawling (ed.), *Popular Literature and Social Change* (Macmillan, 1984); and Donna Harraway, 'A manifesto for cyborgs: science, technology and socialist feminism in the 1980s', in Linda Nicholson (ed.), *Feminism/Postmodernism* (Routledge, 1990).

34 Modris Eksteins, *Rites of Spring* (Black Swan, 1990), Chapter 8.

35 See Joli Jensen, 'Fandom as pathology, the consequences of pathologisation', in Lisa Lewis (ed.), *The Adoring Audience: Fan Culture and Popular Media* (Routledge, 1992), pp. 9–29.

36 On this, see again Sabin, *Adult Comics*.

37 On this, see the battle currently being waged, particularly in the pages of the American *Comics Journal*, over the growth of 'collector-driven' publication. See, for example, Gary Groth, 'Comics: the new culture of illiteracy', *The Comics Journal*, 152 (1993), 3–6.

38 The concept of a 'stereotype' has a troubled history, as I have tried to show in my *Comics: Ideology, Power and the Critics*, Chapter 9. Recent work on it has certainly made it more complex, but without in my view removing the taint of older social-psychological understandings of it.

39 See, for representative work, Lisa Lewis (ed.), *The Adoring Audience*, and Henry Jenkins, *Textual Poachers: Television Fans and Participatory Culture* (Routledge, 1992).

Repeatable pleasures:
notes on young people's use of video

It is plausible that escape from self-awareness is an underlying goal in other recreational activities, including spectator sports, watching movies and taking drugs.

Roy F. Bannister, 'Masochism as escape from self'[1]

To a greater extent than many other media technologies, video has raised central questions of access, regulation and control. Much of the public anxiety which has surrounded video use has been directed particularly at young people, and has renewed perennial concerns about their apparent vulnerability. The 'problem' of video is that it seems to offer young people much easier access to material from which many adults feel they should be protected. Yet at least for some young people, certain types of video viewing appear to be regarded as an aspect of 'youth culture', a peer-group activity whose meaning and pleasure depend precisely on the fact that it is seen to exclude adults who might potentially disapprove.

This chapter focuses particularly on research with working-class, teenage boys living in the inner city, which was part of a longer-term project undertaken for the British Board of Film Classification. In addition to the 'ethnographic' aspects described here, the research also involved school-based interviews and small-scale surveys of a wider sample of young people from various parts of the south-east of England. The broad aim of the research was to investigate young people's views about what they watched on video (with a particular emphasis on feature films) and the circumstances in which they did so. One major focus of the research was on the inter-generational tensions and struggles around young people's leisure, and more specifically the kind of parental scrutiny and control that surrounded the use of video, particularly in working-class homes.

The growth of home video

Although video-cassette recorders (VCRs) first became available in the late 1970s, they did not become widespread until the unit price dropped in the early 1980s. While television is now available in an estimated 98 per cent of homes in Britain, the penetration of video is increasing rapidly, with over 75 per cent of families with children now owning or renting one or more VCRs.[2] As previous research has indicated,[3] however, the advent of video has coincided with the development of other 'new' media technologies such as cable and satellite. Clearly, there is likely to be a limit to the total amount of time we can spend in front of our screens, and it would seem that these new media forms are only likely to expand at the expense of curtailing each other's audience shares.

Levy and Gunter[4] indicate that VCRs were initially used mostly for later replay of broadcast programmes ('time-shifting'), secondly to build home libraries of programmes (mainly feature films) and thirdly to play tapes rented or bought from shops. There is some evidence from trade figures that the market trend is now away from rental and towards 'sell-through' (or outright purchase) of feature films on video. Trade opinion is that the home rental market has now peaked, and that sell-through will keep the industry going through the 1990s.

Such technological innovations inevitably generate new research questions. Perhaps one of the most basic in this case is whether video is better viewed as a dependent cultural form – in other words, as an adjunct of TV – or as fundamentally different in kind. Yet the apparent degree of control afforded by video – the possibility of viewing and re-viewing at one's own pace – raises further questions. If the video is to become 'the paperback of the twenty-first century', as some popular critics have suggested, what implications will this have for the balance between visual and verbal literacy?

Yet there is also a risk here of adopting a totalising view of video. Such broader speculation about the implications of the medium needs to be informed by small-scale studies which concentrate on the social contexts and practices which surround video use. Following recent research on the use of television within the family,[5] we need to consider *how* video is used, and to understand video viewing as a social practice in its own right.

Young people and the regulation of video

The early 1980s saw a major furore over the impact of so-called 'video nasties' on young people.[6] Although the vast majority of the population had never seen any of the films in question, the issue was taken up by a number of national newspapers, and became a vehicle for a much more generalised concern about the apparent vulnerabilities of the young. Indeed, the research which (despite being widely challenged) largely informed the subsequent legislation was centrally concerned with the impact of such material on children.[7]

One consequence of the 'video nasties' scare is that video is now a highly regulated medium. Interestingly, before the legislation which became the Video Recordings Act (VRA) was passed by parliament in 1985, a working party from the video industry had proposed a voluntary code of practice, although this was eventually rejected as insufficient. Indeed, the VRA runs counter to the broad trend which has continued throughout this century for decreased state censorship of the arts.

While the VRA, which is used by the British Board of Film Classification (BBFC) as the basis for classifying and occasionally censoring video content, affects adults' access to video, there is an underlying assumption that video cannot be policed, and is potentially available to all ages. Certainly, in some of the inner-city neighbourhoods in which our research was conducted, it appeared that the Act had only had a real impact on high street stores, and was persistently undermined at street level by piracy and the duplication of pre-VRA tapes.

As this suggests, the 'video nasties' scare also resulted in a 'cleaning up' of the video industry, not least in order to preserve its profitability. The industry has sought to escape from its 'back street' reputation and move towards a 'family' image – as evidenced, for example, by the development in the late 1980s of large chains of high-street retailers, with their standardised bright plastic store liveries and cross-merchandising of popcorn and the like. Their idealised image of their clientele, seen on some publicity material, is of a nuclear family sitting on a big sofa watching a 'family film' together.

The BBFC's certification of video – 'family films' are usually rated PG (Parental Guidance) – must be located within these general forces shaping video consumption, but has to proceed from an assessment of the content of the works submitted. In the process, there is a separation of powers, and a notion of independent expertise comes into play. The BBFC thus stands 'between' the industry and the public, although it is usually keen to efface its role.

However, both the 'official' response to the popular uptake of video (particularly of films on video) and these developments in the video industry appear to be based on a set of underlying assumptions about young people, and on unarticulated developmental notions of 'readiness'. This may partly explain the rather elaborate nature of the system. For example, of the six classifications that the BBFC applies to video submissions – U/c, U, PG, 15, 18 and R18 (with a 12 certificate probably on the way) – four concern products usually associated with young people or families (which implies the presence of the young). There is no attempt to divide up the years from the age of maturity onwards, probably because this would be perceived as undue interference (although some countries such as New Zealand do have a 21+ certificate). In practice, the majority of renters from video shops are 16–24 year olds (the same age group that forms the majority of cinema audiences)[8] and they mostly watch 15- and 18-rated tapes.

Ultimately, however, nobody really knows if video classification 'works' – although it probably does keep the most violent and sexually violent material away from mainstream outlets. It remains unclear whether the detailed system of age-bars and recommendations is understood, supported or particularly obeyed by the public. Interestingly, the BBFC has recently commissioned as-yet-unpublished market research into some of these issues, prior to the introduction of yet another category (the 12, which has applied to films in the cinema since 1988).[9]

Nevertheless, as I have noted, the need for this interface between the industry and the public appears to rest on the presumed vulnerabilities of the young. Of course, this is seen to be especially the case in relation to the 'censorable elements', traditionally sex and violence. For Britain in particular, one would have to add certain issues relating to manners and 'decency' – particularly 'bad language' (often prevalent in Hollywood films, of course) – which can be enough in themselves to effect a prohibition for younger viewers. (At the time of writing, two utterances of the word 'fuck' in dialogue automatically means that a film or video is rated for fifteen years or above.)

In our research, young people themselves were very keen to talk about their favourite videos, although they often seemed slightly baffled as to why an adult should be so interested in a leisure pursuit that they assume is essentially 'theirs'. However, their views on the classification system, which obviously applies much more directly to them than it does to adults, were more contradictory. For those who had been thwarted by it – for example, in being refused a rental tape by a shop-owner – it was often mildly resented: 'grown-ups just like to boss us', said one twelve-year-old girl. On the whole, however, such experiences were rare, especially in urban areas, where the system is easily circumvented.

One interesting factor that recurred in several interview groups was that classification, at least in relation to certain genres, appeared to produce a reverse effect. For example, with horror, a popular genre with young teens, the classification appeared to be used as an index of desirability. PG-rated horror – which is, almost by definition, mild and is rare anyway – was often looked down upon. 15-rated horror was better, but 18 was definitely the best. Indeed, there was an impeccable logic in their use of the system: it served very definite functions for them, albeit rather different ones from those it might serve for other audiences.

Thus, by rating horror films on a scale which implies greater or lesser 'strength', the classification system has the unintended effect of identifying 'forbidden fruit' for age-groups below the one stipulated. In this way, horror films have come to be seen by many young people as something to 'test yourself out on'. Those which are more challenging or disturbing – for example in terms of their 'strong' images, graphic special effects or treatment or repressed or taboo topics – are rated higher accordingly. In this way, certain sorts of video viewing can be seen as a form of 'youth culture', in which a familiar dynamic of control and evasion is played out.

Many of these themes emerge in the following description, which attempts to convey something of the atmosphere of an after-school horror-viewing session which I observed during the research. The boys concerned were all fourteen years old, and lived on a large working-class council estate.

'A really bad vid'

It is agreed that after school the boys will go back to Colin's house to 'watch a vid'. Colin has been boasting that his mum and dad are both away and his little sister (Ella, aged nine) has gone to stay with his 'nan'. It strikes the boys as unlikely that a fourteen-year-old like Colin would be left in charge, but they let it pass. The point is that the place is theirs.

Four o'clock comes and the friends spill out of the school gate and head for the nearest sweetshop/tobacconist to stock up. I meet them on their way out. By 4.20 we are in Colin's parents' flat on the big estate that virtually backs on to the school. Three of the boys, John, Martin and Dave, pile on to the one old sofa and start fighting for a comfortable seat. Steve and Mark negotiate the other two chairs, leaving Colin (who is putting in the tape) and I to find a space on the floor.

Colin has chosen the video – Stephen King's *It* – which he now owns, having got it as a birthday present. We start to watch, and Colin immediately grabs the remote and starts fast-forwarding. With the conch-like remote in his hand, Colin becomes the spokesperson, explaining what sort of film it is. 'It's a really bad horror,' he tells us enthusiastically. In fact, the boys know all about it, because although only Colin has seen it before, it has been a favourite with this age-group for some years, and a common topic of playground talk.

It is easy to see why the video connects with their experience. The convoluted teleplay plot (it was made for three one-hour slots on US cable) jumps between present and past time. The main scenes concern a group of seven mid-teen adolescents, all outcasts in some way, who have to out-face a protean evil force that has possessed their small, 1950s suburban town. From the opening credits, the familiar iconography of horror is on display, and it seems to whet the boys' appetites. Over dreamy, almost wistful, vocals and music, the camera pans slowly across happy childhood photographs and discarded dolls – images of innocence just waiting to be tainted. Finally, there are the monster's sudden, galloping point-of-view shots, illustrating the preternatural speed with which it can attack its stunned victims. The monster usually takes the form of an early twentieth-century clown called Penny Wise – except for the fact that this clown has sharp, dog-like teeth, and that other familiar signifier of evil, a manic laugh. Also, in a direct parallel to the even more popular Freddy Kruger series (*Nightmare on Elm Street* I-VI), he appears in the protagonists' daydreams, where they have to fight him by finding the will to refute his existence.

A couple of warning snarls from the monster (as the camera zooms in to a mouth crowded with teeth) has the boys howling and baying. By now, all but one are smoking and the air in the small living room is a dense fug. Steve takes his cigarette and pushes the lighted end towards the screen, as if to ward off the monster. 'I'd burn him, man ... aaargh!'

Soon, we arrive at Beverly's flashback scene, which is dragged back for a replay by popular vote. Beverly is the token girl in the seven-person group. Early scenes in the film establish that she has a pattern of seeking out dominating men. In the first part of the flashback, we see her, aged about fourteen, being wooed in a puppyish way by two members of the gang. She goes indoors, leaving her two suitors, to be confronted by her 'couch potato' father, who demands to know if she has been flirting with boys, 'just like her mother'. The father raises his hand to her before the camera cuts away. Then we cut back to Beverly as a grown woman in a office, being told off and slapped round the face by her boyfriend, who is also her boss. In the next scene, in their apartment, the row continues: this time the man goes to fetch a belt and wraps it threateningly around his fist.

'Go on, give her one!' blurts out John. Martin and Dave giggle, partly because they know the remark is 'wrong' (they have been 'learning about sexism' in school), and that the audience is supposed to be on Beverly's side. But at the same time, there is a tension here between two conflicting subject positions. The scenes reflect predictable fantasies of male dominance. One could argue that the boys, as male viewers, are partly behind that striking hand: the deep vein of anger at, and fear of, women that is one of the mainstays of patriarchal culture almost forces them into identification with the striker. Yet Beverly is a main character, and the scene is structured in such a way as to place the viewer in her shoes as well, hence the satisfaction when she finally turns the tables. Given the boys' initial reaction, part of the subsequent pleasure may be inflected with relief (the super-ego censuring the impulse to misogyny just in time). Back in the video, the sleazy boyfriend is calling her a 'little girl' and saying, more menacingly, that she has 'forgotten her lessons'. Beverly starts to assert herself. She throws heavy ornaments at the stunned man, one of which hits him in the head and knocks him down. She warns him that if he ever comes near her again, she will 'kill him'. At this point, Colin lets out a loud counter-cheer. It is a deliberate, jokey provocation to Martin and Dave, rather like shouting for your 'side' and against the opposition, as one would at a football match.

In the following scene, we are back to Beverly as a fourteen-year-old. She is introduced to the all-male gang, and a 1950s-style song sequence cuts in, while they work on building something together. The style of song is familiar to the boys through countless revivals and rip-offs in TV and cinema advertising for jeans and soft drinks. There is a brief argument about whether they should spin the song, and John answers by grabbing the remote control. A brief fight ensues in which ashtrays, crisp packets and insults fly. John overshoots the end of the song, and is shouted at again and punched by Mark. The video is partially rewound and started again.

This time, we are with Beverly, still as a girl, but three months before the last scene. The father is slumped in front of the TV, beer in hand. Beverly goes upstairs and hears a weak voice from the bathroom saying 'help me!' She bends over, only to find a red bubble – like a clown's nose – growing out of the plug-hole. It bursts and splatters blood over the sink – to laughter and cries of disgust from the boys watching.

Her screams bring her irate father up from downstairs. Merely bemused by his daughter's hysterics, he dips his finger in the liquid to test it and ends up smearing it on her face. 'What's all that about then?' asks Martin, as the scene is finishing. 'It's like she's on the blob [menstruating], isn't it?' says Colin with matter-of-fact sexism and obvious contempt for Martin's slowness – yet although the 'suddenness' and quantity of the blood do carry those connotations, the implication he draws is much less overt than he seems to suggest.

The video progresses by fits and starts, and the banter and jeering rise and fall with the intensity of the action. The creepier moments are spun to, partly because it is long (180 minutes) but also to intensify the product and to shorten the *longueurs*.[10] At points, the boys seem to be 'completing' the text, or attempting to transform it into a 'stronger' experience than it actually is – for despite the occasional shocks, there is little by way of outright carnage or visceral special effects, and the video is in fact rated at 15.

Once the viewing is over, some of the boys affect disappointment that it was not 'stronger': 'I thought you said it was bad', says Steve. Colin defends his choice, but Steve has the advantage of taking a more macho stance. 'It was a fucking tea party!' he says. 'And they was like poofs.' Steve is referring here to the fact that the male characters do a lot of American-style 'bonding', getting into big huddles at various stages – although it had struck me earlier how these on-screen cuddles mirrored so closely the way the three friends were sitting almost on top of each other on the sofa.

The boys briefly discuss whether the video is 'any good', not just as a horror film but as a Steven King work. They have noticed that King's name is marketed as a sort of brand-name. 'It always says Steven King's so-and-so, doesn't it?' says Mark. 'Yeah, but he doesn't make 'em,' says Colin. 'He must be so fucking rich!' chips in John, and they go on to fantasise about what they would do if they were rich. Later, Colin returns to the topic of how 'faithful' this telemovie is to King's style, and claims to have read the book. It turns out that most of the boys have read something by King. I remembered the conversation I had had with their English teacher when I had told him we were planning to see this film. 'Steven King! Well, that's it. English teachers love him,' he exclaimed, with self-mocking irony. 'Have you tried to get these boys to actually *read* a book after the fourth year? And yet they'll plough through King's stuff. You see them swapping the books in the playground like videos.'

Handling horror

There are significant methodological issues raised by this kind of participant observation of young people's viewing. The presence of a middle-class adult in a context like the above is bound to change it. From the moment one is invited into such a situation, the experience comes to be *about* one's interactions with the participants, and one's 'reading' becomes partly a reading of their readings. Ultimately, it is impossible to gain unmediated access, or to know what it would have been like if one had *not* been there. Such accounts of participant observation are inevitably partial, and need to be complemented with other approaches – not that one can simply triangulate in order to achieve a fixed 'truth' about viewing practices. Nevertheless, they may at least begin to offer insights into what might have been going on for the participants, in a way that may be harder to achieve through interviews, for example.

At the same time, this kind of observation also represents a form of surveillance, and might well be perceived in this way by the participants themselves. As a researcher, I am necessarily in a similar position to some of the other adults (notably parents and teachers) who want to gain access to aspects of young people's viewing – aspects which, as I have indicated, gain much of their significance from the fact that they exclude outsiders and confirm peer-group identities.

I was interested in following up this comparatively 'spontaneous' group viewing, and in finding out more about the boys' attitudes to horror videos and their responses to adults' attempts to regulate their viewing. While group viewings of the kind I have described may be 'typical' in their way, there is definitely a sense in which (as I have implied) the presentation of self in such situations is heavily influenced by the need to live up to peer-group expectations. Was it possible that Colin, for example, was actually more afraid of horror films than he was letting on? And what sort of yardstick did he have to measure this against?

About a week later, I got to interview him on his own. It turned out that he had watched much 'stronger' films, made available through the black market connections that so many working-class young people in the inner city seem to be able to tap into. Here are some extracts from that interview:

> *JW:* Did you see lots of strong stuff when you were younger then?
> *Colin:* I saw them all – *Texas Chainsaw Massacre, Evil Dead, Driller Killer*, all them. They were pirates mostly.
> *JW:* Did you enjoy them?

Colin: Yeah // Except one. I think it was *The Burning*.[11] That bit with the shears got me.

JW: Where he cuts fingers off kids in the summer camp?

Colin: Yeah. It was weird, that. I suppose it gave me a few nightmares. (...) Different things get different people, I suppose.

JW: Did any of the cassettes have certs on them?

Colin: What's that?

JW: You know, 15, 18 ...

Colin: Oh like in the shops now? Didn't notice any.

JW: Do you notice them in the shops now?

Colin: Not really, except to see if it's any good. Like I mean, 18's better, more in it.

JW: Did you ever get refused by the men in the shop when you tried to get 18s?

Colin: Not really. Mark did. He looked young. The man [in the video store] asked him to get a letter from his dad saying he let him see 18s. Then it was all right.

JW: How old was Mark then?

Colin: About 12, 13, I suppose. (...)

JW: Is there any point to it [certification]?

Colin: Yeah, it winds us up! No, seriously, I suppose little kids shouldn't be watching nothing too strong or too scary.

JW: Such as?

Colin: I don't know. *Texas Chainsaw Massacre*, or something like that.

JW: But you watched that when you were only 10 or 11, you say.

Colin: Yeah, I suppose so.

JW: It's banned on video anyway, so maybe it's not a good example.

Colin: Oh, is it? Yeah, but you can get it if you want it. You can get anything you want really.

It is a big leap to say that Colin's views of horror were typical of his age and social class, although in the absence of other research, it seems fair to conclude that they were at least not untypical. While the audience for horror may in fact range much more widely – and the genre may well hold particular pleasures for female viewers[12] – there is clearly a subculture around horror which consists essentially of young, working-class, inner-city males. In this respect, perhaps, the video nasties campaign can be seen as more than merely a media hype. Teenagers like Colin *are* drawn to horror, and the coming of cheap, widely-available video versions in the 1980s simply provided the means of access – although in fact the 'worst case' horror viewers identified by the newspaper articles of the early 1980s were largely pre-teens.

As Colin's comments suggest, for some young people horror viewing almost takes on the status of a *rite de passage* in the early teenage years. (After that age, other activities such as trying to get into pubs and dating generally take over.) Certification, in so far as it is noticed at all, appears to exert a largely contradictory effect here, serving to mark out the 'stronger' material which is most valued. This is largely a video phenomenon. While there is obviously a long history of young people attempting to trick their way into cinemas to see 'forbidden' films, the current price of tickets effectively rules out the cinema as a regular leisure pursuit, at least for working-class kids in their early teens. On the other hand, television programming policy in Britain, especially up to the coming of Channel 4, was quite protective. Horror films would only be shown later in the evening – although of course time-shifting soon defeated that. Some horror films like *The Exorcist* or *Texas Chainsaw Massacre* (both still officially unavailable on video) would not be shown on television, but pirate video copies imported from America and Europe seem to be widely available, at least in cities. As Colin indicates, there are certainly shops that take a half-hearted, token approach to enforcement – although it may be comparatively few that really do carry 'banned' titles. Even less formal black-market networks are themselves affected by the passage of time, and by trends in the mainstream market.

All of Colin's friends said they had seen at least one of the *Nightmare on Elm Street* series (all of which are rated 18), though only two laid claim to more than three. However, the general consensus here was that Freddy Kruger was a 'wanker'. 'It's just for little kids, innit?' said Colin. 'All right when you're about ten or eleven,' added Steve, as if this was decades rather than a few years ago. Of course, horror is quintessentially the sort of material that one has to 'dare to see' (hence the time-honoured film poster campaigns along the lines of 'Don't watch this alone!') As a result, it is seen to be 'cool' to suggest that you have seen more horror films than you actually have and that you were not 'affected' or scared at all.[13] In so far as 'effects' are presumed to occur, these tend to be displaced (as they are by Colin here) on to 'little kids' much younger than oneself. Nevertheless, in this case, the videos the boys discussed were popular, legitimately available, commercial horror products, and there is little reason to suppose that they were unable to get hold of them.

Regulation in the home

As this suggests, official attempts to regulate horror viewing through certification and censorship are very difficult to effect. Without active parental effort, and the possibility of more 'failsafe' devices such as encrypting mechanisms for VCRs, video is effectively impossible to police – and the evidence suggests that such efforts are not widely made. It is possible that most parents consider regulating their children's access to video as a fairly low priority, even where they do not actively oppose it. The other struggles involved in bringing up teenagers are likely to appear much more important. Nevertheless, in considering parents' regulation of video use, one can glimpse the time-honoured game of parental control and adolescent resistance.

To the young people in this research, this was typically part of the broader struggle to get enough space, to get away from the demands of family life, and from the chores that busy parents try to pass on to them – and, above all at this age, from being asked to *talk* about problems and to reciprocate emotional overtures. As Dave said, when asked about his relations with the rest of his family, 'it all comes down to them not giving me hassles: if they'd just leave me alone, I wouldn't give them none.'

Although I was unable to observe family viewing at first hand, I did manage to gain some insight into this issue through interviews. The following account is based on interviews with Mark, one of the boys in the viewing group described above, and with his mother. I had told Mark to tell his mother that I was 'writing an article', although it is hard to say how Mrs Ford herself would have perceived this. As with the boys, the very notion that you are coming in to 'find out' something about them sets up expectations and establishes a power-relationship which inevitably determines what takes place.[14]

I visited Mark's council flat in the early evening. He had helped to arrange the interview, but had mysteriously been 'called away' when I arrived (I learned later that he had gone to the park to play football). The two-bedroom flat gave the appearance of being cluttered but cosy. An ironing board with a still-warm iron was set up in the middle of the living-room, but Mrs Ford was dividing her time between cooking a meal in the small adjoining kitchen and talking to me. A large old colour TV, with a rented video underneath, was left on while we talked. The six o'clock news was just finishing, but the sound was so low that it could not be heard. A small collection of videotapes, in leatherette 'bound book' style cases, was propped up against the television.

I asked about the videos. At first, Mrs Ford seemed to be saying that they weren't hers but her sons' (in addition to fourteen-year-old Mark, she had another son aged seventeen, who was out at work). However, as the conversation progressed, it turned out that several of them were hers: TV mini-series of the bodice-ripper, rich-and-famous variety, which she had taped from the TV with her son's help. 'He's very good with the machine,' she said, 'much better than I am. Well, they've grown up with it, haven't they? I get mixed up sometimes ... all the numbers.' Had Mark watched the mini-series while they were taping them? 'He watched a bit. They're not his sort of thing. He prefers fighting films – that and the sport.'

Later, I was able to ask Mark about these mini-series. He said he had watched quite a lot of them 'because they was there', but in the end had found them not to his taste. Quite possibly a key factor in persuading him to stop watching them, at least in the presence of his mother, was the way the scenes foregrounded a 'sophisticated' notion of passionate sex. Even if, in obeying the codes and conventions of the genre, as well as the fairly prudish moral constraints of American TV, the sex scenes were 'beginnings only' and relatively brief, they were too intrusive for Mark:

> *Mark:* They kept 'doing it' all the time! There was only one woman in it, she was a right whore, [she] kept whipping her clothes off everywhere, even in this bloke's office. She was old too. [The actress was in her early forties.]

Was there something specific about these familiar 'clinch and cut to bedroom' scenes – or was it more the viewing context, the danger of watching such scenes with his mum present, the threatening possibility of arousal breaking strongly held taboos about privacy and familial desires? Hence, perhaps, the afterthought on the age of the actress – the age of the male characters did not apparently seem to be relevant – as Mark's mother herself would probably have been in her late forties. I suggested to Mark that such scenes might be more fun if watched with his peers only. But that seemed to be missing the point too. The genre in which they came would not really appeal to him or his friends – the films were more an object of curiosity than staple viewing. Yet the highly stereotypical view of 'passion' (not really sex, as the films tend to avoid explicitness) seemed to be far from comforting to Mark. The 'impossible' bodies of the men, their designer suits, their unshakeable confidence with attentive, beautiful women – all of these seemed a very long way from the world of a slightly insecure fourteen-year-old living at home. Far from being some sort of 'ego ideal', the male leads were resented or satirised: the impossibility of 'competing' with them led Mark into a self-protective resistance to the text.[15]

However, Mark's actual viewing diet was more diverse than his mother's remark, quoted above, might suggest. Like his mother, Mark initially claimed that he watched sport and action films, and was surprised when he got a more empirically accurate idea of his viewing through a viewing diary. In terms of broadcast programmes, for example, it appeared that he still watched children's TV after school on a fairly regular basis. But it was the long Sunday afternoons in front of *The Big Match* – usually orchestrated around the wishes of his older brother, who also rented most of the Kung Fu films – that Mark's mum identified as 'typical' masculine viewing.

The other genre that featured regularly in the family's viewing was comedies, often the safe middle-ground for disparate viewers:

> *Mrs Ford:* I like the funny shows, we watch them together quite a lot. That David Jason [in *Only Fools and Horses*], he's funny. He's got such a cute face. I don't like swearing, though, especially from women. It [*Birds of a Feather*] goes too far sometimes.

Mark also confirmed that he liked *Only Fools and Horses*: it was his favourite show, 'all things considered'. He could not really remember watching *Birds of a Feather*, though he thought his mum liked it.

So did Mark feel that his mum attempted to shape or regulate his viewing? He couldn't really think of anything. 'Except blue stuff,' he added. 'She had a row with [the elder brother] once when she found he had some.' Did Mrs Ford have a sense of imposing limits?

> *Mrs Ford:* No, I don't mind really. He's sensible, doesn't get into fights or nothing. I don't mind if he watches TV. It keeps him out of trouble, doesn't it?

The 'obviousness' of this remark belies its compacted nature. In terms of the interview situation (see above), it positions me as some sort of teacher or social worker, who might need reassuring that Mark is not out of control. But there is also a sense of one parent talking to another – an assumption that I will understand implicitly how necessary it is to have a safe, reliable time-consumer/baby-sitter when the kids could otherwise be under your feet, or out on the streets, possibly bringing shame and hassle back into the home. Compared with the problems that young people are perceived to be prey to in their leisure, having them lolling about on the sofa is a small price to pay. The TV and the video come to be seen almost as a haven in a heartless world.

Video – a postmodern technology for a postmodern subject?

Ultimately, the driving force behind the increasing availability and use of video in recent years has been the market-led tendency towards reduction in the unit cost. However, as Raymond Williams has argued,[16] new technologies do not arise simply from 'internal' processes of research and development, nor are they simply generated by abstract 'market forces'. If we are not to lapse into a view of young people as merely passively manipulated by the leisure industry, we need to pay much closer attention to their *cultural* investments in contemporary media, and to the social processes in which they are situated. As Paul Willis *et al.* have argued, young people's use of cultural media in everyday life is characterised by diverse forms of 'symbolic creativity': 'The point for us is to try to understand the dynamic, precarious, virtual uses of symbols in common culture, not understanding the everyday through popular representation, but understanding popular representation in and through the everyday.'[17] Video comes into play, then, in a field where social agents (in this case, young people) are already creating meanings, rather than waiting to be 'filled up' or merely distracted.

Nevertheless, the *rate* of technological changes, and the concomitant speed with which young people adapt and react to them, need to be addressed in their own right. I am reminded of a conversation I had recently with an academic friend about my research into video. 'Video!' she said, mockingly. 'That's a bit out of date, we're at least three technologies on from that!' Although said half in jest, this does capture something that modern Western city dwellers may recognise – the sense that the world somehow seems to be 'speeding up' and, as it does so, there is less chance to grasp anything like the totality, or even the schematic outline of a totality. This 'nostalgia' for coherence and legibility is often cited as a key symptom of the 'postmodern condition'.

What underlies this discussion is of course the notion of video as a distinctively postmodern technology – a notion which has implications not merely in terms of the sites and practices of video (the 'where' and the 'how'), but also in terms of broader debates about changing conceptions of subjectivity. On the first of these issues, for example, Sean Cubitt's somewhat breathless – and definitely postmodernist – account of 'video culture'[18] usefully draws attention to the general shift from 'mass' forms of entertainment and recreation (for example, ballroom dancing, cinema and some sporting events) to more atomised, privatised forms such as television and video. Although video may occasionally be seen in the context of pub jukeboxes or 'rave' parties, and cassettes are traded and rented from high-street chains, Cubitt's argument that video is primarily a domestic, private medium is well taken.

The broader question of video's role in changing notions of subjectivity is inevitably harder to pin down. Marsha Kinder,[19] for example, argues that the new 'interactive media systems' made available by such things as advanced computer games represent very different processes of subject formation, that make TV *per se* seem almost 'nostalgic', while the cinema is prehistoric. As Angela McRobbie explains in her review of Kinder's book:

> Alongside this is a continual weaving of genres which enables the young viewer to experience the media complex not as discrete sets of segments and programmes, but as an endless flow of intertextual images and micro narratives. This process addresses him/her not as the idealised subject of Lacanian psychoanalysis but as the mutable, protean subject of postmodernity.[20]

Similar arguments might be made in relation to video (or, more accurately, video and allied technology), as making possible a different kind of 'text' which in turn calls forth a different kind of viewer. As Geoff Wood suggests: 'The alliterative techniques of fast-forward, rapid rewind, freeze frame, all make possible a different kind of viewing subject, so that narrative no longer offers the same kind of integrity.'[21]

Nevertheless, it is important to exercise some caution here. These notions of 'interactivity' and 'micro-narratives' do have some empirical purchase, as anybody who has played with a remote control would agree; and there is a tempting homology with the now-canonical idea of the split and de-centred subject. Nevertheless, there is a familiar risk here of overestimating the power of the media, and aggrandising its role in the constitution of subjectivity. The larger, partly institutionalised structures of the family, work, schooling, the economy, and so on may well serve as a counterweight to the atomising effects of the media, at least as posited here. Yet it is quite possible to agree with Wood that video offers the possibility of a different '*viewing* subject' without assuming a totally protean quality to all aspects of lived experience – in other words, to investigate the notion of a 'video sensibility' without necessarily extending that back to subjectivity itself.

As I have indicated, young people's use of video has become a focus of popular anxiety largely because it often occurs in situations where adults are actively excluded. In a sense, however, the same may be true of the much grander forms of theoretical speculation about 'video culture' and postmodernity alluded to here. As in so many other areas of media research, young people have become a focus of forms of concern and debate which often seem to bear little relation to the concrete realities of their lives, or to take account of their perspectives on the issues. In this respect, the growing phenomenon of video requires much more detailed, situated study of the kind begun in this chapter.[22]

Notes and references

1 *Journal of Sex Research*, 25: 1 (1988), 28-59.

2 See I. Reid, *Social Class Differences in Britain* (London, Fontana, 1989).

3 See Mark Levy and Barrie Gunter, *Home Video and the Changing Nature of the Television Audience* (London, Independent Broadcasting Authority, 1988); Mark Levy (ed.), *The VCR Age* (Newbury Park, Sage, 1989).

4 Levy and Gunter, *Home Video*.

5 For example, David Morley, *Family Television: Cultural Power and Domestic Leisure* (London, Comedia, 1986); James Lull, *World Families Watch Television* (Newbury Park, Sage, 1990).

6 See Martin Barker (ed.), *The Video Nasties* (London, Pluto, 1984).

7 G. Barlow and A. Hill (eds), *Video Violence and Children* (London, Hodder and Stoughton, 1985).

8 See the journal *Cultural Trends* (London, Policy Studies Institute, 1991).

9 British Board of Film Classification, *Annual Report* (1989).

10 More research is needed on the use of video remote controls. Although using replay and fast-forward facilities can enable the audience to 're-make' the text (see Geoff Wood, 'Frenzies of the visible', *Economy and Society* 21: 1 (1992), 58-74), this rarely saves much in terms of total viewing time. There is certainly an argument for this being seen as an activity in its own right, like 'channel hopping' or 'grazing'.

11 There is some irony here in the fact that the BBFC is about to pass *The Burning* on video. It will be the UK cinema version (which was itself cut), with only a few further cuts. The version that will be passed is therefore not significantly different from the film that circulated a decade ago, and that the VRA was partly designed to combat. At the moment, other notorious horror titles are being unearthed (such as *Zombie Flesh Eaters*) and some shops are already sporting display racks labelled with the category 'banned'.

12 See Carol Clover, *Men, Women and Chainsaws* (London, British Film Institute, 1992).

13 In the 'video nasties' research, Barlow and Hill (*Video Violence*) appear to have taken such claims at face value, although subsequent research has suggested they were very likely to be misleading (see Barker, *Video Nasties*).

14 Similar points apply here as in the account of the boys' video viewing. Valerie Walkerdine's account of viewing the film *Rocky II* with a working-class family makes some crucial points in this respect about the role of the researcher. She argues that the intellectualised view of popular culture and the voyeuristic approach to working-class viewers characteristic of this kind of research forms part of the 'will to truth' which both falsifies *and* validates the researcher's discourse. See 'Video replay: families, films and fantasy', in V. Burgin *et al.* (eds), *Formations of Fantasy* (London, Methuen, 1986); and see also Walkerdine's Chapter 4 in this volume.

15 There is more work to be done here on the pleasures for males of texts that are traditionally regarded as 'feminine': see, for example, Steve Craig (ed.), *Men, Masculinity and the Media* (London, Sage, 1992).

16 Williams, *Television: Technology and Cultural Form* (Glasgow, Fontana, 1974).

17 Willis *et al.*, *Common Culture: Symbolic Work at Play in the Everyday Cultures of the Young* (Milton Keynes, Open University Press, 1990), p. 6.

18 Cubitt, *Timeshift* (London, Comedia/Routledge, 1991).

19 Kinder, *Playing With Power in Movies, Television and Video Games* (Berkeley, University of California Press, 1992).

20 McRobbie, 'Game boys and girls', *Sight and Sound* (March 1992), 34-5.

21 Wood, 'Frenzies of the visible'.

22 One additional issue here relates to the part played by structures of power and privilege in structuring research agendas. While this chapter has lamented the scarcity of situated accounts of working-class video use, there are even fewer accounts of middle-class viewing practices. For example, it is possible that middle-class parents are significantly more anxious about regulating their children's viewing, and that this struggle intensifies as examinations loom and the danger of children 'dropping out' or otherwise failing to take their place in the elite comes to be perceived as a possibility. Indeed, for some media researchers, there may be an inevitable element of bad faith about this, not to say a dual standard: there may even be an implicit notion that if working-class kids either can't or won't 'better themselves' (for example via education), they might as well watch TV.

Conclusion:
re-reading audiences

A vital imaginative life, and the deep effort to describe new experience, are found in many others besides artists, and the communication of new descriptions and new meanings is carried out in many ways – in art, thought, science and in the ordinary social process. ...

The emphasis that matters is that there are, essentially, no 'ordinary' activities, if by 'ordinary' we mean the absence of creative interpretation and effort. Art is ratified, in the end, by the fact of creativity in all our living.

Raymond Williams, *The Long Revolution*[1]

Raymond Williams's argument here for the creativity of 'the ordinary social process' represents one of the founding principles of Cultural Studies. Williams rejects views of 'art' as something 'special and extraordinary', which should be set apart from everyday processes of communication and human interaction – views he sees as characteristic of modern, industrialised societies. Yet rather than arguing for the need simply to spread 'civilisation' to the masses, he offers a broader conception of art and creativity, that is not confined to the activities of a narrow elite. In this way, Williams argues, it may be possible to reconcile the more specialised notion of culture as 'creative activity' with the broader, anthropological notion of culture as 'a whole way of life'.

In this sense, Williams's argument is much more *radical* than those of his contemporaries – for example, the attempts to import critical standards derived from the traditional arts to the study of popular culture, or to distinguish between the authentic (or organic) forms of 'folk culture' and the artificial (or imposed) forms of 'mass culture'.[2] On the contrary, Williams insists on the importance of studying 'creative human activity, not only in art and intellectual work, but also in institutions and forms of behaviour', and of addressing 'the relationship between elements in a whole way of life'.[3] Yet at the same time, he does not seem to

suggest that notions of artistic or social value should simply be jetti-
soned: rather, he wants to change the terms by which these values are
defined in the first place.

However, Williams's observations are not merely a set of recommendations for academic study. They form part of a more comprehen-
sive project for political change, and an attempt to define the role that
culture might play within it. For Williams, this will involve a fundamental democratisation of cultural institutions, including those of the 'mass'
media. Yet it is public education in its broadest sense, 'designed to
express and create the values of an educated democracy and a common
culture',[4] which lies at the very centre of that project. In this concluding
chapter, I want to draw upon the studies contained in the book in order
to indicate some of the possibilities and limitations of this emphasis on
everyday 'creativity', and to consider its political implications in terms of
both research and education.

Creative audiences?

In their recent book *Common Culture*, Paul Willis and his colleagues
mount an argument for the 'symbolic creativity' of everyday life which
has a great deal in common with that of Raymond Williams.[5] Drawing
on work undertaken by a team of researchers for the Gulbenkian Foundation enquiry into 'the cultural activities of young people',[6] the book
adopts a broad conception of culture, which extends well beyond a
concern with artistic or media texts, to encompass a very wide range of
social practices.

Willis asserts that by insisting on a 'self-interested view of elite
creativity', the traditional 'high' arts, and the institutions which support
them, have served to exclude the majority of young people. By contrast,
he argues,

> we insist that there is a vibrant symbolic life and symbolic creativity in
> everyday life, everyday activity and everyday expression – even if it is
> sometimes invisible, looked down on or spurned. ... Young people are all
> the time expressing or attempting to express something about their poten-
> tial or actual *cultural significance*. This is the realm of living common
> culture.[7]

This 'symbolic creativity' is one of a number of forms of 'necessary
symbolic work', which are seen to be a condition of human communication, and thus of humanity itself. Symbolic work and creativity, Willis
argues, involve the production of new meanings and identities (both

individual and collective), and thereby 'develop and affirm our active senses of our own vital capacities, the powers of the self and how they might be applied to the cultural world'.[8]

Yet it is primarily in the domain of leisure, in the attempt 'to find and make identity outside the realm of work',[9] that this creativity is expressed. In their use of commercial cultural forms, and more generally through pleasure and 'fun', young people are seen as creatively seeking 'to establish their presence, identity and meaning'.[10] This is a dynamic, sensuous process, based on what Willis calls 'grounded aesthetics' – 'a process whereby meanings are attributed to symbols and practices and where symbols and practices are selected, re-selected, highlighted and re-composed to resonate further appropriated and particularized meanings'.[11]

Thus, Willis argues that young people's use of 'cultural media', such as television, video and magazines, needs to be regarded as an essentially active process. The notion that texts contain fixed messages which are simply imposed upon audiences is therefore rejected. Meanings are made in the process of reception, and are thus diverse and unpredictable: 'Viewers, listeners and readers do their own symbolic work on a text and create their own relationships to technical means of reproduction and transfer. There is a kind of cultural production all within consumption.'[12] Willis accordingly rejects what he calls 'armchair semiotics' based on textual analysis, in favour of the *situated* study of 'the social relations of consumption' – 'not understanding the everyday through popular representation but understanding popular representation in and through the everyday'.[13]

These broad arguments would probably be accepted by the majority of Cultural Studies researchers. *Common Culture* acknowledges, in my view very productively, some important cultural and technological developments in young people's relationship with the media.[14] It draws attention to the potential of new digital technologies, for example in the fields of music and video, which offer significant opportunities for young people to become cultural producers rather than 'merely consumers'. It rejects the notion of young people as dupes and victims of the 'culture industry', arguing that they are 'the most sophisticated "readers" of images and media of any group in society',[15] and points to the ways in which their growing sophistication has been recognised by the media industries themselves.[16]

Yet *Common Culture* is also symptomatic of some of the broader problems with the view of young people as 'active readers'. Although the book does not consistently indulge in the kind of simple-minded celebration of popular culture that has been widely condemned in recent years,[17] it does at times come alarmingly close to it. Willis's highly rhetorical arguments about the 'inherently democratic impulses' of common culture, and his description of the way in which symbolic work and creativity 'eat away at traditional and received certainties', producing 'the possibilities of oppositional, independent or alternative symbolizations of the self'[18] are far from adequately supported by the evidence he presents. By and large, the ethnographic data is used unproblematically, as a form of illustration that somehow speaks for itself: the social context of the research, and the social differences between subjects, often disappear in favour of broad assertions about 'young people' as a whole.[19] Despite the insistence on remaining 'grounded', the theoretical arguments repeatedly take off into the ether, leaving the evidence well behind. As a result, Willis's generalised enthusiasm for young people's 'vitality', 'imagination' and 'discrimination', and his claims for its political significance, carry a distinct air of wishful thinking.

At the very least, this insistent emphasis on 'creativity' runs the risk of understating the *routinised* nature of cultural activity, and the extent to which a great deal of media use is casual and uncommitted. Far from being characterised by enormous amounts of emotional or intellectual investment, for much of the time the media are merely a form of 'moving wallpaper' or background noise, a way of passing the time when you are too tired – or just can't be bothered – to do anything else.[20] While *Common Culture* occasionally acknowledges the boredom and frustration which characterise the lives of many young people (and particularly the growing numbers of unemployed), it tends to assume that their attempts to overcome this are automatically effective. *Personal* psychological forms of empowerment (for example through fantasy or symbolic 'experimentation' with new identities) are implicitly seen to be synonymous with collective *political* empowerment.[21]

These problems are particularly apparent in those sections of the book that deal directly with aspects of the everyday life of young men. While Willis acknowledges that 'pub culture', street fighting and sports may serve as arenas in which 'conventional gender identities and definitions' are reproduced, his final insistence is on the 'creativity' that they involve.[22] The ways in which these activities exclude and constrain the lives of young women appear to be a secondary consideration. 'Creativity' – like 'pleasure' – comes to be seen as something which is inherently positive, while 'everyday life' becomes an unproblematic site of 'cultural production'.

The contrast here with Willis's earlier work *Learning to Labour*[23] is particularly striking. There, Willis pointed to the way in which working-class boys' resistance to schooling represented *both* a rejection of 'official' values and a kind of preparation for a life of manual labour. In a sense, the 'lads' were actively socialising themselves into class membership: their 'resistance' to dominant power-relationships led not to a transformation of those relationships, but on the contrary to their reinforcement. By contrast, *Common Culture*'s emphasis on the 'creativity' of working-class culture runs the risk of underestimating the ways in which it has been formed by its relation to the dominant culture – and of ignoring, both at an individual and a social level, the 'hidden injuries of class'.[24] Compared with the more complex account provided by *Learning to Labour*, the later book has a much weaker sense of the *political* contradictions and limitations of working-class 'youth culture'. In this respect, its enthusiasm for young people's everyday creativity runs the risk of being merely patronising.

Similarly, Willis's argument for a positive re-evaluation of the market raises more problems than it solves – and here the contrasts with Raymond Williams's arguments are particularly marked. While it may be true to say that 'the main seeds for everyday cultural development' are to be found in 'the commercial provision of cultural commodities' rather than in the institutions of 'high art',[25] it remains important to consider other alternatives. Does it still make sense to talk, for example, in terms of democratising the media, or in terms of social responsibility, diversity or even 'quality'?[26] What role might media institutions play in struggles to being about a society in which young people's 'creativity' is more fully recognised and supported? While the 'cultural optimism' of Willis's argument is at times uplifting, it could easily lead to a form of political complacency, in which the struggles for media representation and access which have traditionally been the concern of the left come to seem irrelevant, if not pointless.

In responding to some of these points, Willis argues against those 'old-fashioned Marxist rectitudes' which see the vanguard party 'unmasking' the masses and thereby bringing about the socialist millennium. He argues for the importance of leisure as a site of political activity, as against the traditional leftist focus on work, asserting that 'ordinary people must make themselves as culturally producing citizens before they make socialism'.[27] Yet if such changes are necessary (and Willis seems to assume they are), how are they to be brought about?

Ultimately, the wider political project which is offered here is one which may relate much more directly to the class and institutional position of left-wing academics than it does to the realities of political change. Demonstrating the 'creativity' of 'ordinary people' is only relevant if it is assumed that the opposite argument has any purchase. In this respect, the celebratory approach adopted by *Common Culture* and some other recent work in this field is explicitly intended to counter a view of young people as dupes of the media, helplessly subordinated by the 'dominant ideology'. It is a response, in effect, to the legacy of elitism on the left – a move in a debate which is internal to the left, and mainly to left academics at that. In the case of Media Studies, for example, the legacy of *Screen* theory provided a definition of academic theorists and avant-garde cultural producers as a kind of vanguard party of cultural struggle. Yet the imaginary solidarity with 'the people' that is apparent in some recent work – albeit a solidarity expressed in language that most people would find wholly incomprehensible – is merely the opposite side of the same coin.[28] The rhetoric of this work is one in which the testimony of 'ordinary people' is often used unproblematically, as a guarantee of the truth of the academic theorist who claims to speak 'on the people's behalf'. It is assumed that 'they' need 'us' to defend them: and yet 'we' also need 'them' to validate our political credentials.

So where does this defence of 'ordinary people' take us in terms of political strategy? And what role might 'ordinary people' themselves play in such a strategy? In accordance with the aims of the project on which it is based, *Common Culture* makes some general suggestions for changes in arts funding policy, and describes a few specific instances of the new kinds of institutions and 'cultural exchanges' that might emerge.[29] Yet the implications of such developments for the lives of the majority of young people would be at best marginal. What is effectively absent here is any sustained attention to those institutions – schools and colleges – in which young people are compelled (and in some cases actively choose) to spend significant amounts of their waking lives. Here again, the contrast with Williams is striking. Education seems to be defined too easily as a site of social reproduction, and as simply irrelevant to the concerns of working-class youth.[30] Willis is rightly scathing about the use of media in schools as a way of 'keeping kids quiet by feeding and doping them up with popular cultural forms'.[31] But media education, as it has developed in schools and colleges over the past twenty years, has been much more constructive and effective than this would suggest. Of course, education is not the only possible form of engagement here, but it is undeniably one of the most significant. And while it would clearly be naïve to suggest that education is an empty space, in which political interventions can be made directly and unproblematically, it would seem equally naïve to ignore it. These are issues to which I shall return in the final section of this chapter.

Situating audiences: some implications for audience research

In arguing for the analysis of culture to address 'the relationship between elements in a whole way of life', Raymond Williams was attempting to widen the focus beyond a narrow concentration on artistic productions or texts. By implication, he points to the need to study those forms, not in the abstract, as objects of 'aesthetic appreciation', but in the context of their social circulation and use. At the same time, he cautions against a deterministic approach: it is not merely, he suggests, 'a question of relating the art to the society, but of studying all the activities and their interrelations, without any concession of priority to any one of them we may choose to abstract'.[32] In practice, Williams's own analysis tends to concentrate much more on the *institutional* contexts of cultural production and reception.[33] Yet the outline of cultural analysis that he offers clearly points to the need for the *situated* study of popular culture, and of media audiences, as part of this broader project. Despite its limitations, *Common Culture* does represent an important instance of this approach, and one which is at least partly based on detailed empirical research.

The studies collected in this volume illustrate this situated approach in different ways. The analyses of 'family viewing' by Chris Richards, Valerie Walkerdine and Marie Gillespie, for example, or the participant observation account of video use provided by Julian Wood, contain evidence gathered through direct observation. In other cases – for example, in the chapters by myself and Gemma Moss – the account is 'at one remove' from the activity itself: here, the emphasis is on how the meanings of reading or viewing are defined in peer-group discussion, and the social functions those definitions serve in that context. Yet what unites the contributions is a sense that reading – *and* talking about what we read – are social processes. The meanings and pleasures readers derive from texts are thus partly determined by the social contexts in which they are consumed and circulated, and by the ways in which readers themselves define those contexts (which of course include the context of research itself). As these studies indicate, these contexts are characterised by power-relationships of various forms – for example between adults and children, between boys and girls, between older and younger children, and indeed between researchers and their subjects.

Broadly speaking, therefore, the approach adopted here reflects the gradual shift of attention in audience studies, away from 'readings' of specific texts towards an emphasis on the social contexts in which reading (or viewing) is situated. As advocates of this approach have argued, media use cannot be seen in isolation, as a 'variable' whose influence can be extracted from other aspects of social life. More recently, however, this move has extended into arguments for a much more inclusive 'ethnography of everyday life', in which media use is seen in the context of a wider range of other 'cultural determinants'[34] – although there has been very little research which has actually come close to fulfilling this ambitious brief.[35]

However, the danger here is that important distinctions between different aspects of this process may become blurred. In the case of *Common Culture*, for example, essentially the same set of arguments about 'symbolic creativity' is sustained across accounts of a very broad range of activities, including watching TV and video, reading magazines, playing and listening to music, making and shopping for clothes, playing sports, fighting in the street and drinking in pubs. Likewise, John Fiske develops an account of popular culture as a form of 'resistance' to dominant ideology which runs through such diverse phenomena as video games, shopping malls, ripped jeans, pop videos and TV quiz shows.[36] Yet, at the risk of stating the obvious, these are clearly very different *kinds* of activities, and we need to be wary of collapsing the distinctions between them.

Thus, however much we may want to argue that cultural 'consumption' is in fact an active, productive process, it is clearly different in kind from cultural production. For example, playing music, whether in the privacy of your bedroom or in public in a band, is very different from listening to music, which is different again from dancing to it. New technologies may have blurred some of these distinctions, but they have not abolished them: there remains an important difference between compiling a cassette of songs to listen to on your Walkman and 'sampling' a bass line or a drum pattern to use in your 'own' piece of music. Of course, it is possible to analyse young people's cultural productions in their own right, or as a means of gaining insights into their readings of other cultural products, as Julian Sefton-Green does here.[37] In the case of some media forms, it may be a realistic option for some consumers to become producers, as Martin Barker indicates in his case-study of 'Alan'

– and this may well play a more general part in forming readers' relationships with the medium, even where they do not themselves pursue this option. Nevertheless, these options are clearly more possible with some media forms than with others, for reasons which are ultimately to do with technological and institutional constraints.

Likewise, it is important to insist on the difference between representation and reality. The media may well afford opportunities for experimentation with alternative identities, as Willis and his colleagues suggest, but they do so primarily at the level of *representation*. For example, Valerie Walkerdine points to the ways in which the fantasies of the film *Annie* offer the Porta family a way of dealing with difficult aspects of their lives – although they can only offer a negative judgement of the mother's role. Likewise, Martin Barker describes the ways in which 2000 AD offers 'Mary' a sense of hope which goes beyond the 'pessimistic structure of feeling' of the text – yet he is careful to describe this as 'an act of *personal* empowerment'. These accounts offer powerful explanations of what such texts 'do' for their readers. Yet, as in the case of *Common Culture*, we need to avoid the easy assumption that these semiotic struggles and resistances have political consequences, and that those consequences are necessarily 'progressive'.

Furthermore, it is important to distinguish between one's experience of the media and one's representation of that experience to others.[38] For example, as a number of these studies indicate, what children say about what frightens or disturbs them may not correspond to what they felt at the time of viewing. There may be a considerable social pressure to claim that one was unaffected, as may be the case for example for the boys in my own study, or for Julian Sefton-Green's young writer, 'Ponyboy'. On the other hand, as Chris Richards implies, talk itself may be a particularly useful way of 'handling' readings or responses which we may find uncomfortable or unpleasant. As John Fiske suggests,[39] there is likely to be a dynamic interplay between 'individual' and 'social' readings, and one might well argue that the distinction is theoretically and methodologically impossible to sustain. In the end, we may simply be unable to gain access to 'individual' readings, even through observation: certainly in the case of group viewings, as Julian Wood's account implies, how individuals behave may not necessarily be any more reliable than what they say 'after the event', whether to each other or to a researcher.

On one level, this reinforces the need for self-reflexivity in research, and the need to take account of the research context. Despite their theoretical commitments, Cultural Studies researchers have often adopted an empiricist approach, in which audience data – and particularly talk – is taken at face value, as 'evidence' of how people think or behave.[40] In some instances, data is reduced to the level of illustration, and the connections between theory and evidence are asserted rather than developed through a close analysis of the material itself. By contrast, many of the studies in this volume take a more cautious approach, demonstrating how the power-relationships between researchers and their 'subjects' – and between subjects themselves – influence the status of the data that is produced. Close interrogation of the data points to inconsistencies and contradictions, which relate in turn to the different 'subject positions' and 'discursive strategies' speakers adopt.

Nevertheless, one of the obvious problems with this emphasis on 'situating' the audience is that it runs the risk of neglecting the *specificity* of the media, both at the level of texts and of the institutional contexts in which they are produced and circulated. There is a danger that the media become almost incidental, a mere pretext for a much broader study of discourse and social relationships. Yet, for some of the reasons I have indicated, there is surely a meaningful distinction to be maintained between an inclusive sense of culture as a 'whole way of life' and a narrower view of culture as (for example) 'symbolic forms'.[41] We need to avoid simply collapsing the specific properties of 'media' into the broader, and inevitably less precise, concept of 'culture'.

Indeed, as media researchers pay ever closer attention to the texture of everyday life, there is a danger that some of the other 'elements' Raymond Williams refers to will be ignored. As I noted in my introduction, debates about the 'power of the media' have become increasingly polarised in recent years. Audience studies have become increasingly divorced from other forms of media analysis, and there is a considerable amount of mutual caricature.[42] Disciplinary specialisms are inevitable, of course. Yet the urgent need at present is to attempt to reintegrate the various concerns of media research – with institutions, texts and audiences – and to acknowledge the dynamic, shifting relationships between them. As Graham Murdock has argued, 'we need to conceptualise the relations between the material and discursive organisation of culture without reducing one to the other'.[43]

Indications of this move are inevitably very partial here. Nevertheless, far from neglecting 'the power of the text', many of the studies in this collection pay close attention to the ways in which texts invite (or indeed seek to prevent) particular meanings and pleasures. The studies by Marie Gillespie, Martin Barker and Valerie Walkerdine, for example, certainly attribute 'power' to the text, although they suggest that this will be dependent on the institutional contexts in which it is read. In the case of Marie Gillespie's Hindu family, for example, the mother actively uses the text in what amounts to a pedagogic process, designed to reinforce its particular cultural values. By contrast, Valerie Walkerdine's analysis suggests that the video *Annie* serves as a 'relay point' for psychic tensions and conflicts within the family, and that the mother seeks to resist the version of events that it offers. In other cases, the institutional parameters of the context in which the text is read and discussed (for example of the home or the school) may result in an apparently 'subversive' celebration of pleasures (for example in 'violence') which are distinctly less than 'progressive'.

Nevertheless, this is also true in the case of studies that are less obviously 'led' by single texts. The romantic fiction chosen by Gemma Moss's readers, or the 'masculine' texts described by the boys in my own and Julian Sefton-Green's studies, clearly speak to established gender identities, and set parameters on how they are defined. Yet what also emerges here is a rejection of the behaviourist notion that texts simply 'condition' young people into fixed gender identities. As Chris Richards notes, this process may involve active choices, and the conscious rejection of alternative possibilities. Yet these identities are never simply achieved once and for all: there is a constant process of negotiation, in which contradictions and insecurities have to be managed or avoided, and in which the media may offer challenge as well as reinforcement. Furthermore, as Gemma Moss argues, individuals have 'reading histories' that will inevitably be diverse, and in which particular texts or genres become part of a broader 'social system' of reading.

The institutional forms of production and distribution also exert constraints on these processes, although they are inevitably perceived here in rather more distant ways. Martin Barker, however, argues strongly for the need to situate the phenomenon of 'fandom' in the broader context of changes in the comics industry, and its attempts to define and control its relationship with readers. Similarly, Julian Wood locates the social use of video within the context of wider commercial and technological developments, and points to some of the contradictory effects of state regulation.

Taken together, then, these studies point to the limitations of viewing texts as infinitely 'polysemic' and of assuming that audience readings automatically 'resist' or exceed the intentions of producers.

They should caution us against an easy celebration of the 'symbolic creativity' of audiences, and the assumption that this 'creativity' necessarily produces political consequences – let alone those that might be seen as 'progressive'.

Learning cultures: some implications for education

Advocates of Cultural Studies have often been keen to present it as an essentially *political* project, whose relevance extends beyond the narrow confines of the academy. Yet an illusory identification with 'the people' can easily become a form of political posturing, which is no more effective than the vanguardist position which it has increasingly come to replace. Celebrating the 'creativity' of ordinary people may appear to be a more positive approach than lamenting their helpless subordination to the 'dominant ideology'. At least, it might make 'us' feel better about things – although whether it makes any difference for 'them' is certainly debatable. Yet there remains a risk here that more concrete and immediate possibilities for political intervention will continue to be neglected. In particular, Cultural Studies has been remarkably reluctant to reflect upon its own status as an *educational* practice. The pedagogical relationships between academics and students, the ways in which students are 'socialised' into the subject and indeed the ways in which they read Cultural Studies texts have effectively been ignored. Yet students are also members of educational 'audiences' – and they may often be much more 'active' and 'resisting' than their teachers might wish.[44]

However, the kind of work represented in this book also has particular implications for the teaching of Media and Cultural Studies to young people in schools. In this context, many of the dilemmas I have outlined take on a different, and more urgent, light. Against the background of increasingly reactionary developments in educational policy – for example, the impending revision of the National Curriculum for English – it is even more vital to insist on the importance of popular cultural media in young people's lives, and the need to abandon atrophied and elitist notions of art and culture. Yet the debate about the teaching of culture in schools needs to move beyond the narrow preoccupation with questions of artistic value in which it is currently framed. It is not a matter of having to 'choose' between Shakespeare and situation comedy, as Tory commentators appear to suggest. On the contrary, there is a need for a much more fundamental reconsideration of the *purpose* of teaching about either.

Teaching about popular culture has often been regarded as a form of 'inoculation'. For the literary critic F. R. Leavis and his colleagues,[45] teaching about advertising and the popular press was seen as a central element in 'the training of critical awareness'. By exposing the 'crude emotional falsity' and 'illusory values' of popular culture, it was argued, students would come to recognise the inherent superiority of great art and literature. Yet despite their rejection of Leavisism, many advocates of media education appear to have adopted a similar approach. The 'radical' version of media education which was prevalent in the 1970s and 1980s was largely based on a view of young people as passive victims of ideological manipulation. Media education was seen as a form of 'demystification', which would remove the veils of illusion from before their eyes and reveal 'alternative realities' suppressed by the media.[46] This approach inevitably implies a 'traditional' teacher-centred peda-gogy: only by training students in the 'objective analysis' of media texts and providing them with information about the covert operations of capitalist media institutions would it be possible to free them from the false ideologies the media were seen to contain and promote.

This 'radical' version of media education has often coexisted with a more 'progressive' approach. Far from regarding young people as 'dupes' of media ideologies, this approach has much in common with the celebratory account partly represented by *Common Culture*. Media education is regarded here as a 'validation' of aspects of students' cul-tures which are traditionally excluded from the school curriculum. This approach is much more student-centred: the students are now the 'ex-perts', while the teacher is no longer the main source of authority. The emphasis here is on 'experiential learning', on students exploring their own subjective responses through collaborative group work and practi-cal media production.

Debates about the pedagogy of media education in schools have often been caught in a tension between these two contrasting positions[47] – although predictably, very little of this debate bears much relation to the realities of classroom practice.[48] Here, and in syllabuses and teaching materials, there are often awkward tensions between these two ap-proaches – for example, between the insistence on an 'objective' body of radical knowledge and the attempt to adopt more open-ended teaching strategies. Teachers are often careful to assert that 'there are no right answers', while clearly believing that there are.[49] The emphasis on 'de-mystification' has tended to result in a propagandist style of teaching, in which 'politically correct' analyses are simply imposed on students. This approach is all too often perceived by working-class students as an attack on what they regard as their 'own' cultures – as yet another instance of middle-class teachers seeking to command assent to their views of the world, while simultaneously claiming to be acting on the students' behalf.[50] Yet the 'progressive' approach has often seemed to confirm students' (and indeed other teachers') perceptions of media education as a 'soft option': while students may find it enjoyable, it is rarely seen to involve much 'real work', let alone much actual learning. While teachers may perceive themselves to be 'validating' students' cultures, it is not at all clear that students themselves perceive this to be happening, or even to be necessary in the first place. Furthermore, giving space to students to explore their own cultural concerns often results in material which is ideologically (and indeed practically) very hard to handle.[51] Ultimately, this approach runs the risk of simply leaving students where they are.

However, recent classroom-based research and curriculum development work in media education has begun to indicate the possibility of a more productive approach to teaching and learning, which in some respects moves beyond this tension between 'radical' and 'progressive' perspectives. This approach is based on a more dynamic and dialectical relationship between theory and practice, and between different language modes: it stresses the central importance of reflection as a means of enabling students to make their existing knowledge explicit, and to begin to reformulate and move beyond it. The work of the Russian psychologist Vygotsky, in particular, has been seen to offer a theory of learning and a model of the development of conceptual understanding which is of considerable relevance in this respect.[52]

Nevertheless, one of the most significant absences here is of any detailed understanding of what young people *already* know about the media, and how this might relate to the new knowledge made available by teachers. As I have implied, both 'radical' and 'progressive' approaches to media education appear to be based on simplistic theories of young people's relationship with the media. While the 'radical' view of young people as passive victims in need of ideological salvation is no longer as prevalent as it used to be, the celebratory approach adopted by 'progressive' versions of media education does not ultimately appear to offer a satisfactory alternative.

For these reasons, empirical research into young people's relationship with the media, of the kind represented in this book, should play a central role in the development of such new approaches to media education. Yet the value of such research will depend crucially on the extent to which it is able to explain and respond to the concrete dilemmas of teachers and indeed of students themselves. Ultimately, such dilemmas will not be resolved by mere abstract theorising, or by research which remains at a safe distance from the messy complexities of classrooms and of students' lives. Cultural Studies has often retreated from such complexities, preferring the grand rhetoric of 'cultural struggle' and the seductive generalities of theory. It is time for it to recognise its responsibilities, not just as an academic or political practice, but also as an *educational* one.

Notes and references

1 Williams, *The Long Revolution* (London, Chatto and Windus, 1961), pp. 24, 37.

2 See, for example, Stuart Hall and Paddy Whannel, *The Popular Arts* (London, Hutchinson, 1964) and Richard Hoggart, *The Uses of Literacy* (London, Chatto and Windus, 1959).

3 Williams, *The Long Revolution*, pp. 42, 46.

4 *ibid.*, p. 115.

5 Willis *et al.*, *Common Culture: Symbolic Work at Play in the Everyday Cultures of the Young* (Milton Keynes, Open University Press, 1990).

6 The report to the Gulbenkian Foundation was published simultaneously as Paul Willis and team, *Moving Culture: An Inquiry into the Cultural Activities of Young People* (London, Calouste Gulbenkian Foundation, 1990).

7 Willis *et al.*, *Common Culture* p. 2.

8 *ibid.*, p. 22.

9 *ibid.*, p. 16.

10 *ibid.*, p. 2.

11 *ibid.*, p. 21.

12 *ibid.*, p. 20

13 *ibid.*, p. 6.

14 For further discussion of this, see David Buckingham, *Changing Literacies: Media Education and Modern Culture* (London, Tufnell Press, 1993).

15 Willis *et al.*, *Common Culture*, p. 30.

16 See also Mica Nava and Orson Nava, 'Discriminating or duped? Young people as consumers of advertising/art', *Magazine of Cultural Studies*, 1 (1990), 15-21.

17 Notably, of course, in the debates around John Fiske's recent work: see my introduction, note 35.

18 Willis *et al.*, *Common Culture*, p. 139.

19 For critiques of this tendency, see David Harris, *From Class Struggle to the Politics of Pleasure* (London, Routledge, 1992), and David Buckingham, 'What are words worth? Interpreting children's talk about television', *Cultural Studies*, 5: 2 (1991), 228-44. In line with the tradition of youth culture studies, *Common Culture* barely considers the very different position of middle-class youth.

20 See Conrad Lodziak, *The Power of Television* (London, Frances Pinter, 1986); Joke Hermes, 'On media, meaning and everyday life', paper delivered to the International Television Studies Conference (London, 1991).

21 Again, this is a recurring issue in the debate around Fiske: see particularly Jim Bee, 'First citizen of the semiotic democracy?', *Cultural Studies*, 3: 3 (1989), 353-9.

22 For example, Willis *et al.*, *Common Culture*, p. 115.

23 Paul Willis, *Learning to Labour: How Working Class Kids Get Working Class Jobs* (Farnborough, Saxon House, 1977).

24 R. Sennett and R. Cobb, *The Hidden Injuries of Class* (Cambridge University Press, 1972)

25 Willis *et al.*, *Common Culture*, p. 129.

26 These issues do get raised briefly in *Common Culture* (for example, on pp. 37-8), although the tone here is somewhat at odds with the overall argument. For a thoughtful discussion of these issues, see Charlotte Brunsdon, 'Problems with quality', *Screen*, 31: 1 (1990), 67-90.

27 Willis *et al.*, *Common Culture*, pp. 159-60.

28 This tension is particularly apparent in Lawrence Grossberg, Cary Nelson and Paula Treichler (eds.), *Cultural Studies* (London, Routledge, 1992): see particularly the contributions by John Fiske and Simon Frith.

29 These are spelt out in slightly more specific terms in Chapter 8 of Willis *et al.*, *Moving Culture*.

30 Willis *et al.*, *Common Culture*, pp. 147-8.

31 Willis *et al.*, *Moving Culture*, p. 60.

32 Williams, *The Long Revolution*, p. 45.

33 For example, in Williams, *The Long Revolution* and *Television: Technology and Cultural Form* (Glasgow, Fontana, 1974).

34 These arguments are made, for example, in Janice Radway, 'Reception study: ethnography and the problems of dispersed audiences and nomadic subjects', *Cultural Studies*, 2: 3 (1988), 359-76; Roger Silverstone, 'Let us then return to the murmuring of everyday practices: a note on Michel de Certeau, television and everyday life', *Theory Culture and Society*, 6: 1 (1989), pp. 77-94: and Ien Ang and Joke Hermes, 'Gender and/in media consumption', in James Curran and Michael Gurevitch, *Mass Media and Society* (London, Edward Arnold, 1991). The influence of the French social theorist Michel de Certeau is apparent here: see his *The Practice of Everyday Life* (Berkeley, University of California Press, 1984).

35 The recent work of David Morley and Roger Silverstone probably comes closest: see their piece 'Domestic communication: technologies and meanings', *Media, Culture and Society*, 13: 1 (1990), 31-55.

36 John Fiske, *Reading the Popular* and *Understanding Popular Culture* (both London, Unwin Hyman, 1989).

37 See also Greg Philo, *Seeing and Believing: The Influence of Television* (London, Routledge, 1990) – although, as Julian Sefton-Green notes in his contribution here, Philo's study tends to collapse these distinctions, taking production data as evidence of the ideological effects of consumption.

38 In his contribution here, Martin Barker argues for a tripartite model of 'reading', as does John Corner in his article 'Meaning, genre and context; the problematics of "public knowledge" in the new audience studies' (in Curran and Gurevitch, *Mass Media and Society*). The problem with this, it seems to me, is both theoretical and

methodological. Studies of children learning to read, for example, have questioned this separation of 'top-down' and 'bottom-up' processes (see, for example, the work of Frank Smith or the Goodmans). Quite how these processes could be isolated for the purpose of study is also problematic.

39 In *Television Culture* (London, Methuen, 1987), for example on pp. 105-7.

40 See Buckingham, 'What are words worth?'

41 See John B. Thompson, *Ideology and Modern Culture* (Cambridge, Polity, 1990).

42 See Buckingham, *Children Talking Television*, Chapter 11.

43 Graham Murdock, 'Cultural studies at the crossroads', *Australian Journal of Communication*, 16 (1989), pp. 37-49. For a parallel argument, see Thompson, *Ideology and Modern Culture*.

44 Harris, in *From Class Struggle to the Politics of Pleasure*, makes some important and amusing observations on this issue.

45 See, for example, F. R. Leavis and Denys Thompson, *Culture and Environment: The Training of Critical Awareness* (London, Chatto and Windus, 1933); Denys Thompson (ed.), *Discrimination and Popular Culture* (Harmondsworth, Penguin, 1964).

46 See Len Masterman, *Teaching About Television* (London, Macmillan, 1980) and *Teaching the Media* (London, Comedia, 1985). For critiques of Masterman's approach, see David Buckingham, 'Against demystification', *Screen*, 27: 5, 80-95: and Cary Bazalgette, 'The politics of media education', in M. Alvarado and O. Boyd-Barrett (eds), *Media Education: An Introduction* (London, British Film Institute, 1992).

47 For overviews of these debates, see David Lusted, 'Why pedagogy?', *Screen*, 27: 5 (1986), 2-14; and David Buckingham, 'Media education: from pedagogy to practice', in D. Buckingham (ed.), *Watching Media Learning, Making Sense of Media Education* (London, Falmer, 1990).

48 See Buckingham, *Watching Media Learning*.

49 See David Buckingham, Peter Fraser and Netia Mayman, 'Stepping into the void: beginning classroom research in media education', in Buckingham, *Watching Media Learning*

50 For discussions of this issue, see Judith Williamson, 'How does girl number twenty understand ideology?', *Screen Education* 40 (1981/2), 80-7; David Buckingham, 'Against demystification'; Phil Cohen, 'The perversions of inheritance', in P. Cohen and H. S. Bains (eds), *Multi-Racist Britain* (London, Macmillan, 1988). Here again, however, it is important to acknowledge that these processes will be very different for middle-class students; James Donald, for example, suggests that media education may be perceived by such students as 'simply an initiation into the new elect of justified sinners, the culturally undoped' (in his review of Allen, *Channels of Discourse* and Fiske, *Television Culture* in *Screen*, 31: 1 (1990), 113-18).

51 For an eloquent discussion of this issue, see Chris Richards, 'Teaching popular culture', in Ken Jones (ed.), *English and the National Curriculum: Cox's Revolution?* (London, Kogan Page, 1992), p. 75.

52 Lev Vygotsky, *Thought and Language* (Cambridge, MA, MIT Press, 1962) and *Mind and Society* (Cambridge, MA, Harvard University Press, 1978). For developments of this argument see my 'Towards a theory of media learning', in my *Watching Media Learning*, and 'Media education: the limits of a discourse', *Journal of Curriculum Studies*, 24: 4, 297-313. These issues will be considered in greater detail in David Buckingham and Julian Sefton-Green, *Cultural Studies Goes To School* (London, Falmer, forthcoming).

INDEX

academics 155, 206-7, 213, 216
Action 160-1, 180n
Action Force 140, 142
advertisements 38
age differences 15, 31-2, 95-6, 120, 162-3
'Allo 'Allo 31
Anderson, D. 20n
Ang, I. 21n, 156-8n, 217n
Annie 74, 78-87, 210, 212
Ariès, P. 22n
art 202-3
Askew, S. 113-15n
A-Team, The 146

Bad Company 142
Bains, H. 218n
Ballard, C. 72n
Bannister, R. 184
Barker, M. 18, 20n, 22n, 116-19, 121-2, 134n, 200n, 209-12, 217n
Barker, M. 180n
Barlow, G. 200n
Barrs, M. 26-7, 46n
Basinger, Kim 107, 109
Batman 140, 145, 147-8
Batsleer, J. 134n, 156n
Baywatch 105-6, 109
Bazalgette, C. 218n
Bee, J. 22n, 217n
Beezer, A. 180n
Benjamin, W. 182-3n
bestsellers 126-9
Beuf, A. 113n
Bhagavad Gita 53, 55, 67
Bharucha, R. 66
Big Match 197
Billig, M. 181n
Birds of a Feather 197
Blue Peter 32
Blume, Judy 128-9, 131-2
Blyton, E. 125-6

Bond, James 142-3
Bourdieu, P. 38-9, 40, 47n, 114n, 173, 182n
Brake, M. 22n
Briggs, S. 75, 87n
Bristow, J. 157n
British Board of Film Classification 184, 186-7, 200n
Brookside 36
Brown, R. 20n
Brunsdon, C. 21n, 217n
Bryant, J. 20n
Buckingham, D. 19-22n, 114-15n, 158n, 216-18n
Burning, The 193, 200n
Burton, R. 181n
Butterflies 42

Care Bears 40
cartoons 5, 26, 93-6
censorship/certification 186-8, 193-4
Centre for Contemporary Cultural Studies 11, 22n
Chambers, I. 20n
Charles, Prince 3, 19n
Chetwynd, J. 113n
childhood 4-5, 12, 24
children's books 124-6
Chodorow, M. 27-9, 46
Christian-Smith, L. 134n
Clarke, G. 22n
class 12, 25, 39, 43-5, 74-7, 80-1, 85, 87-8n, 123, 161, 192-4, 201n, 214-15
Clifford, J. 23n
Clover, C. 200n
Cobb, R. 169, 182n, 217n
Cohen, P. 137-8, 156n, 218n
Collins, Jackie 128
Collins, Jim 157n
computer magazines 131
Connell, I. 20n
content analysis 8